THE

THEATRICAL 'WORLD'

FOR

1893.

THE

THEATRICAL 'WORLD'

FOR

1893.

BY

WILLIAM ARCHER.

BENJAMIN BLOM  New York/London

First Published 1894
Reissued 1969 by
Benjamin Blom, Inc., Bronx, New York 10452
and 56 Doughty Street, London, W.C. 1

Library of Congress Catalog Card Number 77-82818

Printed in United States of America
at Westbrook Lithographers, Inc.
Westbury, New York

AUTHOR'S NOTE.

———·◆·———

My thanks are due to my ever courteous and
sympathetic Editor and friend, Mr Edmund Yates,
for his sanction of the following reprint; likewise to
the Editors of the *Illustrated London News*, and the
Pall Mall, *Westminster*, and *St James's Gazettes*, for
their permission to reproduce one or two supple-
mentary papers. The articles are reprinted almost
verbatim, even the most trivial mention of this or
that performance being retained, in order that, with
the aid of a full index of names, the book may serve
as a record and work of reference. Musical performances do not come within my province, and matinées
are seldom noticed; but for the rest I believe few
productions of any moment at the West End theatres
are entirely unrecorded. In one or two instances,
short passages have been restored which had been
"crowded out" of the columns of the *World*. I have
recorded in a foot-note the date of the first *and last*
performances of every important play, so that the
reader may see at a glance how far my estimate of its
merits coincided with that of the public.

CONTENTS.

EPISTLE DEDICATORY

TO

MR ROBERT W. LOWE.

———

My dear Lowe,

It is by accident, not design, that your name figures in the second sentence of the first article of this book; for when I wrote that article I did not dream that it would ever be reprinted. But it was a happy chance which made you my " first foot," as we say in Scotland, on the threshold of 1893 ; and, accepting the omen, I now inscribe your name, not " in my haste " but " at my leeshure," in the forefront of the little volume. Our unfaltering friendship of twenty years was cradled in the theatre. Our love of the theatre is the common ground on which, despite many divergences of opinion and of habit, we can still meet with unfailing pleasure. You did not precisely implant this love in me—of that I must acquit you—but your sympathy and companionship fostered and

confirmed it, and you are therefore in some
measure responsible for the fruits it has borne.
I hope, as you turn the following pages, you
may not find this burden of responsibility lie
too heavy on your soul.

The one merit which I can confidently claim
for these pages, and which you, at least, will
allow them, is that they are the outcome of a
very genuine passion for the art, or rather the
arts, with which they deal. " Passion ! " some
people will say—" Call it mania or craze, and
you will be nearer the mark." Perhaps they are
right ; but does not some touch of insanity, or
at any rate of unreason, enter into all love that
is worthy of the name ? Does the painter care
for nothing in art but its rational, definable,
defensible glories and achievements ? Is not
his primary impulse a mere childish, irrational
desire to scribble with a pencil and dabble in
colours ? What lover of literature confines his
love to masterpieces ? Ultimately, on realising
the shortness of life and the length of the
British Museum Catalogue, he may read by the
light of reason ; but he is no true bookman if his
love of literature did not grow out of a mere
unreasoning passion for books, an itching of the
fingers to turn the printed page, a lust of the

eye after everything—except draught-boards—
bound and lettered on the back. Who says
" love," in short, says " unreason,"—it needed no
Schopenhauer to tell us that. To love rationally is not to love at all. Love is essentially a
mania, a craze, for something or other—for
books or colours ; for flowers, for birds, for
animals ; for the sea or for the snow-peaks ; for
home or country ; for man, for woman, or for
child. Of all crazes the most irrational is the
craze of a man for a woman, a woman for a
man ; yet who does not know that behind its
unreason may lurk the highest wisdom ?

We need " take no shame " to own, then, that
our love for the theatre has been a craze, a fine
frenzy. With me, it was not only unreasonable,
it preceded reason in the order of development.
I was a country-bred child, and none of my
family had any connection with the stage, or
took any particular interest in it ; yet I cannot
remember the time when the word "theatre"
had not a strange fascination for me. I did not
in the least know what a theatre was, but I
knew it was one of the things I most wanted to
know. " Pepper's Ghost," with a dumb-show
representation of the story of Faust and Margaret, was the first theatrical entertainment I

ever saw, and it made an epoch in my experience.   Thenceforward, for years, my great
ambition was to possess a toy theatre.   The
ambition was never realised, for I could no
more have bought one than I could have bought
Drury Lane, and my mechanical genius was
quite inadequate to constructing one.   I got the
length, however, of tracing the costume-plates
in Knight's *Pictorial Shakespeare*, pasting them
on cardboard, colouring them, and cutting them
out; but, alas! the cardboard invariably curled
up, so that not only Richard the Third, but
my whole dramatic company, seemed afflicted
with incurable spinal curvature.   I must have
been twelve or thirteen before I saw the inside—
or for that matter the outside—of a real theatre.
My father had promised to take me for a short
yachting cruise in the Solent.   We were to lie
for some days in Portsmouth Harbour, to visit
the "Victory" and the "Duke of Wellington,"
to see a volunteer review, and, in short, to
partake in all manner of delights.   The whole
experience — the sailing, the living on board
ship, and everything—was heaven itself to me;
but I knew there was a theatre at Portsmouth,
and what I had chiefly set my heart on from
the moment the trip was mentioned was to per-

suade my father to take me to it. He did;
we saw Wallace's *Maritana;* and the daring
and wit of Don César de Bazan seemed to me
incomparable—almost superhuman. Then, on
a visit to London, I was taken to the Strand
Theatre, and saw John S. Clarke in *Toodles* and
Among the Breakers, with *The Field of Cloth of
Gold* as an afterpiece. But the full glory [of
the mimic world did not burst upon me until I
saw a Drury Lane Pantomime—*Beauty and the
Beast*, with Fred Vokes as the Beast, and his
sister Rosina as Beauty. To the eternal discredit of my taste, it was not with her that I
fell in love, but with another lady in the cast. I
still see this lady from time to time, and wonder
whether she would feel flattered to know that
she was the object of my first affection. She
would scarcely discover the fact, I fear, from an
obituary notice of her which I once wrote (and
published) when she was falsely reported to be
dead.

It was not till some years later that you and
I first met, in that city which, like our dear and
illustrious fellow - townsman, the author of
Catriona, we must ever think of as our home.
You are a somewhat older playgoer than I. If
I mistake not, you have seen Charles Kean, and

remember Helen Faucit when she was still on
the stage : I saw her only once, in an occasional
performance, long after her retirement. My
memories go back no further than to Phelps,
Charles Mathews, and Sothern—actors, one may
say, of yesterday. Our common mania quickly
made us friends. You—shall I remind you of
this ?—were an amateur actor of some note. I,
curiously enough, never even imagined that I
had any talent for acting, or felt the smallest
wish to figure personally on the boards ; but if
you were to put me on oath, I could not swear
that I did not write a play in which you took
the "juvenile lead," though what it was all
about I cannot for the life of me remember.
We must have spent hundreds of hours together
on our favourite back seat of the Princess's pit ;
and they were among the pleasantest hours, and
certainly not the least profitable, of my life.
(The Theatre Royal, you remember, had just
been destroyed by fire ; and you may or may
not remember that among the burnt-out actors
in that fatal pantomime was one whose remarkable name, already familiar to us at that date,
has since become still more familiar, and occurs
pretty frequently in the following pages—Mr A.
W. Pinero to wit.) It was a dingy, malodorous,

little den that Princess's Theatre, yet to me
its memory is fragrant. I have just been going
over a bundle of my old playbills (each about
four feet long, and still sticky with printers'
ink), and I find that there, in the course of
a couple of seasons or so, we saw *Hamlet*,
Macbeth, *Othello*, *The Merchant of Venice*, *As
You Like It*, *Romeo and Juliet*, *Antony and
Cleopatra*, and *Cymbeline*, to say nothing of *She
Stoops to Conquer*, *The School for Scandal*, *The
Lady of Lyons*, *Richelieu*, *Money*,—in short, the
whole standard repertory of the English stage.
A tolerably liberal education, was it not? And
we not only saw, we studied most of these plays.
We were learned in " readings " and " business,"
critical of emphases, intransigeant on questions of
metre. I have sometimes been accused, in these
latter days, of slighting and undervaluing Shakespeare. Well, I will not say that I *appreciate* him
—who dares make such a boast?—but you and I
know how we loved him. I have probably received
more pure, unmixed pleasure from *As You Like It*
than from any other play that ever was written ;
but *Romeo and Juliet* runs it hard in my affections. How often have we seen these plays, I
wonder? There was a time when I am sure we
could have " taken up " any cue in them, and

given the substance, if not the words, of the
following speech. The trouble with us now-a-
days is not that we undervalue Shakespeare, but
that we approach his works with definite ideas,
or prejudices if you will, as to how they should
be rendered in detail, and are therefore, perhaps,
unreasonably hard to please. We belong in
this respect to the Old School, the school for
which rhetoric was rhetoric, and verse was verse.
In these days, the critic thinks his duty amply
fulfilled when he has given a picturesque account
of the general impression produced by this or that
sumptuous revival, without condescending upon
a single detail of any sort. In the good old
days of our *Lehrjahre*, we were prepared with
whole treatises on a wrongly-accented syllable,
and dissertations on a pause misplaced.

Of course the classic drama was not our only
fare. We browsed at large on all that was
"going" in those days—farce, burlesque, comic
and grand opera, and melodrama. All
Robertson's comedies we saw, even the less
known ones ; and do you remember the delight
with which we first savoured the wit and sentiment of that wasted genius, James Albery, in
Two Thorns, *Two Roses*, *Apple Blossoms*, and
Forgiven ? The Haymarket company was then

in its decline ; Kendal and " Madge Robertson " had already left it ; but there was still old Chippendale to render us (I fear) unjust to any subsequent Sir Peter, Sir Anthony, Mr Hardcastle, or Adam ; there was Compton the incomparable in Touchstone, Mawworm, and Sam Savory ; and Buckstone's oily chuckle was still as delightful in Tony Lumpkin as in some other parts it was offensive. By this time, too, we were fully alive to the humour as well as the glamour of the stage. Oh, what deliciously bad acting we have seen in our time !—not the colourless incompetence of to-day, but the elaborate, the strenuous, the exquisite execrableness of the third-rate stock-company actor. It is the mark of your true devotee of the drama that he takes almost as much pleasure in characteristically bad as in good acting, and that the vilest performance of the wretchedest play will sometimes afford him rare entertainment, simply as a quaint scene from the human tragicomedy. The play within a play is often much more amusing than the play the author wrote. Our experiences, too, were by no means confined to Edinburgh. Together (you remember ?) we saw Salvini's Othello at Drury Lane, when he first visited England ; together

we delighted in *Trial by Jury* during its first
run at the Royalty.   And shall we ever forget
that evening in the parterre of the Français,
when Bornier's *La Fille de Roland* was the
novelty of the hour ?   It was our first visit to
Paris, and we knew nothing of the French
stage ; so when Roland's Daughter glided upon
the scene, a snow-white, willowy figure with
lustrous eyes, we looked at our programme with
a sudden access of curiosity, and read for the
first time the name of Sarah Bernhardt.

Soon after this, our paths in life diverged, and
so, in a measure, did our interests in the stage.
You came more and more to make the theatre
of the past your province ; I remained " adscript "
to the theatre of the present.   Yet the diver-
gence was more apparent than real ; for though,
as a student of stage-history, I can at best hold
a candle to the editor of Cibber and of Churchill,
the author of *A Bibliographical Account of
English Theatrical Literature*, I in nowise yield
to you in my passion for these old *and happy*
far-off things, and triumphs long ago.   Ah ! how
those philosophers waste their emotion, who pity
the actor for the evanescence of his achievements !   Even the bad actor is enviable as
compared with the third-rate painter and the

mediocre poet, in that his failures do not survive
him, to be the weariness or the scoff of posterity.
But the good actor, the actor who has once
succeeded in touching the emotions and stimulating the imagination of his contemporaries—what
artist so happy as he ? Does he not act on for
ever in the imagination of those who come
after, a fit audience and not so very few ? It
is his faults, his mannerisms, his failures that
" evanesce " ; his sublimated genius lives on in
that region of the ideal where critics cease from
troubling and rivals are at rest. We read of the
" Garrick fever " which broke out in Dublin one
very hot summer, when Garrick, in the first
flush of his popularity, visited that city ; and the
incident was truly typical. That Garrick fever
lasts, by infection, to this day ; and every great
actor begets a particular bacillus which pro-
pagates itself from imagination to imagination,
and is like to do so to the end of time. I have
passed through the Siddons fever, the Kean
fever, the Talma, the Rachel fever, and many
others ; and they are apt to return upon me at
any moment. What a relief and refreshment
it is, from time to time, to escape from the elec-
tricity and oxy-hydrogen of to-day, and relight
in fancy the candles of Betterton's or Garrick's

Drury Lane, or of Molière's Petit-Bourbon! And then, apart from its interest as the home of a great literature and a fascinating art, how delightful is the theatre of the past simply as a social institution! To follow our theatrical annals from the Restoration downwards is to live in company with the finest wits, the quaintest characters, the most famous men and the most beautiful women in our literary and social history. Cowley and Buckingham, Dryden and Congreve, Addison and Steele, Goldsmith and Johnson, Sheridan and Byron, were all actually "men of the theatre," and for a century and a half the play-house was one of the chief foci not only of intellectual but of fashionable life. How we smile when Lord Braybrooke, the first editor of Pepys, gravely apologises for transcribing the immortal gossip's notes of his visits to the King's and the Duke's Houses, and of the lip-homage (literal, not figurative) which he paid to "Nelly," that "mighty pretty soul," who "acted the great part of Celia very fine, and did it pretty well"— as though these things were not the very jewels of the whole treasure-heap! And the wits and characters aforesaid did not merely congregate in the pit and boxes: they were at home in the

green-room as well.   Quin and Foote, actors
both, were undoubtedly among the very foremost wits of their century.   Was a happier
retort ever made than that of Quin to Warburton, which so delighted Horace Walpole?
"Bishop Warburton, in company at Bath,
spoke in support of prerogative.   Quin said:
'Pray, my lord, spare me; you are not acquainted
with my principles.   I am a republican; and
perhaps I even think that the execution of
Charles the First might be justified.'   'Ay!'
said Warburton, 'by what law?'   Quin replied:
'*By all the laws he had left them.*'"   I like to
remember, too, how the most exquisite compliment ever paid to woman was paid to an actress
and belongs to theatrical history.   When Sir
Joshua Reynolds had finished his portrait of
Mrs Siddons as the Tragic Muse, he placed his
signature on the border of the drapery,—"For,
madam," he said, "I am resolved to go down to
posterity on the hem of your garment."   Was
ever a phrase uttered more entirely worthy of
the man who spoke it or the woman to whom it
was addressed?   Truly, truly, my dear Lowe,
we have no need to blush for our craze, our
mania, for the stage of the past.   I sometimes
look along my bookshelves, and wonder which

book, if the house were on fire, I would first rush
to save.   There are a few books of some little
money value, and one or two of a value not
measurable in money, since they are marks of
friendship from men whose friendship is beyond
price ; yet I have very little doubt that the book
of all others which I would risk my life to rescue
would be the ten-volume *History of the Drama
and Stage in England from 1660 to 1830*, which
we owe to the ever-blessëd industry of the
Reverend John Genest.   It is not a *written*
book at all : there is not a single coherent or
punctuated sentence in all its seven or eight
thousand pages : yet I am sure Charles Lamb
would have prized it as you and I do, and would
never have classed it among his *biblia a-biblia.*
I wonder if he knew of its existence ?   It
was published some time before his death,
but seems to have fallen still-born from the
press.

Perhaps you do not catch the drift of this
long vindication of an enthusiasm which has
never seemed to you, I daresay, to need any
vindication whatever.   But I assure you I am
not revelling in the Pleasures of Egotism simply
for their own sake.   This train of thought has
been very naturally suggested by the little book

which I here inscribe to you. A little book it
is, but it represents the better, or at any rate the
larger, part of the thoughts and labours of a
whole year; for to the time occupied in writing
these articles must be added the hundreds of
hours spent in the theatres in preparation for
them. I might, then, adapting the epitaph of
the Licentiate Pedro Garcia, inscribe on the
title-page of this volume " Aqui està encerrada
el alma del año 1893." The soul of my life for
the past year (and for many years) has been
given up to the service,—or, if that begs a
question, let us say to the consideration—of an
art to which many people deny the name of art,
and of which we are all apt to speak with an
apologetic accent, as of something frivolous and
childish. I myself, in moments of intellectual
snobbishness, have talked of "this poor, tawdry,
claptrap art of the theatre," and affected a sub-
lime superiority to the passion of my life. It is
precisely this snobbery that I here abjure and
protest against. The theatre is the meeting-
place of all the arts and all the philosophies. It
has a glorious past, a fascinating present, a
future rich in possibilities. If this book is slight
and trivial, 'tis because of its inadequacy to its
great argument. If I have buried my soul in

the theatre, I can only hope that it may not seem too unworthy of so august a tomb.

Some may think—though I am sure you will not—that I have given away my case in confessing that my passion for the theatre preceded any rational conception of the meaning of the word. Let us recur to the analogy of the painter and the bookman. Do they realise what art is, and what literature, when they first fall under the fascination of line and colour or of the printed page? Not at all—they simply obey an instinctive foreboding which tells them that along this line of interest, of study, of endeavour, lie vague but splendid possibilities towards which their souls yearn. What is all worthy education, in matters of art, but the process of disengaging a high ideal from among the crude instincts, proclivities, and enthusiasms of the neophyte? If every art were childish which inflames the imagination of a child before he can realise its essential beauty and nobility, I know not where we are to look for a virile art. Sculpture itself, in all its chill and abstract austerity, has its baby devotees. Who has not seen infants in the strict sense of the word— children who cannot speak articulately—happily absorbed in "moggling" in clay? Yet stay!

there is one art which, by this test, may fairly
lay claim to virility—the art of criticism. It
leaves the childish imagination cold enough;
and yet, by a curious paradox, it sometimes
seems to have the property of prolonging the
intellectual nonage of its professors.

When we think of it, is not this habit of
depreciating the dramatic art a strange form of
unreason? No one denies that the very masterpieces of the world's literature, and that in
almost every language, were written for the
stage. Enumerate the great poets of Greece,
Spain, France, Germany, England, and you will
find playwrights in a clear majority. Shakespeare, the crown and summit of English
literature, Molière, the supreme glory of France,
were not only playwrights but managers and
actors. All this is notorious and beyond dispute; yet here am I, at this time of day,
apologising, in the very act of vowing I will not
apologise, for abasing my fine genius to the consideration of the art or arts to which Shakespeare devoted his life! What is the origin of
this insanity? Partly, no doubt, it is a legacy
of Puritanism, for it is much less marked in
France and Germany than in the land of
Shakespeare—and Milton. But there are other

and more immediately operative reasons for it, which will readily occur to you.

In the first place, we have the fact that the masterpieces of dramatic literature do not always and entirely gain by stage presentation, and that, conversely, great actors have often won their finest triumphs with very inferior literary material to work upon. That, as you know, was Charles Lamb's famous contention. He slightly overstated his case, as one naturally does in maintaining what was in his day a heresy; but in the main his facts are undeniable. What deduction, then, shall we draw from them? Because certain portions of certain works of Shakespeare transcend in subtlety and sublimity the highest potentialities of stage-expression, are we to conclude that the art of the stage is utterly base and despicable? That was not Lamb's conclusion, at all events. Who has loved the stage, and celebrated it, better than he? True, he has also protested against certain excesses of the actor-worship which was less disproportionate, perhaps, in his day than in ours; but he would have been the first to admit that these very excesses are nothing but an additional evidence of the unequalled potency of the actor's art to move and sway the minds of men. Those despisers of the stage, moreover, who appeal to the authority of Lamb, in order to make a virtue of their intellectual limitation, thereby show an imperfect understanding of the existing conditions of the case. The dramatic art of to-day is a totally different thing from that of eighty, seventy, even fifty years ago. Lamb's authority cannot apply to a theatre which he no more foresaw than he foresaw the "kodak" or the phonograph. He may, indeed, be validly cited as an, or rather *the*, authority on the romantic drama and old comedy ; but nothing that he says can make either for or against *Francillon, Hedda Gabler*, or *The Second Mrs Tanqueray*, for the simple reason that they belong to a form of art, both literary and theatrical, which in his day did not exist. We do not cite Wellington on machine-guns or Nelson on torpedo-boats.

Again, you may say, I seem in danger of giving away my case. In asserting the majesty of dramatic art, I make a great flourish of the name of Shakespeare ; and then, after admitting that the theatre cannot do the fullest justice to his greatest works, I proceed to argue that the modern drama, the drama with which the modern

stage must of course be chiefly concerned, differs
in its very essence from the Shakespearian
drama, and indeed from all the great dramatic
literatures which have been the glory of the
stage, from Æschylus downwards. I might
reply that the theatre does not stand or fall by
the modern drama, and that in this very record
of 1893, Sophocles and Shakespeare hold a prominent place. But I scorn the subterfuge. In
my opinion, the theatre *does* practically stand or
fall by the modern drama. I am, as you know,
deeply attached to the drama of the past ; I
would fain see it more systematically and intelligently cultivated than it is at present on the
English stage ; but that does not alter my conviction that the theatre which provides no
adequate representation and criticism of contemporary manners and thought is in a parlous
state, and does not fulfil the most vital part of
its natural function. If the modern drama is
despicable, then we who live in, by, and for the
theatre, are indeed wasting our lives.

But who can read the contents-list of this
little book, and say that the modern drama is
despicable ? No doubt a great deal of despicable
matter comes within the record ; but make a full
record of a year's doings in any art whatsoever,

and you will scarcely have to register mere
masterpieces. This brings me to a consideration, often overlooked, which goes far, I think,
to account for the illusion of an essential in-
feriority in the dramatic art, as compared with
the other arts of our modern world. It is one of
the mechanical disadvantages, so to speak, of
the theatre, that it admits of no obvious discrimination between the various grades of accom-
plishment in the works it presents. It is a
gallery in which every picture is hung on the
line, the worst with the best ; and the enormous
size of the canvases makes it very difficult for
the amateur to seek out his elective affinities.
When you enter a picture-show, a very rapid
glance around enables you to pitch upon the three
or four works which have anything to say to you,
and the rest, so far as you are concerned, cease
to exist. Not so with the drama. Unless you
can find a critic, a professional " taster," whose
palate exactly agrees with your own—and that
is improbable—you run the risk of taking a
good deal of trouble, and incurring some expense, only to find yourself bored or irritated by
a mediocre or vulgar play. After half-an-hour
of a bad novel, you fling it aside, and return it
to Mudie's ; but it takes a great deal more than

half-an-hour, and costs almost as much as a year's subscription to Mudie's, to "sample" a bad play ; and meanwhile, perhaps, the two or three plays of the season which are capable of affording you keen artistic delight, may have had their day and ceased to be before you have even heard of them.   To the true lover of theatrical art, even a bad play has its interest, and generally its compensation in the shape of some happy episode or clever piece of acting ; but to many people, of course, a good quarter-of-an-hour seems poor compensation for a weary evening.   The upshot appears to be that a man of fastidious taste, who is inaccessible to the mere amusement of theatre-going, insensible to the exhilaration of light and colour and human companionship, and unprepared, in short, to take the rough with the smooth,—such a man perhaps does well to hold aloof, in the main, from the theatre.   But let him not plume himself upon what is at best a mere idiosyncrasy, if not a positive limitation.   Let him not conclude that there are no high, and intense, and exquisite artistic pleasures to be found in the theatre, simply because he cannot be at the trouble of going to seek for them.   Life is too short, and faculty too limited, to allow the

average man to get the best out of every art;
but it is a paltry consolation for those who cannot climb a mountain to sneer at the glories of
the prospect from the summit.

You will agree with me, I am sure, that one
of the chief uses of an endowed or subsidised
theatre would be to serve, so to speak, as "the
line" in a picture gallery—the post of honour
where one should naturally look to find, not
always the best work, but always work of a
certain importance, dignity, and distinction.
This, however, is too large a subject to be more
than indicated here.

And now let me admit that I was not playing
quite fair in refuting our imaginary scorner of
the stage by a reference to the muster-roll of
1893. The very reason for the existence of this
book is that the past season has been altogether
exceptional, a veritable " annus mirabilis," in the
history of the modern stage. Never within my
recollection—not often, surely, in the whole
annals of the English theatre—has the student
of the stage had so much to " break his
mind upon " in a single season. We have
had one play of Sophocles, three of Shakespeare (not counting Lyceum revivals), two of
Tennyson. We have had a new play by

Ibsen, and performances of five of his older
works. We have had the whole company, and
practically the whole current repertory, of the
Théatre-Français to pass in review, including
five or six plays by the masters of the contemporary French stage, Dumas and Augier. We
have seen in Eleanora Duse certainly the most
interesting and delightful artist who has risen
over the dramatic horizon since Sarah Bernhardt
first dawned upon us. The Independent Theatre
has presented at least three original works of
genuine interest. Mr Henry Arthur Jones has
produced two ambitious dramas ; Mr Oscar
Wilde, Mr Sydney Grundy, and Mr Louis
Parker, have each given us a play " of some
importance " ; and Mr Pinero has made the
year memorable by the production of a tragedy
which (not to enter here on the question of its
merits) has at least excited more interest and
discussion than any other English work of our
time. Was it not what Alan Breck would call
" a true observe " when I said that if this book
is slight and trivial, it is because of the inadequacy of the writer to his themes, not because
of any unworthiness in the themes themselves ?

Indeed, it would be the height of arrogance
in me to suppose it probable that I could deal

adequately with all the multitude of problems
—technical, philosophical, sociological, psychological, æsthetic—presented by the theatrical
"output" of such a year. (I might have added
"physiological" to the roll of problems, for the
critic who cannot talk of "neurasthenia" is nowhere. I take this opportunity of apologising
for the absence of that blessëd word from my
memorial.)   Whatever may have been the
glories of "the palmy days," it is certain that
the critic of those times did not require anything like the multifarious intellectual equipment
demanded of his latter-day successor. He was
bound to know something of Shakespeare, and
of the traditions of "legitimate" acting; but
this knowledge he could scarcely fail to acquire
in the very act of attending the theatre. We,
too, have occasion some three or four times a
year for similar erudition, while we have far less
opportunity of acquiring it. "The legitimate"
apart, there was no necessity for either knowledge
or thought in dealing with the trumpery, conventional, dead-alive tragedies, comedies, and
farces which formed the staple of the contemporary drama. You related the plot, you
quoted with praise or blame a few lines of
fustian, you passed judgment on the acting, and

there was no more to be said. A play that
opened up any serious philosophical, moral, or
æsthetic question was the rarest thing in the
world. Take for instance Hazlitt's *View of the
English Stage*, published in 1818, and covering
the previous four years. It contains, as every
one knows, the luminous and penetrating
criticisms which made the reputation of
Edmund Kean ; it contains interesting notices
of the last appearances of Kemble and
Mrs Siddons, of the performances of Miss
O'Neill, and of the early efforts of Macready ;
but in the contemporary drama there is absolutely nothing for a writer like Hazlitt to
"break his mind upon." It is pitiful to see him
condemned to deal seriously and sedately with
"a new piece, in five acts, called *Smiles and
Tears ; or, The Widow's Stratagem*," or with "a
very tedious and nonsensical farce" entitled *My
Landlady's Nightgown*. The book, in short, is
still profoundly interesting for its criticisms and
descriptions of acting ; but, so far as literary
appreciations are concerned, it is "Shakespeare
und kein Ende," or rather "Shakespeare und
weiter Nichts." Imagine—I will not say *Rosmersholm*, or *Le Gendre de M. Poirier*, or *Denise*
—but such a play as *A Woman of no Import-*

ance or *Gudgeons*, produced in 1815! What a vivid, vital, palpitating masterpiece it would have appeared beside the *Widow's Stratagems* and *Landlady's Nightgowns* of the day! To Hazlitt, it would have come as an electric shock, stimulating his every faculty. Imagine, again, the intellect and style of Hazlitt applied to *The Master Builder*, or *Francillon*, or *The Second Mrs Tanqueray!* But no—on second thoughts I must beg you not to imagine anything of the sort—it would render you too intolerant of the following pages. All the same, if talent and opportunity were always commensurate in this excellent world, there is no doubt that I should have lived in Hazlitt's time, and Hazlitt now. The loss to the beginning of the century would have been more than compensated by the gain to the end. But I am heartily glad that fate has ordered it otherwise, not only because I prefer to "break my mind," such as it is, on the problems of to-day, but because I can to-day subscribe myself, my dear Lowe,

Ever your sincere friend,

WILLIAM ARCHER.

2nd January 1894.

THE

THEATRICAL "WORLD"

FOR

1893.

———————

I.

THE PANTOMIMES—"UNCLE MIKE"—
"EAGLE JOE."

4th January.

WHY does not some theatrical antiquary write a *Short
History of Christmas Pantomime?* Here, Mr Joseph
Knight or Mr R. W. Lowe, is "a subject made to
your hand." For they have a curious and somewhat
intricate history, these monster extravaganza-spectacles
which flare forth each Boxing-Night all over England,
like the beacon-fires that heralded the Armada. The
late Mr Dutton Cook has given a brief sketch of the
origin of pantomime, as we now know it, in an article
entitled "Harlequin & Co.," reprinted in his *Book
of the Play.* He shows how the Court masque grew
into the ballet; the ballet was enlivened by the introduction of certain stock figures from the Italian
comedy; and thus a sort of trick-spectacle was

evolved, consisting of scenic surprises, magical trans-
formations, comic antics, tumbling and dancing, all
conducted in dumb-show. This was the pantomime
of last century, the pantomime of the great John Rich.
Then Harlequin, ever apt at such manœuvres, split
into two parts, representing the magical and the
mischief-making sides of his character. The magi-
cian and dancer, retaining the name of Harlequin,
did not don until the year 1800 the parti-coloured
eel-skin suit which now seems almost literally in-
separable from him. Meanwhile the mischief-making
element was embodied in the Clown, whose present
costume and characteristics were invented by Joseph
Grimaldi, not without some hints, of course, from the
French Pierrot. The "opening" was devoted simply
to the introduction, the genesis as it were, of Harlequin and his crew. In *Mother Goose*, produced in
1806, there were four scenes in the "opening" and
fifteen in the harlequinade. It was not until Planché
—founding partly on the old burlesque tragedies,
such as *Bombastes Furioso*—had invented and popu-
larised musical extravaganza, that the "opening"
began to swallow up the harlequinade, and political
and "topical" allusion became one of the recognised
features of pantomime. Then Planché with his
costumes, and Beverley with his imaginative and ingenious scenery, helped to bring the spectacular element into greater and greater prominence with each

successive season. It is at this point that Mr Dutton
Cook's sketch breaks off. He leaves an infinitude
of details to be filled in ; he does not attempt to
trace the spread of pantomime throughout the provincial theatres ; he takes no account of the music-
hall invasion, which in his time had barely begun,
if, indeed, it was not altogether a thing of the future.
Why does not some one, I ask again, elaborate Mr
Cook's sketch into an illustrated volume ? The
growth of a national art-form—or perhaps I had
better say a national institution—is always worth
studying, and the book might be made no less entertaining to the general reader than valuable to the
student. In France it would have been written long
ago.

But even more interesting than the past of pantomime is its future. That it has, and deserves to have,
a future, I am quite convinced. It is, in its essence,
an invaluable art-form, far superior to the French
revue. When the Aristophanes arrives for whom we
are all (intermittently) yearning, he will almost certainly write pantomime. There is room within its
infinitely flexible, expansible framework for all sorts
of ingenious and delightful developments—for poetry,
fantasy, parody, satire, sense, nonsense, the most
ingenuous nursery babble and the most penetrating
criticism of life. The ideal pantomime should charm
the senses, stimulate the imagination, and satisfy the

intelligence.   It should be an enchanting fairy-tale
to the young, to the old a witty, graceful, genially-
satiric phantasmagoria.   It has this immense advantage over burlesque, that it does not necessarily in-
volve the degradation of anything noble and beautiful.
The nursery folk-lore in which it finds its traditional
subjects presents just the requisite blending of the
graceful with the grotesque.   It is painful to see
Lancelot and Guinevere, Faust and Margaret, grin-
ning through a horse-collar ; but the grace and pathos
of the Babes in the Wood and Cinderella might quite
well remain intact, while the Wicked Uncle and the
Robbers, the Cruel Stepmother and the Proud Sisters,
might be handed over to Fantasy as butts for its most
impish humours.   The fact that it is, or ought to be,
primarily an entertainment for children is the justification, and will one day be the salvation, of pantomime.   There is something essentially undignified
and humiliating in the spectacle of a theatre-full of
grown men and women settling down solemnly and
intently for a long evening of sheer tomfoolery, even
if it were of a wittier sort than that which prevails in
our three-act burlesques.   But at the children's season
we can be childish with a good grace ; and there is
no reason in the world why poetry, wit, and wisdom
should not be blent with our childishness.   Let me
give one indication of the tone of the ennobled pantomime which I foresee.   The past year has taken from

us a great poet, one whose name should be familiar
to every English-speaking child; for he had at his
command the simplest, sweetest melodies, no less
than the loftiest and most complex harmonies. What
more natural and fitting than that the pantomimes
of 1892 should contain some mention of the great
national event of the year, some tribute, poetic, plastic,
or pictorial, to the divine genius of Tennyson? That
such a tribute would have been very much out of
place in the existing pantomimes, I fully admit. What
I dream of—what I venture to foretell—is a pantomime in which an episode of serious emotion should
not be felt as an incongruity; a pantomime in which
it should be possible to invoke the greatest memories
without fear of smirching them by contact with what
is common or unclean.

It is high time that I should turn from pantomime
as it might be to pantomime as it is. Mr Oscar
Barrett, one of our most skilful Christmas caterers,
has this year given us two really beautiful fairy-plays
in *The Babes in the Wood and Bold Robin Hood* at
the Crystal Palace, and *Dick Whittington* at the New
Olympic. For children, I think I should prefer the
Palace production. I know one youthful playgoer
who stoutly maintains that he enjoyed *Whittington*
most, but that, I think, is simply because he saw
it last. The Alphabet Procession in *The Babes in
the Wood* is a singularly happy inspiration—pretty,

humorous, effective; and the Noah's Ark scene, concluding with a delicious quadrille danced by Mr and Mrs Noah and their progeny, is a pure joy to the youthful mind and eye. The Snow Ballet, too, is exceedingly pretty, and the transformation-scene, "The Seasons," is charming. Mr Horace Lennard's libretto is pleasant and unpretentious, setting forth the story in a rational, comprehensible fashion. The acting, too, is almost entirely inoffensive, and in some cases really clever. Miss Kitty Loftus and Miss Rosie Leyton are bright and genuinely childish as the Babes. They dance very prettily, and Miss Loftus sings three verses of Mr Kipling's "Tommy Atkins" with excellent effect. Such an interlude is one of the things that would certainly find a place in my ideal pantomime. Male comedians in petticoats would as certainly be excluded; but it is only fair to own that Mr Mat Robson, as the Baroness, is one of the least objectionable of his tribe, while Mr Sam Wilkinson, as the Baron, is genuinely funny. The two robbers, Tarara and Boomdeay, find blood-curdling representatives in Messrs Arthur Watts and Watty Brunton; and Robin Hood and Maid Marian are brightly played by Miss Elsie Irving and Miss Laura Linden. Don't fail to wait for the second scene of the harlequinade, the gambols "On the Roofs," invented by Mr Charles Lauri, which were so popular at Drury Lane last year.

In *Whittington*, at the Olympic, likewise written by Mr Lennard and arranged by Mr Oscar Barrett, the spectacular element is more elaborated. A more brilliant, ingenious, and tasteful spectacle than the " Blue Ballet " scene it would be impossible to desire. The effects are piled up with genuine art. Every moment you think, "This *must* be the culminating point"; but no ! Madame Katti Lanner gives another turn to the kaleidoscope, and evolves some still more dazzling combination. The pantomime as a whole is distinctly entertaining. Mr Victor Stevens, who plays Fitzwarren's cook, reminds me too much of Mr Herbert Campbell to be altogether pleasing to my personal tastes ; but Miss Edith Bruce, as Whittington, once more proves herself one of the best "principal boys" on the stage, and Mr Lauri makes an inimitable cat. Mr Barrett's pantomimes have always one great advantage in the fact that the music is selected and arranged by himself. The popular airs of the day are fully represented, but they are pleasantly varied by snatches of good ballad music, with a strain here and there from classical sources. There is even a touch of wit in what may be called the allusive appropriateness of these accompaniments.*

---

* Sir Augustus Harris's Fourteenth Drury Lane Pantomime, *Little Bo-Peep, Little Red Riding-Hood, and Hop-o'-my-Thumb*, must not pass unrecorded. Sir Augustus did not invite my attention to it, and there seemed to be no reason why I should

Miss Florence Warden's four-act comedy, *Uncle Mike*,* now running at Terry's Theatre, displays much ability and still more inexperience. It is worth seeing, however, if only for the scenes between Mr Terry as the soft-hearted Shylock, and little Madge and Midge Stapleton-Turner, charmingly played by Miss Annie Hill and Miss Lucy Webling. Mr Herman's *Eagle Joe*, at the Princess's, is a picturesque and fairly interesting drama of passion, revenge, and necromancy,

---

force my appreciations upon his sensitive soul. At this distance of time, however, one may perhaps remark, without absolutely braving the terrors of the law, that the production gave evidence of even more than the usual profuseness of expenditure, and no more than the usual economy of brains. It would be futile to look to Drury Lane for the regeneration of pantomime. The traditions of the theatre and its size are equally unfavourable to any experiments in the direction of literary grace and artistic refinement. In the meantime, there is much that is worthy of admiration in the gigantic and gorgeous spectacles devised year after year by Sir Augustus Harris. I am not even disposed to quarrel with his practice of going to the music halls for his company. It is because performers of the pantomimic class now take to the music hall instead of to the theatre (greatly to the advantage of both) that the theatre is compelled at Christmastide to seek reinforcements from the music hall. The principal "artistes" engaged in the Drury Lane pantomime of 1892-93, were Miss Marie Loftus, Miss Marie Lloyd, Miss Ada Blanche, Mr Dan Leno, Mr Herbert Campbell, and "Little Tich." The production ran from Boxing Night until March 25, two performances a day being given during a great part of the time. The Olympic pantomime ran until March 11, and the Crystal Palace Annual until February 18.

* December 8, 1892—January 7.

fully up to the average of its class. It has doubtless
been relieved of a good deal of superfluous talk since
its first performance on Boxing-Day.* The leading
parts are vigorously and effectively played by Mr
Rollo Balmain, Mr Bucklaw, Miss Sara Mignon, and
Mr W. H. Day.

II.

" HYPATIA."

11th January.

ONE looks forward with fear and trembling to the
production of a blank-verse play on the English stage.
In nine cases out of ten, the blank verse is either
sheer uneducated balderdash, neither verse nor prose,
neither grammar nor sense—I have seen Mr Beerbohm
Tree himself figuring in at least one production of
this nature—or else it is stilted, stodgy, pseudo-
Shakespearian stuff, with all the vices of Sheridan
Knowles, and without his florid energy. A scene or
two of Mr Stuart Ogilvie's *Hypatia*,† at the Haymarket, sufficed to relieve one's mind of the worst
apprehensions. Mr Ogilvie writes like a man of
education and a man of sense. That he is a great
dramatist or a great poet I should be sorry to affirm ;
but he has given us an intelligent, competent piece
of work, which does no discredit to the Haymarket

---

* It had a very brief run.   † January 2—April 15.

stage. I have had no opportunity of reading his text ; but I venture to say that he writes blank-verse much better than the majority of his interpreters speak it. I made "snap-shots" at several snatches of his dialogue, and on deciphering my notes I find them confirm my impression that he has a very pretty knack of turning out resonant, polished, somewhat monotonous iambics, occasionally falling into platitude, but very seldom guilty of the much graver sin of fustian, bombast, and inflated verbiage. Let me quote one or two scraps, as I find them in my tablets. When Philammon looks down from Cyril's upper chamber upon Hypatia passing in the street, he sees her with an aureole round her head

> " Like that bright light which burned upon the brow
> Of Moses on the Mount of Sinaï."

The Jew, says old Issachar, is content

> " To stand aside in ambush, while his hand
> Still slyly shapes the Gentiles' history."

Rome, remarks Hypatia (more sonorously than accurately),
> " Has ever been
> A civil, not a sacerdotal, state."

Of the pagan ideals, again, she declares that

> " These, these alone are certain ; these the stars
> That steer life's shallop o'er the darkling seas."

Strictly speaking, the stars do not steer the shallop any more than the compass does ; but ladies are

proverbially lax in their notions of navigation. " If
thou couldst but know," cries Hypatia in another
place,

> " How we, who sing the gods' high psalmodies,
> Crave for an echo from our listeners."

When Philammon is beginning to realise that there is
a great deal of human nature in man, he says :

> " My stars are setting fast.   Above me breaks
> The leaden dawn of disillusionment."

It appears that Mr Ogilvie is very fond of lingering,
polysyllabic cadences ; but perhaps it is because I
too am fond of them that so many have dwelt in my
ear.   He rather overdoes the trick, I think, in such a
line as the following :

> " One word from thee, and Africa is freed
> From the rank blight of Christ-ee-an-i-tee."

In all my notes I find no single instance of the weak
endings, technically so called, the light eleventh
syllables so characteristic of our best dramatic blank
verse—and also some of our worst.   If Mr Ogilvie
should write another metrical play—not that I would
incite him to the attempt—he would do well to use
the light ending with Shakespeare, not abuse it with
Fletcher.   On the whole, his versification is so work-
manlike that I have no hesitation in attributing some
impossible lines and sequences of lines, which
occurred here and there, to the British actor's well-
known contempt for the trammels of metre.   Mr

Fernandez, in particular, seemed to think it incumbent on the Bishop of Alexandria to speak in improvised Alexandrines. Neither the inspiration nor the improvisation was happy.

What, now, of the drama as drama? Let me first make a clean breast of it, and own that my notions as to where Kingsley ends and Mr Ogilvie begins are gained at second-hand from the newspapers and from obliging friends. Once upon a time I read *Hypatia* with great delight. I remember thinking Raphael Ben Ezra, up to the point of his final surrender, a monstrous fine fellow—and that is practically all I remember about it. Some years ago I tried to read it again; but after a very few pages, "above me broke The leaden dawn of disillusionment." I read no further; and not even my Spartan sense of duty could now tempt me to recommence the experiment. From all I can gather, it would appear that Mr Ogilvie has taken his history, his local colour, and his leading characters from Kingsley, but that his plot and situations are practically his own. If this be so, Mr Ogilvie has evidently a fair share of constructive faculty. Each scene, taken by itself, is well enough devised, and executed with intelligence, if with no great originality of dramatic resource. And yet the effect of the whole picture is somewhat indefinite and disappointing, for a reason which is not very far to seek. The fact is, Mr Ogilvie has attempted to do too much. In the effort to create a commanding part for Mr Tree, he has written two plays instead of one. What he ought to have shown us—the subject was quite large enough to satisfy any reasonable playwright—was the clash of adolescent Christianity with outworn Paganism. There is no more pathetic, no more dramatic, subject in the history of the world; and here, on a fairly plausible historic basis, we find it presented in its most dramatic phase. We have a young ascetic, a fanatic, an eremite in the literal sense of the word, suddenly transplanted from his wilderness into the artistic capital of the ancient world, the headquarters of all that remains of the pagan joy of life. He is confronted with that joy of life, with the pride of intellect and the glory of art, in their most fascinating incarnation : a beautiful, eloquent, and noble woman. His senses and his intelligence leap suddenly to life. He recognises the hideous inadequacy of his ideals. If he sees the corruptions along with the splendours of paganism, he sees still more vividly the corruptions of the Church. In Hypatia alone he finds not only sweetness and light, but the beauty of holiness. His whole nature goes out to her; and yet he cannot surrender himself to the charm. The pessimism of Christianity has sunk into the very fibre of his soul. Even his awakened reason tells him that the Christian metaphysic has in it more of the true secret of the universe than the

hectic Apollonism of Hypatia. And she, on her
side, awakens to a realisation of the hollowness, the
factitiousness, of her allegorising creed. She recognises that Great Pan is dead, that the world has
outgrown Hellenic paganism, which has sunk on the
one hand into sensual indifferentism, on the other
into an academic cult, an æsthetic hypocrisy. She
has glimpses of a depth of feeling, if not of thought,
in the despised Syrian superstition, for which she
looks in vain in her beloved poets and sages. Yet
her soul revolts against Christian dogma, no less than
against the fanaticism and obscurantism of Christian
politics. The new doctrine seems simply to have
darkened and befouled the happy sunlit civilisation
of Hellas. She feels, justly enough, that humanity is
relapsing into barbarism ; and not having realised that
everything is for the best in the best of all possible
worlds, she is not in a position to

> " Forecast the years,
> And find in loss a gain to match,
> And reach a hand through Time to catch
> The far-off interest of . . ."

disillusionment. Their love, in a word, leads Philammon and Hypatia, by different routes, to a common
standpoint—to the melancholy certitude attained a
few years earlier by Julian the Apostate (the Julian of
Ibsen, if not the Julian of history), that " The old
beauty is no longer beautiful, and the new truth is no

longer true." Their spiritual no less than their
material situation is pregnant with tragedy ; and for
the development of this tragedy the most skilful
dramatist might well have found the conventional
five acts but a "scanty plot of ground." What, then,
does Mr Ogilvie do ? Not content with exhibiting
the struggle between Paganism and Christianity, he
must needs bring Judaism into the field, and treat us
to a "triangular duel of three." The result is a
deplorable complication of the political motives of the
action, and an elbowing-aside of the two protagonists
in order to make room for the subsidiary plot in
which the picturesque Hebrew—who happens to be
the actor-manager—is engaged. A good enough plot
it is, in itself ; but since Corneille did not find five
acts too much for *Polyeucte*, one does not see why Mr
Ogilvie should imagine that he can run *Polyeucte* and
Le Roi s'amuse into one, and treat them adequately
in four acts. As a matter of fact, neither is adequately
treated ; even the comparatively commonplace seduc-
tion-story deserved a larger development. As for the
love-story, not to say the spiritual tragedy, it is simply
nowhere. It seems scarcely credible, but it is nevertheless a fact, that Hypatia and Philammon have only
two very brief conversations in the whole play, one of
them occupying the three or four minutes before their
assassination. They meet in public and look at each
other both in the first act and in the second ; but for

the exchange of sentiments and ideas they are allowed
only some three minutes in the third act.   A rather
exiguous arena this whereon to fight out the battle
of antiquity against mediævalism, of the old beauty
against the new truth.   Seven-eighths of the space at
the dramatist's command are devoted to the subsidiary plot and to political combinations of very
mediocre interest.   Issachar, to put it briefly, is the
ruin of the play as a work of art.   If his Goshenite
forefathers were such meddlers and muddlers as he,
one fully understands the anti-Semitic policy of the
Pharaoh who knew not Joseph.   How ludicrous, for
example, is the position of Orestes the Prefect in his
wooing of Hypatia, when he stands aside mute as a
mackerel, and allows the irrepressible Issachar to do
all the talking !   No doubt this is a touch of Hebrew
character.   Issachar reminds me for all the world of
Sugarman the Shadchan, or marriage-broker, in Mr
Zangwill's *Children of the Ghetto*—the most powerful
and fascinating book, by the way, that I have read for
many a long day.   But we don't go to Alexandria in
the fifth century to learn that the Jew is an inveterate
match-maker.   What we look for is the clash of
ideals, the tragedy of two noble souls in the grip of a
Time-Spirit which, so far as they can see, is working
darkly towards dolorous ends.   This is what we demand
from the poet who seizes upon such a theme as that
of *Hypatia ;* and I can't help thinking that some one,

some day, will see that we get it. He will have to find
an actor-manager who wants to play Philammon.

Even as it stands, however, the play is stirring,
picturesque, and not unattractive. Mr Tree makes a
stately and striking figure of old Issachar, and plays
at some points with real originality, though at others
his attitudes savour of staginess. Miss Neilson looks
the part of Hypatia admirably, bears herself with a
grace she does not always exhibit in other characters,
and speaks her lines with fair intelligence and conviction. Mr Fred Terry makes the most of Philammon ;
Mr Lewis Waller is a swarthy and sinister Orestes ;
Miss Olga Brandon finds little to take hold of in the
terribly "sacrificed" part of Ruth ; and Mr Piffard
deserves a word of praise for his energetic performance of the small part of Jonadab. The scenery is
beautiful in design, but not altogether happy in
execution. It lacks solidity ; there is too much
flapping canvas about it ; and the "flats" do not
always "jine." In Hypatia's lecture-theatre, for
example, the illusion was sadly marred on the first
night by a yawning fissure in the marble gradines.
The costumes are splendid, and the stage-pictures,
as a whole, are brilliant and animated. One word
more : the comic relief ought to be altogether
abolished. It is perfunctory and dismal ; and besides,
Issachar provides all the comedy we can reasonably
require.

III.

"ROBIN GOODFELLOW"—"A WHITE LIE"—
"KERRY."

18th January.

IN the Elizabethan sense, and without the slightest
reflection upon Mr Carton's modesty, I am fain to
describe *Robin Goodfellow* * at the Garrick as a "ples-
aunt conseated comedye." Its dialogue is one tissue
of conceits, and its plot is simply a conceit on a
larger scale. Were I inclined to be philosophical, I
think I could show, in some fifteen or twenty columns
of *The World* (which would of course be conceded
me with alacrity), that Mr Carton, at the close of
"this so-called nineteenth century," is suffering from
a literary disease which broke out all over Europe
somewhere in the fifteen-hundreds, and which has
ever since run in the family of our English comedy-
writers. Marini in Italy, Gongora in Spain, and John
Lyly in England, were practically contemporaries, and
Marinism, Gongorism, and Euphuism are all, I take
it, phases of the same disorder. But in Italy and
Spain (I write under correction, and from merely
second-hand knowledge) the disease was incident to
what, since "conceits" are in question, I may perhaps call the decadent renaissance. In England, on
the other hand, Euphuism, or at any rate the habit of

---

* January 5—February 11.

mind of which Euphuism was the extreme manifesta-
tion, caught the renaissance at its prime, and profoundly modified its whole development. It was all
very well for Shakespeare and the younger Elizabethans to deride and caricature the affectations of
Lyly ; they were themselves all tarred with the same
brush.   Artifice, not nature, is the note of their
comedy dialogue. They are for ever on the hunt
after word-plays, similes, tropes, and figures of all
sorts—in brief, those quaintnesses of thought and expression which, adopting the Italian term, they themselves described as conceits.   No doubt society, as
well as the stage, was to some extent infected with
these fantastic habits of speech.   But we cannot suppose that the playwrights, in their orgies of quip and
crank and whimsicality, had any thought of repro-
ducing the actual conversation of their age.   Sometimes, as aforesaid, they burlesqued the extravagances
of a small group of writers and speakers, the "æs-
thetes" of the day ; but their burlesque dialogue is
not in reality more artificial than much of the comic
dialogue which they put forth without the least satiric
intention—it is only more foolishly artificial.   And
this habit of artificiality, of conceit-hunting, has been
handed down from one comedy-writer to another,
even, in the fulness of time, to Mr R. C. Carton.   It
is *the* characteristic of English comedy.   We call it
"wit," and glory in it—in some cases with very good

reason. Just think how little wit, in our sense of the word, there is in Molière! You will find more similes, more epigrams, more quaint departures from ordinary habits of conversation, in one scene of Con-greve or Sheridan—ay, or of Mr Carton—than in a whole comedy of Molière. The aim of his dialogue is to give absolutely just and absolutely finished ex-pression to character—to sublimate, not fantasticate, everyday speech. And, exceptions apart, this con-trast holds good throughout the whole theatrical his-tory of the two peoples. French comedy drew its inspiration from the Latin, while French farce was largely founded on the Italian *commedia dell' arte*, a popular, not a literary, product, whose origins are lost in remote antiquity. Thus the French stage, deriving from classic sources, and developing somewhat later than ours, escaped the infection of Marinism or Gon-gorism, and adhered firmly, even in its wildest buf-fooneries, to "l'école du bon sens." We, on the other hand, chose romantic themes for our comedies no less than our tragedies, and made our comic dialogue a very carnival of *concetti*, which may be de-scribed as the *confetti* of style. Even when classical influences reached us through France, and the comedy of manners supplanted the comedy of cape and sword, the habit of fantastic dialogue survived, and we continued to strive after "points" rather than to seek for those comic effects which grow naturally out of character and situation. I do not mean, of course, that we have entirely neglected character and situation, or that the French are absolutely guiltless of verbal and artificial wit. What I mean is that when an English playwright sits down to "write dialogue," he instinctively tries to produce something as *un*like as possible to ordinary conversation, overlaying the dramatic tissue with a heavy embroidery of quaint fancies and "good lines." The result is, that whereas French conversation is, on an average, incontestably wittier than English, English stage-dialogue does its best to be far wittier than French, and succeeds in being far more artificial. There is no stranger perversion of fact than our national superstition which denies humour to the French while granting them wit. In the lighter French comedy-writers, with the inimitable Labiche at their head, there is a great deal more humour than wit; whereas, in such a writer as H. J. Byron, for example, there is a great deal more wit than humour—only that the wit happens to be of a very miserable quality. When we come to a higher level, we find in Dumas a writer whose tendency to "faire de l'esprit" in and out of season, is unsparingly denounced by his critics; but Dumas's dialogue, polished and sparkling though it be, is far less *fantastic*, far less remote from ordinary conversation, than, let us say, Mr Pinero's. It would need a volume to prove (with the necessary exceptions and reservations) this theory of what I may perhaps call the hereditary Euphuism of English comedy ; and I fear it would take much more than a volume to persuade English playwrights that the time has come when they must "go to nature" for their dialogue. They either will not understand, or else they understand too clearly, that it is much more difficult to write simply and dramatically, than to write brilliantly and theatrically.

So much by way of defining, or rather accounting for, the particular convention which governs the quaint and pleasing art of Mr Carton. Over the surface of life, as he presents it, there plays a sort of shimmering iridescence of verbal fantasies and felicities. Almost all his characters are professional humorists, carefully selecting their words with an eye to comic effect. Sometimes his "good lines" come off, sometimes they don't ; but, take it all in all, his wit is no less piquant than it is persistent. For my part, I have a keen relish for this graceful facetiousness ; it does not bore me a bit ; and on tracing it to its origins, as I have tried to do in the preceding paragraph, one cannot but allow it a certain historic dignity. And then Mr Carton has the art to temper his plot to his dialogue. Not until they intrude into passages of serious import (as, for example, in *The Profligate*) do conceits become really annoying. Now in Mr Carton's delicate fairy-tales (I am tired of using the term, but it imposes itself in this connection) there are no passages of serious import. "What are you all playing at?" cries Mrs Bute Curzon when the imbroglio of *Robin Goodfellow* is at its height; and that is really "the word of the situation." Mr Carton's personages are simply playing at life; and the art of the author lies in keeping his audience in the humour for joining in the game. If his quips and cranks fail for five consecutive minutes to keep us amused, we cry, "We won't play!" and the game is up. But in *Robin Goodfellow* there is no such gap in the tissue of fantasy. We surrender ourselves open-mouthed to the mild excitement of the fairy-tale, knowing full well that the good fairy will ultimately baffle the powers of darkness with their powers of attorney, and that every one will "live happy and die happy, and never need to drink out of a dry cappy," as the old Scotch formula runs. Once or twice, indeed, the conduct of the good fairy becomes so flagrantly immoral that we are half inclined to cry, "We won't play!" It would be hard to conceive anything weaker and wickeder than her complicity in the machinations of the necromancer, her father. To avert a problematical risk to the life of her respected grandmother, she is prepared to stand by and see four young lives irretrievably ruined! That is the plain statement of the case; and I decline to accept as an extenuating circumstance the fact that her own life is

one of the four.   The thing might pass at a pinch, if
the grandmother were such an exceptionally delightful
old lady as to make us feel that, at all hazards, she
must live ; but, frankly, " je n'en vois pas la néces-
sité."   The morality of fairy-tales, however, is a thing
apart ; and I am serenely confident that no young
lady among the Garrick audiences will be tempted to
follow the example of Grace Barbrook in immolating
the happiness of all around her on the altar of—her
grandmother.

Mr Hare's Valentine Barbrook is a delightful piece
of acting, which would lend attraction to a much
duller play than *Robin Goodfellow*.   It is not the
first character of the same type which Mr Hare has
presented to us ; but the beauty of the thing lies in
the delicacy of its differentiation from its predecessors.   Mr Forbes Robertson's part is deplorably
unworthy of his talent.   How this somnolent, ineffectual Hugh Rokeby ever earned the nickname of
Robin Goodfellow I am at a loss to conceive.   Robin
Goodfellow, I take it, is a busy, tricksy, benevolent
sprite, actively helpful to those who deserve his good
offices ; whereas Hugh Rokeby does nothing at all in
the whole course of the play, but drifts passively
about, and, if anything, helps to muddle matters by
his rank stupidity.   Mr Sidney Brough is manly and
pleasant, Miss Kate Rorke womanly and pleasant,
Miss Norreys charming, Miss Compton incisive and

clever, Mr Donald Robertson amusing, and—and really my stock of adjectives has run out.

It is very seldom that the second state of an imperfect play is better than the first, but Mr Grundy's *White Lie** at the Avenue is the exception which proves the rule. He has expanded the three acts into four, eliminated the scenes of sentimental drama, and made the whole play a comedy of intrigue. And an ingenious and amusing intrigue it is. The situation at the end of the third act is so effective that we readily overlook some improbabilities in the leading up to it. For instance, if Kate Desmond could have escaped from the inn while Sir John Molyneux was dozing, why should escape become impossible the moment it appears that Lady Molyneux also is there? And where, indeed, is the necessity for any escape at all, when the two ladies find themselves there together? There is nothing to prove that they did not come together, which they would scarcely have done had the motive of either been unavowable. Kate Desmond, too, knowing very well that Sir John Molyneux is following at her heels, would never go about her explanation with Captain Tempest in such a gratuitously leisurely fashion. A few trifling improbabilities like this are surely worth correcting. It would be easy, at any rate, to make Sir John Molyneux, for

---

* First produced in London at the Court Theatre, May 25, 1889. Revived at the Avenue, January 7—February 28.

once in his life, refrain from falling asleep while waiting for his audience with Captain Tempest.   Mrs Kendal returns to us* with no diminution of her extraordinary vividness and variety as a comedy-actress. One has rather to complain, now and then, of an inartistic over-exuberance of style ; but that I am quite willing to attribute to the nervous excitement of a first-night in London after so long an absence.   In Sir John Molyneux, Mr Kendal finds one of those John Mildmay parts in which he is always admirable ; and Miss Annie Irish is pleasant as Lady Molyneux. Mr Cecil M. Yorke seemed to make of Captain Tempest an unnecessarily obtrusive " bounder " ; but a certain measure of offensiveness is essential to the part.   The production was received by the audience with evident enjoyment.

Boucicault's version of *La Joie fait Peur*, entitled *Kerry*, now precedes *The Churchwarden* at Terry's Theatre.   Mr Terry's rendering of the old Irish major-domo is a really remarkable piece of character-acting.

IV.

"THE SPORTSMAN"—"OVER THE WAY"—
"THE BURGLAR AND THE JUDGE."

25th January.

THE new farce at the Mendacity Theatre—situated,

---

* From America.

as all the world knows, in Panton Street, Haymarket
—is one of the funniest and least offensive of its innumerable tribe. The formula is almost nauseously
familiar—Act I., The Lie Preparatory; Act II., The
Lie Damnatory; Act III., The Lie Exculpatory—but,
in the present instance, the tangled web is woven with
a certain exuberance of fancy which renders many
passages irresistibly ludicrous. I gather, from the
evident gusto with which those who had seen the
French original narrated its humours, that Mr Lestocq
has shown a good deal of expurgatory skill in his
adaptation. He has certainly provided *The Sportsman** with some bright and telling dialogue for which
he can scarcely be indebted to *Monsieur Chasse*.
The success of the farce was for a moment endan-
gered by the childish and inept conclusion of the first
act; but the second and third acts were received with
shouts of laughter. Mr Hawtrey's effrontery is as
delightful as ever, and he is excellently supported by
Miss Lottie Venne, Mr Charles Groves, Mr W. F.
Hawtrey, and Miss Annie Goward.

The weakest portion of the new triple bill † at the
Court Theatre is undoubtedly the comedietta by
T. W. Robertson, entitled *Over the Way*, which has
been injudiciously dragged to light. It is evidently a

---

* January 21—April 15, at the Comedy Theatre.
† January 20—February 25.

hasty adaptation of a fifth-rate, mid-century, French vaudeville. *The Burglar and the Judge*, on the other hand, goes even better than it did at the Haymarket.* There is real humour in the conception, the execution is spirited, and the acting of Mr Brookfield and Mr Weedon Grossmith is exceedingly funny. These two gentlemen are also the life and soul of the perennial *Pantomime Rehearsal*, which has put forth some fresh blossoms — a topical song among the rest—and promises to flourish exceedingly.

V.

"THE BAUBLE SHOP"—"THE GUV'NOR."

1st February.

THE whole essence of my criticism of *The Bauble Shop* †—Mr Henry Arthur Jones's new play at the Criterion—can be concentrated into very few lines. Mr Jones has baulked us, if not of the *scène à faire*, at least of the *mot à faire*. Through two acts and a half we waited longingly to hear Viscount Clivebrooke bid Mr Stoach, M.P., "Go to the devil!"—and had he used an even curter formula to the same effect, I don't think the Censor himself could have objected. Instead of taking this simple, obvious, and probably effectual course, the noble Viscount, like the 'coon of

---

* Where it was produced, November 5, 1892.

† January 26—June 14.

the legend, chooses to whimper forth, " Don't shoot,
Colonel! I'll come down!" And he *does* come
down! He grovels, he writhes, he whines, he abases
himself to the dust before a contemptible scandal-
monger at whom, in the circumstances stated, the
country would simply have jeered. Mr Jones, in
reply, may point to two recent and unhappy instances
of great political careers blasted by the breath of
scandal; but in these cases the circumstances were
entirely different and infinitely more serious. No
doubt there is material for a fine drama—nay, for
several fine dramas—in the question of private morals
in their bearing on public life; but it is futile to present a case in which no question of private morals
actually arises. Midnight is certainly an undesirable
hour—one would have supposed it peculiarly inconvenient for a Leader of the House of Commons—at
which to take afternoon-tea with a pretty shop-girl
and her papa. The world — both Mr Stoach's and
Lord Clivebrooke's own—would doubtless be apt to
misinterpret such visits. But, after all, Lord Clivebrooke is a bachelor; the young lady is of full age;
even on the worst interpretation there is no cruelty
or criminality in the case; and it does not appear
that the Public Morals Bill, which Lord Clivebrooke
has in charge, is to the full as drastic as that Viennese
statute which, in *Measure for Measure*, condemned
Claudio to the scaffold. It may be doubted, indeed,

whether even that *Law against Lovers*, as Davenant
called it, would have handed over to Abhorson a
gentleman convicted of no more heinous offence than
consuming tea on unlicensed premises, and after clos-
ing-time. "But," says Mr Jones, "the absolute
merits of Lord Clivebrooke's position are neither
here nor there; the question is whether Mr Stoach,
by whispering in the lobbies, or even stating in the
House, that Lord Clivebrooke keeps a mistress, could
secure the rejection of the Bill he is piloting." Well,
that is a question I must leave to "old parliamentary
hands"; all I can say is that to me, an outsider, Mr
Jones has failed to make the thing seem probable.
Admitting, however, that it is conceivable, I cannot
make the same admission as to Clivebrooke's behaviour in the difficult situation in which he finds
himself. If ten Bills, twenty Governments, fifty
careers had been at stake, no man of reasonable
spirit would have humiliated himself before the adversary as Clivebrooke does. There are men, it is
true, to whom a political career seems such a necessity of life that they will do anything and suffer
anything rather than relinquish their footing on the
parliamentary ladder. Had Clivebrooke's conduct
been satirically presented—had he been held up to
us as a deplorable example of this mania—no one
would have denied the accuracy of Mr Jones's
observation. But his intention is the reverse of

satirical. He thinks Clivebrooke no end of a fine
fellow, and would have his very abjectness pass for
heroism; as though there were any Bill or any
Government worth preserving at the total sacrifice
of one's dignity as a human being. "But hold!"
cries Mr Jones. "You quite mistake the situation.
It is not the Bill or the Government that Clivebrooke is fighting for; it is a woman's reputation,
which he holds himself bound in honour to protect."
Well, I grant that a conjuncture might have been
devised in which this plea would hold good; but I
submit that Mr Jones has not devised that conjuncture. As Mrs Alving puts it, do not let us talk
in general terms; do not let us ask whether any
sacrifice is justifiable in order to save "a woman's"
reputation, but whether we can conceive Clivebrooke
licking the dust at Stoach's feet in order to save
the reputation of this particular woman, this Jessie
Keber? It is a large thing to say, but say it I
must — no more wooden lay-figure was ever presented to a confiding public in the guise of a
heroine. Beside her, Little Nell seems positively
human. What do we know of her? Absolutely
nothing. Her character, her culture, her social
position are all left equally in the vague. Is she
a shop-girl? She neither dresses nor speaks like
one. Is she, in the conventional sense of the word,
a lady? Then she must surely be aware that it is

a trifle unusual for ladies to accept idyllic country
residences from casual gentlemen, upon whose generosity they have no avowable claim. All we really
learn about her — for she says so herself — is that
she has no friends, and lives, with her dipsomaniac
father, a life of absolute seclusion. What can we
possibly care for the "reputation" of such a puppet?
Reputation, I take it, is the esteem in which one is
held by the social circle to which one belongs. But
Jessie Keber belongs to no social circle; and if she
did, would not her reputation be as hopelessly ruined
by her acceptance of the cottage in the country as by
anything Stoach can say or do? If Clivebrooke had
compromised a woman whom we *knew*—a woman in
his own rank of life (Lady Kate for instance), or
any flesh-and-blood woman in any social *milieu*
whatsoever—we might have sympathised with him
in his struggle to "keep her name out of the
papers." But can we conceive a statesman humiliated and an Administration overthrown for the sake
of the fair fame of a porcelain doll? That is the
true description of Miss Jessie Keber. If the other
mechanical toys turned out by Matthew Keber were
not more life-like than she, I think his genius must
have been over-rated.

There is only one word—and that, unfortunately,
a French one—to describe the whole conception and
execution of the play : it is incurably *naïf*. Mr Jones

is a disciple of Matthew Arnold: can he really imagine that his Earl of Sarum and Viscount Clivebrooke fairly represent the "barbarians" of that delicate observer? So far as they are human at all, they are middle-class to the finger-tips. Conceive (let us say) the late Duke of Devonshire, at a time when the present Duke was leader of the House of Commons, going about the lobbies and buttonholing all and sundry to tell them how he heard a workman by the roadside saying, "My pal, Lord Hartington, is going to give 'em beans to-night," and how he tipped the noble fellow half-a-sovereign! The worst of it is that the workman is as improbable as the peer. He does not know his own language. A "pal" is essentially a personal acquaintace, a mate, a crony.* The word is not used as a term of esteem, or even affection, for a man, be he peer or peasant, who is known to the speaker only by repute. And it is gravely proposed, in the room of the Leader of the House, that this precious evidence of popular enthusiasm shall be "sent round the party." Send it round the party, forsooth! Send it round the Marines! If Lord Sarum were to send round the

---

* The *Century Dictionary* says:—" PAL, partner, mate, chum, accomplice.

'High-born hidalgos
With whom e'en the king himself quite as a pal goes.'"
—*Ingoldsby Legends*, II., 63.

hat in order to recoup himself for his outlay (of half-a-sovereign) on behalf of his party, the whole incident could not be more preposterous.   Yet it is not in the least out of keeping with its surroundings. I know nothing and care nothing about the minor details of parliamentary life.   I don't know whether it is probable that the Leader of the House should move the second reading of a Bill after nine o'clock, any more than I know whether the windows of his room look out on the Clock-Tower. Mr Jones might be mistaken in every single touch of this order, and I should not think one ha'p'orth the worse of the play. His notions of parliamentary procedure matter nothing at all ; it is against his notions of human nature that I feel bound to pro-test. Or rather I don't "feel bound" to protest—I do so whether I will or no. From the middle of the second act onwards, a voice within me keeps on crying out in spite of myself: "No! no! things do not happen like this! These are not men and women, but sentimental situation-makers! Unob-served! theatrical! false, false, false!—and not very cleverly false either !"

The contrast between *The Bauble Shop* and *The Crusaders* is, to me, dispiriting ; and I think Mr Jones himself must smile a little bitterly as he reads the eulogies showered upon his present effort, and remembers the treatment meted out to his last.

The earlier play is, in my judgment, incomparably the better, the more intelligent of the two. There is character in it, there is fantasy, there is poetry of a sort. Cynthia Greenslade is a live woman, Una Dell an ideal figure of real grace and tenderness; Palsam is subtlety itself compared with Stoach, Lord Burnham and the Hon. Dick Rusper are ten times more credible than Lords Sarum and Clivebrooke. The whole action of *The Bauble Shop* is a sort of monstrous enlargement of the feeblest incident in *The Crusaders*—Lord Burnham's promise to renounce horse-racing if Palsam will hold his tongue about Mrs Greenslade. Supposing, however, that I am unjust to *The Bauble Shop;* supposing that it is of equal merit with *The Crusaders* (and I am sure Mr Jones himself will maintain no more): how are we to account for the difference of their reception at the hands of the critics? The explanation is obvious, though not reassuring. *The Crusaders* happened to be presented to a captious and unruly first-night audience, and it was not supported by the prestige of an actor-manager; therefore the critics, with very few exceptions, did not take the trouble to look for and discern its essential merits. *The Bauble Shop*, carried on the shoulders of a popular actor-manager, meets with unstinted first-night applause; therefore the critics either cannot or will not recognise its essential weaknesses. The moral is—to adapt that wise saw with which Mr Jones has adorned his play-bill—"Critics are only human; sometimes very human." But the reflection is scarcely exhilarating for a dramatic author who is not content to sell his soul to the actor-managers.

In the present case, I cannot tell what may have been Mr Wyndham's influence upon the conception of the play; as regards its presentation, Mr Jones has every reason to be grateful to him. It was not only his prestige, but his vigour and conviction, that carried the play through to popular success. He was now and then a trifle too theatrical in attitude and gesture; but on the whole his portraiture of the pitiable Clivebrooke was by far the strongest piece of serious acting he has as yet given us. Another excellent performance was Mr W. H. Day's Matthew Keber; and Miss Fanny Enson was so good as Lady Kate Ffennell that one could not but regret the smallness of the part. Miss Mary Moore was pretty and sympathetic as Jessie Keber, and Mr Somerset, though I thought him less happy than usual in the earlier scenes, certainly contributed largely to the effect of the final situation.

Pray let it not be supposed that I grudge Mr Jones his success. On the contrary, I should have been sincerely sorry if the play had failed. With all its

faults, it is above the average of contemporary
English playwriting. Its first act is exceedingly
bright, clever, and promising, and even its later acts
are not tedious. It is far better worth seeing than
many plays which one passes over with facile praise,
simply because they are not worth serious analysis.
But it is one thing to admit that the play is worth
seeing, as plays go, and quite another to proclaim it
an artistic success. The day will come, I am sure,
when Mr Jones himself will class it among his errors
of judgment. In *The Crusaders* he had well-nigh
achieved intellectual distinction; in *The Bauble Shop*
he has relapsed for the moment into commonplaceness, not to say commonness.

Encouraged by the success of *Our Boys,* the
Brothers Gatti have revived at the Vaudeville
another play of the old James-and-Thorne repertory
—*The Guv'nor* * to wit. Though no author's name
has ever been publicly attached to this piece, it is
understood to be a joint production of two playwrights, both of whom are now deceased—Messrs
H. B. Farnie and Robert Reece. It is a very unpretending piece of work, old-fashioned both in plot
and dialogue; but, played with plenty of conviction
by the excellent Vaudeville company, it keeps the
audience thoroughly amused. Mr David James, of

---

* January 28—February 21.

course, resumes his old character of the deaf boat-builder,* and other parts are filled by Messrs W. Farren, E. W. Gardiner, Reeves Smith, and Charles Ashford; Miss Sophie Larkin, Miss Annie Hughes, Miss May Whitty, and Miss Abington.

VI.

"THE COUNTY COUNCILLOR."

8th February.

OF *The County Councillor,* † by Mr H. Graham, which has gone into the evening bill at the Trafalgar Square Theatre, I can only repeat, what I said at the time of its afternoon production, ‡ that it is an unpretentious, rollicking farce, with a certain happy audacity in some of its situations. It is played with any amount of vigour and conviction by Miss Fanny Brough, Mr E. W. Garden, Mr Yorke Stephens, Mr Mark Kinghorne, and Mr Cyril Maude; and, after a somewhat languid opening has been got through, it keeps the audience in fits of laughter.

---

* This was the last revival in which Mr David James appeared. He died October 2.

† February 4—April 28.

‡ At the Strand Theatre, November 18, 1892.

VII.

TENNYSON AND THE DRAMA: A FOREWORD TO "BECKET."

Westminster Gazette, 6th February.

FORTUNATE in all things else, Tennyson was unfortunate as a dramatist. His non-dramatic works
were, above everything, timely; his dramas were
untimely births. They came at the wrong time in
his career, and at the wrong time in the history of
the stage.

All three of the chief poets of our half-century have
written historical or romantic plays in blank verse.
Tennyson alone is generally admitted to have failed,
because—yes, *because*—he alone came within measurable distance of success. The plays of Browning and
of Mr Swinburne are read (it is believed) by a faithful
few: for the world at large, even the reading world,
they can scarcely be said to exist. The public passes
them by with distant respect. They are as safe from
ridicule as the Pyramids or the Great Wall of China
—and just about as vital. Neither poet possesses any
one of the three essential gifts of the dramatist—the
power to breathe life into a character, to develop a
situation, to tell a story. Browning's personages are
always discussing a dimly-suggested drama, never
acting it; and their thoughts seem to rebound from
each other at every angle except the natural, the con-

ceivable one. In Mr Swinburne's works, again, the
drama is drowned in the overwhelming copiousness of
rhetoric. Like his own Darnley, we are

> "Surfeited . . .
> With winds of wordy weather round our ears."

And yet, as I make these assertions, I feel them to
be not only inadequate, but incapable of proof. The
plays—and this is precisely their advantage over
Tennyson's—set criticism at defiance. They are remarkable, even stupendous, productions, full of all
sorts of literary power, and yet so utterly remote
from the purposes of drama as to elude all critical
standards. Their faults do not lie here and there,
but everywhere or nowhere. They might be flawless
masterpieces if they were not abortive altogether.
Not so with the dramas of Tennyson. They live,
they move—they halt, they stumble. He who runs
may read them, and he who reads may ridicule. The
gallery-boy can jeer at their puerilities, the sporting
critic can scoff at their technical defects. Tennyson
has been hooted on the stage ; his brother poets do
not even stir an audience to the hissing-point. None
of Mr Swinburne's dramas, so far as I know, has
ever been acted ; Browning's *Strafford*, *Blot in the
'Scutcheon*, *Colombe's Birthday*, and *In a Balcony*,
have been recited on the stage and listened to with
respect, but they have never "got over the footlights."
According to some accounts, *Strafford* was hissed on

its first production ; but I doubt whether the pit had
energy enough for any such demonstration. When
the Browning Society produced this and other plays
a few years ago, the enthusiasts applauded, and the
majority of the audience felt no more disposition to
hiss than if they had been listening to a meritorious
performance in an unknown tongue. Tennyson's
plays, on the other hand, get well across the footlights. They seize our attention and challenge our
criticism. They stand or fall by the same tests which
we apply to *Richard III.* or *Coriolanus*, to *Egmont* or
Wilhelm Tell.

Tennyson was sixty-six when he published his first
play. His poetical power was unimpaired, as, indeed,
it remained to the end ; but he was too old to study
and master the mechanism of a new art. He was
content to adopt the simplest Elizabethan formula
—that of the loosely-strung chronicle play ; for-
getting that the modern public, which can go to
books for narrative and detail, requires in drama the
concentrated essence of historic character and situation. Much of the dialogue was inert, superfluous ;
some scenes were feebly humorous, though not more
feebly than the Elizabethan models which suggested
them. The critics and the public, ever ready to
assume that a man who has succeeded in one form
of art cannot possibly succeed in another, found
plenty of faults in the play to justify this assumption.

They "expected to be disappointed"—an attitude of mind by no means peculiar to critics of Hibernian stock—and they were not to be baulked in their expectation. But the sins of *Queen Mary* were sins of excess, not of defect. Within the amorphous mass lay a noble and moving drama, which only required (and requires) to be stripped of its superfluities in order to rank among the classics, not of English drama alone, but of the English stage. The version presented at the Lyceum was unskilfully arranged, and, though it had an ideal Philip in Mr Irving, the somewhat hard and monotonous talent of Miss Bateman —not then so ripe an artist as she now is—did not bring out the delicate lights and shades of Mary's character. That character is one of the finest, even from a theatrical point of view, in the English drama, and it only awaits the advent of a great tragic actress to leap, as it were, to life. It was stated some time ago that *Queen Mary* had been played with great success in Australia. Sooner or later, it must be recognised as one of the dramatic possessions of the English-speaking world.

Mary is undoubtedly Tennyson's masterpiece in character-drawing; his second play, *Harold*, is his masterpiece in point of form. It might be placed on the stage almost as it stands; it *would* be if we had a national English Theatre. Here again we have a chronicle-play, but one in which the political motives shape themselves, almost without effort on the poet's part, into a large and simple tragic drama. In all the leading scenes there is a fine dramatic movement; and there are, fortunately, no episodes of Elizabethan humour. If we should ever possess a really worthy non-commercial stage, *Harold* will certainly take an honourable place in its repertory.

Becket seems to have been conceived soon after the completion of *Harold;* but three minor works intervened before its publication. In *The Falcon* and *The Cup*, which were, or ought to have been, constructed dramas, not long-drawn frescoes like the earlier plays, the poet's lack of dramatic science revealed itself. In both he missed what may be called, in the literal sense of the words, the psychological moment. We see nothing of Ser Federigo's anguish of heart ere he can decide to sacrifice his darling bird; the whole affair is despatched in a brief aside to his servant. We see nothing of Camma's grief and despair, of the growth of her thirst for vengeance, or of her resolution to be avenged. In both plays the true drama passes behind the scenes. Both are exquisitely written, however; and one cannot but wish that Mrs Kendal would give us another opportunity of admiring her noble impersonation of the Lady Giovanna. Some of the too Shakespearian pleasantries of Filippo might, without irreverence, be suppressed. *The Promise of May*, on the other hand,

was the one unqualified and irremediable blunder
of the poet's career.   "The British Drama," he wrote
to Mr Hall Caine after its failure, "must be in a low
state indeed if, as certain dramatic critics have lately
told us, none of the great moral and social questions
of the time ought to be touched upon in a modern
play."   But whatever these critics may have said, it
was not the subject of the play that led to its failure;
it was the total lack of tact with which the subject
was handled.   Edgar, the freethinker, was a mere
grotesque, whose speeches, even as one reads them
in cold blood, are irresistibly comic; and to make
such a caricature the central figure of a serious drama
was simply to court disaster.   There was a certain power
and beauty in the later scenes, but Edgar's opening
soliloquy alone was enough to seal the fate of the play.

The cold reception of *The Falcon* and the failure of
The Promise of May seem to have embittered the
poet against the stage, so that in the working-out of
Becket he deliberately disregarded what he calls, in
the dedication to Lord Selborne, "the exigencies of
our modern theatre."   Yet there are evidences that
he originally conceived it with a direct eye to the
stage, and doubtless to the very actor and actress
who are to-night to embody the leading characters.
Why else should he have done violence to history
by — not precisely interweaving — but jumbling
together the stories of Becket and of Fair Rosa-

mund? In a drama intended for the study, there is no need to "work in the female interest"; that is one of the "exigencies of the theatre." There was ample material for a fine play in the history and character of the Archbishop alone. The Rosamund episode has, in reality, nothing to do with the main theme, and is as improbable as it is unhistorical. Let us hope that its theatrical effectiveness will justify it. As it left the poet's hands, *Becket* is undoubtedly the feeblest of his three chronicle (or fresco) plays. Here again, as in *The Falcon* and *The Cup*, the true drama passes behind the scenes, between the acts. The dramatic as well as the historical interest of the character of Becket lies in his conversion from the soldier-statesman into the theocratic priest; and here the whole change takes place, without a word as to the why and wherefore, between the prologue and the first act. As a result, there is no sense of movement, of progress, in the drama, which (apart from the Rosamund episode) practically resolves itself into a series of indecisive "rounds" between the king and the prelate. Several of the individual scenes, however, are vigorous and striking, and judicious compression has probably done much to correct the sense of languor in the dramatic action. Whatever the result of to-night's experiment, there can be no doubt that in making it Mr Irving shows a worthy sense of the duties of his position, and deserves well of the republic of literature and art.

VIII.

"Becket"—"An Underground Journey."

15th February.

To come to the point at once, Mr Irving's production of *Becket** is one of the triumphs of his career. In point of artistic delicacy and strength, his Becket deserves to rank with his Charles I. So long as he is on the stage, we are interested, fascinated, moved; and if there are one or two bad quarters of an hour when he is *not* on the stage, that is Tennyson's fault, not his.

As for the play—well, on that point there can surely be no two opinions. A good play it is not, and cannot be made. It may even be called an exceptionally, singularly bad play. "Some gents," says the keeper, in *Punch*, to the unsuccessful sportsman, "goes a-wingin' and a-worritin' the poor birds; but you, sir—you misses 'em clane and nate!" With the like delicate tact, criticism can only compliment the poet on the "clane and nate" way in which he has missed the historical interest, the psychological problem, of his theme. What was it that converted

---

* February 6. Performed every evening till April 8, then for some weeks every evening except Saturday, when *Louis XI.* and *The Lyons Mail* were revived. It was repeated occasionally up to the end of the season, in the course of which Mr Irving passed in review almost his whole repertory.

the Becket of Toulouse into the Becket of Clarendon
—the splendid warrior-diplomatist into the austere
prelate? The cowl, we are told, does not make the
monk; but in Lord Tennyson's psychology it seems
that it does. Of the process of thought, the development of feeling, which leads Becket, on assuming the
tonsure, to break with the traditions of his career,
with the friend of his heart, and with his own worldly
interest—of all this we have no hint. The social and
political issues involved are left equally in the vague.
Of the two contending forces, the Church and the
Crown, which makes for good, and which for evil?
With which ought we to sympathise? It might be
argued that we have no right to ask this question, and
that it is precisely a proof of the poet's art that he
holds the balance evenly, and does not write as a
partisan. But as a matter of fact this is not so. The
poet is not impartial; he is only indefinite. We are
evidently intended to sympathise, and we *do* sympathise, with Becket, simply because we feel that he is
staking his life on a principle; but what that principle
precisely is, and what its bearings on history and
civilisation, we are left to find out for ourselves.
Thus the intellectual opportunity, if I may call it so,
is missed "clane and nate"; and the same may be
said of the very fine emotional opportunity presented
by the theme. It seems to have been the case—at
any rate it is quite conceivable—that the mutual love

of Henry and Becket survived their political differ-
ences and underlay their whole contest.   Here, then,
was a truly tragic conjuncture.   What can be more
moving, more intensely dramatic, than the conflict
between inward affection and outward antagonism ?
sorrow for the friend that was, now softening, and
again embittering, resentment against the enemy that
is ?   The poet touches feebly upon this motive in the
Frétival scene ; but for any adequate working out of
it space would have been required, and the better
part of the space at his command he chose to devote
to the fairy-tale of Rosamund.   Of this Rosamund
episode I can scarcely trust myself to speak : the
lapses of a great poet are best passed over in silence.
Let me only say that it is unhistorical, inconceivable,
and profoundly uninteresting.   If even the two themes
—that of Becket and that of Rosamund—were merely
juxtaposed, there would not be so much to deplore.
As it is, in the attempt to interweave them, the poet
manages to exhibit Becket in an equivocal and almost
a farcical light.   All we can do, then, is to *un*twine
them in our minds as much as possible, and to concentrate attention on the two or three really noble,
moving, and dramatic passages in which Becket com
mands the stage.   The Council at Northampton and
the murder scenes are, of course, the culminating
points of the action.   It is futile to deny a certain
order of dramatic faculty to the man who wrote these

scenes. They are very fine examples of that large, pictorial treatment of history which is one of the noblest possibilities of the romantic drama. These two scenes, and especially the debate over the Constitutions, actually moved and thrilled me in the same way, if not to the same degree, as the Meiningen presentation of the murder of Cæsar and Mark Antony's Address used to move and thrill me; and it is many a day since I, for my part, have felt any kindred emotion within the walls of the Lyceum.

It is difficult to analyse the impression produced by Mr Irving's Becket, and decide how much of it is due to artistic intention and effort, how much to mere physical aptitude. The latter element is undoubtedly of great importance. It would be almost impossible for Mr Irving to fail in an ascetic, a sacerdotal character. His cast of countenance, his expression, his manner, are all prelatical in the highest degree. Nature designed him for a Prince of the Church; he would have played the spectacular side of the character to perfection, and I do not think that the diplomatic function would have suffered at his hands. Thus a part of his success as Becket lay in his mere personality, and is to be accounted to him for (artistic) righteousness only in so far as that very personality is a work of deliberate art. Every self-conscious human being is his or her own creator to a certain extent; and this is specially true of actors in general, and of Mr Irving in particular.   But there is much more than his mere personality in Mr Irving's Becket; there is imagination, there is composition, there is—pray, Mr Printer, indulge me with characters adequate to so startling an averment—there is DICTION ! If the actor had relied on his personality alone, and played the part simply as he could not help playing it, there would have been nothing, except details of costume, to distinguish it from his Wolsey. As it is, the two men are clearly individualised—one may almost say sharply contrasted. Wolsey was above all the statesman-priest ; Becket is the hero-priest. Craft, policy, personal ambition, love of power, were the ruling forces in the Cardinal; the Archbishop is animated by an intense, simple-minded, almost fanatical devotion to the Church, untainted by either subtlety or self-seeking. This may or may not be the Becket of history ; it is certainly the Becket of Tennyson, whom Mr Irving embodies with infinite sympathy, fidelity, and charm. Truth to tell, he is no great genius, this Thomas of Canterbury. He impresses us by force of character—by courage and single-mindedness—rather than by vigour of intellect. Though not quite "serafico in ardore," he is such stuff as saints—not cardinals—are made of.   I do not know whether the "holy, blissful martire" is as much esteemed by Roman Catholics of to-day as he was in Chaucer's time ; but if so, both the poet's conception

and the actor's rendering of it must, I should think,
be eminently pleasing to the Ultramontane faction.
To me they are delightful from the point of view of
pure poetry. In the three or four really vital scenes
of the play, Tennyson has sketched a noble and
touching figure, assigning to him many noble and
touching speeches, full of the true Tennysonian
melody. The history may be bad, the dramatic
quality, even of these three or four scenes, is none of
the highest—but the writing is exquisite. And to
this exquisite writing Mr Irving does ample, almost
perfect, justice. Oh, the difference between his
diction in *Becket* and in *Lear!* Here he gives us—
or at any rate gave us on the first night—clear-cut,
beautiful English speech in smooth-flowing, delicately-
cadenced, poetic periods. Many of his lines and
sequences of lines were a joy to the ear—one
regretted the evanescence of their charm. It is true
that Tennyson's blank verse, even in his plays, is not
dramatic in the fullest sense of the word, though he
sought diligently to make it so. It lacks impetus and
strength of wing; it is fragile, delicate, dreamy, rather
than vivid and vehement; it is not quite free from
some of the very undramatic mannerisms of the *Idylls*,
such as, for instance, the trick of chiming repetitions:

> "As when we dwell upon *a word we know*,
> Repeating, till *the word we know* so well
> Becomes a wonder, and *we know* not why."

But, after all said and done, it is quite sufficiently dramatic to present a fascinating problem to any actor with an ear for verse and a faculty for diction. In one way it is obviously suited to Mr Irving, for the very lack of impetus, the short-windedness, so to speak, which I have noted above, is the chief characteristic of his delivery. It might have been feared, however, that he would not succeed in imparting to it the smoothness and finish of phrasing without which it is naught; it might have been feared that he would seek to make it natural by making it spasmodic. But no such matter! Mr Irving shows himself acutely sensitive to the refinement and polish of the verse, delivering it with a smoothness I have never hitherto known him to attain. And let him not imagine that, because this beauty of diction is not consciously recognised by the majority of the audience, it is therefore a thing of no importance. Beauty is beauty, and ugliness is ugliness, however little we may think of analysing or docketing them; and because only a few members of an audience can put into words their sense of the presence or absence of a given quality in a performance, it by no means follows that the others do not *feel* it. If Mr Irving had *spoken* Lear, especially in the later scenes, as beautifully as he speaks Becket, we—well, we might have had longer to wait for this production.*

---

* *King Lear* was produced November 10, 1892.

An able critic, I see,* attributes Mr Irving's success
in Becket to the fact that it is a melodramatic part,
in which "the acting is of more importance than the
thing acted." This is, I think, unjust both to the
poet and the actor. They have co-operated, in the
strict sense of the word, in a character-creation of
remarkable beauty. It cannot, perhaps, be called
tragic, but melodramatic still less. How about
"poetic"? I think that is the word that meets the
occasion ; and, in the slang of the day, it is "good
enough for *me*."

Since Mr Terriss plays Henry, we need not be
inconsolable for the almost total excision of his great
speech in the Northampton scene—by far the finest
piece of rhetoric in the play. It is not Mr Terriss's
fault, but his misfortune, that Becket so entirely
dwarfs Henry, who was, in fact, at least his equal in
intellect and force of character. The same misfortune would befall almost any actor now on the
stage who had to play the Henry of Tennyson to the
Becket of Mr Irving. Miss Ellen Terry is graceful,
tender, and altogether charming as Rosamund, but
the character seems to me so futile and out of place,
that the greatest actress in the world could scarcely
bring it home to my sympathies. Miss Geneviève
Ward is the ideal Eleanor of tradition and of Tenny-

---

* In the *Pall Mall Gazette.*

son ; and of the minor characters, the most noteworthy are Herbert of Bosham and John of Oxford,
excellently played by Mr Haviland and Mr Ian
Robertson respectively.

At a charity performance at the Comedy Theatre
last week, a comedietta by Mrs Hugh Bell and Mr
Charles Brookfield, entitled *An Underground Journey*,*
was performed for the first time. It is a bright little
piece, full of that vivacious dialogue—one does not
quite know whether to call it witty or humorous—in
which Mrs Bell excels. Mr Cyril Maude and Miss
Fanny Brough were excellent as the Duke and the
Cook, who go through a whole tragedy of varied
emotions between Baker Street and South Kensington.

IX.

" DIPLOMACY "—" THE MASTER BUILDER "—
" FLIGHT."

22nd February.

AN evening of tumultuous enthusiasm, and—this is
not always the same thing—of real enjoyment, at the
Garrick on Saturday. It would be stretching a point
to say that *Diplomacy* † is quite all our fancy painted it
fifteen years ago,‡ when it seemed the very summit of

---

* February 9.

† February 18—July 14.   Reproduced November 2—December 16.   *See* Article XL.

‡ First produced in England, Prince of Wales's Theatre, Tottenham Street, January 12, 1878.

all possible dramatic achievement. We have since
then learnt to look for simpler, subtler, and (let me
add) more potent sensations in the theatre. But it
remains a well-made, thoroughly interesting play, in
which strongly-marked character and dexterous situation keep the audience unflaggingly amused. I don't
think a dramatist of to-day would venture to make
Dora quite so humbly and enthusiastically grateful
for Julian's magnanimity in offering to marry her;
and I doubt whether her outburst in the third act,
" Then why is he alive ? " would now be considered
an inspiration of genius. These, and a few other
touches, begin to " date " a little. But what then ?
It merely means that we have a dash of historical interest to eke out the dramatic excitement. It was a
joy to recognise Mrs Bancroft's voice and her crystal-
line laugh, both absolutely unimpaired, even before
she stepped on the stage. Her Lady Henry Fairfax
is an accomplished piece of comedy, and leads one to
hope that this reappearance will not be followed for
many years to come by another protracted disappear-
ance. There is a whole bevy of important characters
absolutely beckoning and calling aloud to Mrs Bancroft. Mr Bancroft's Orloff seemed to me a trifle too
deliberate, but was manly and affecting as ever, and
Mr Arthur Cecil's Baron Stein has lost nothing in
polish and humour. If Mr Clayton had succeeded
Mr Hare in the part of Henry Beauclerc, we should

probably have thought his performance lacking in
delicacy and incisiveness.   As it is Mr Hare who succeeds Mr Clayton, we are apt, in the same way, to
think him a little deficient in authority and colour.
No better Julian Beauclerc than Mr Forbes Robertson could possibly be desired ; and Miss Kate Rorke
and Miss Olga Nethersole as Dora and Zicka, fully
sustain the reputation of our younger generation of
actresses.   Lady Monckton, excellent artist though
she be, is a little too English for the Marquise de Rio
Zarès.   Miss Le Thière was absolutely the woman of
the part.   Mr Gilbert Hare made a bright and pleasant Algie Fairfax, and Miss Helen Luck proved herself one of the best soubrettes now on the stage.
Sum total—general congratulations on a well-deserved
success.

Before this article is in type, the most daring dramatic experiment, even of these experimental days,
will have been tried at the Trafalgar Square Theatre.
How *The Master Builder* will " go " with the British
public it is impossible to predict.   The dress rehearsal
—always a depressing function—has left me anything
but sanguine.   I have no doubt that, take it all round,
the play will be at least as ably presented as any of its
predecessors ; but would the finest acting in the world
induce an English audience to place itself at the right
point of view for the enjoyment of a drama which,
while realistic in form, is in essence as poetic, as

mystic, as fantastic, as *Faust*, or *Peer Gynt*, or *Prometheus Unbound?* A few hours will show ; and meanwhile, as *The Master Builder's* allotted span of life will be over before my next article appears, I may perhaps be allowed to put aside the question of its fitness for the stage, and to state briefly my own impressions of the play in itself.

" It is the great ambition of my life," a poet-dramatist once said to me (not a Scandinavian poet-dramatist, unless, as his Christian name suggests, he is descended from the Norse kings of Leinster)—" it is the great ambition of my life to write a really *obscure* poem." I tried, Socratically, to get at his conception of an obscure poem. Was there to be a real, definite meaning, swathed, as it were, in a veil of words ? Or was the poem to be all veil, with no meaning at all underlying it ? " That is just it ! " he cried, making arabesques in the air with his cigarette, " I would weave a veil so wonderful, so beautiful, so exquisitely wrought, that every one looking at it should say, ' Behind that veil lies MY secret ! ' " In conceiving *The Master Builder*, as it seems to me, Ibsen has been moved by some such ambition. He has set himself, not to enforce this doctrine or that—not even, as in *Hedda Gabler*, to lay bare the inmost fibres of a great type-character—but simply to stimulate our imagination with a work of vital art, in which, as in a fiery sunset, we shall each of us trace different dream-

forms, and read a different prognostic for the coming
day. Has he succeeded, then, in thus stimulating
the imagination? There is only one imagination for
which I can answer, but it, such as it is, responds
with no uncertain note. To my thinking, the story
of Solness and Hilda is the most haunting, the most
fascinating, ever conceived by this great Inventor. I
do not mean that the play is his greatest work; that
is a totally different matter. I mean simply what I
say, neither more nor less. With what consummate
art does he handle the machinery of hypnotism, that
incredible yet undeniable force, hovering (so conveniently for his purpose) over the border-line between
science and superstition! A lesser poet, if, by some
unthinkable chance, he had stumbled on the theme,
would have given us disquisitions (no doubt making
Dr Herdal his mouthpiece) on the possible and impossible in hypnotism, and would have sought to
rationalise the spectacle by showing precisely where
he conceived reality to end and hallucination to
begin. Not so Ibsen. Without apology, without
discussion, he goes straight to the limit of the conceivable, and relies upon our very scepticism as to
what may or may not be physically possible to make
us accept the situation which is poetically necessary.
And what a situation it is! A young girl, just at the
age when the wonder of the world is beginning to
dawn upon her, sees what appears to her childish

eyes an incredibly lofty tower soaring into the air
over the poor little church of her native village. She
is filled with admiration for the Master Builder who
is the informing spirit of so great a work ; and then,
on a sunlit holiday, when she herself and the whole
town are in festal array, she sees the Master Builder
standing forth against the sky, on the very pinnacle
of his own tower, while he hangs a wreath upon the
vane. Now it is a day of crisis in the Master
Builder's own life. He has just arrived at a great resolution ; and standing where he has never dared to
stand before, he communes inwardly with the Master
Builder of the universe, and vows that he will never
again build churches for the Power which has made
pain and devastation the condition of progress. Between Solness and Hilda, each tensely overwrought,
an occult sympathy establishes itself. The defiant
exultation in his mind is transmitted to hers, and
transmuted into music. She thinks she hears him
singing as he stands by the vane ; and it sounds to
her "like harps in the air." Then, the same evening,
he comes to her father's house, and finds her alone.
He recognises in her an imaginative, audacious,
queenly child, and, romancing as one does to a child,
promises to come back for her in ten years, carry her
off like a troll, and make her Princess of the
Kingdom of Orangeland. As they weave this
romance together, he becomes vaguely conscious of

the woman in the child.   It flashes through his mind,
" How if I were to take her in my arms, bend her
head back, and kiss her on the mouth ! "—and once
more the thought flashes, this time in the form of a
picture, from his mind to hers.   Looking back on
this wonderful half-hour with the hero of her imagination, Hilda very soon comes to believe that he actually did seal his promise of making her *his* Princess
by kissing her " many times."   After that evening
she sees him no more ; and he, unconscious of the
occult bond between them, forgets all about her.
She, on the other hand, hears of him from time to
time as the great architect of the day, and goes on
living in her romance.   She will not write to him lest
it should all " vanish away " ; but when the ten years
are up, in a mingled spirit of curiosity, adventure,
defiance, and devotion, she comes to claim " her
kingdom."   She is met, of course, by disillusionment.
Her Master Builder no longer stands free and great
at the summit of lofty towers of his own building.
As an artist, he is sunk in bourgeois materialism,
building towerless houses that are mere breeding-
places for crude humanity, and ruthlessly wrecking
the career of others in order to retain his supremacy
in this paltry craft.   As a man, he is battling ineffectu-
ally with a " sickly conscience," brooding over in-
soluble problems of human responsibility until his
brain reels on the verge of madness, and finding a

"salutary self-torture" in torturing his wife with reti-
cences and misunderstandings. His wife, physically
an invalid, suffers in mind and heart from atrophy of
the maternal instinct, which was the one strong force
of her narrow nature. She is a slave, moreover, to
the ideal of marriage and its "duties," and goes on
struggling to keep up the outward semblance of a
relation of which the soul is long since dead. Into
the dark recesses of these two hapless souls, Hilda's
keen eyes are not long in penetrating. ("There's
scarcely a corner in me safe from you," says Solness
at one point.) She is saddened, but not dispirited.
Her Master Builder shall stand free and great again.
She forces him to abandon his underhand tactics of
intriguing against "the younger generation," depressing their energies and barring the way for their ambitions. She continues to demand her kingdom ;
but her new insight into life, and especially her
glimpse into the desolation of Mrs Solness's soul, has
shown her that her kingdom cannot be of this world.
There is only one sure abiding-place for human happiness, and that she will build along with her Master
Builder. What is it ? Why, a dream, an ideal, a
"castle in the air" ; and in that castle she will dwell
with him, and look down from the topmost balcony
on the swarm below who are building churches and
"homes for human beings." But, by way of proving
the reality of his regeneration, her Master Builder is

to stand great and free once more at the top
of a high tower of his own building.   Infected
with her faith in him, he climbs to the pinnacle.
Once more he stands communing with the Master
Builder on high ; once more she hears " harps
in the air."   But, alas ! the real Master Builder
is not, and never was, the Master Builder of her
ideal.   He is only Halvard Solness with the
" dizzy conscience," and wedded to the ghost-
haunted past.   There, on the top of the poor little
stone - and - mortar tower, he is only, in Hilda's
eyes, laying the foundation of their castle in the
air—when lo ! he turns dizzy, he reels, he falls,
he is dashed to pieces on the common earth !   " I
can't see him up there now," says Hilda, too dazed
to realise what has happened.   " But he mounted
right to the top.   And I heard harps in the air.   *My*
—*my* Master Builder ! "

So ends the weird ironic tragedy.   In the
course of this brief analysis, I have tried to con-
vey, however vaguely, *my* interpretation of it, the
secret which the veil suggests to *me*.   I am far
from maintaining that it is *the* interpretation—the
only, the best, or even the most obvious.   Others
may divine subtler and profounder secrets behind
the veil.   All I dare assert is this—that whoever
looks at it with eyes unclouded by prejudice
(or by that cataract which the gods them-

selves* are powerless to remove) will find adumbrated, in strange and fascinating forms, some of the deepest facts of human life and destiny.

Mr Walter Frith's four-act play *Flight*,† produced at Terry's Theatre last week, is exceedingly improbable in motive and decidedly commonplace in treatment. It contains some pleasant enough writing, but does not at any point succeed in arousing our interest, much less in enchaining our belief. It has, too, this further disadvantage, that the part played by Mr Terry is entirely extraneous to the action. Mr Terry is amusing, however; Mr Murray Carson plays the villain with intense conviction, and Miss May Whitty is clever as the heroine. The first-night audience seemed to take to the play kindly enough, if without enthusiasm.

X.

"THE MASTER BUILDER."

Illustrated London News, 25th February.

THERE can be no doubt that we have made an extraordinary advance of late years in what may, perhaps, be called artistic open-mindedness. Who could have foreseen, five, three, even two years ago, that a play so fantastic in its atmosphere, so recondite

---

* " Mit der Dummheit kämpfen Götter selbst vergebens."
—Schiller, *Jungfrau von Orleans.*

† February 16—February 25.

in its symbolism, so daring in its technique, as *The Master Builder*,* would hold an English audience spellbound and would be received by the Press, not, certainly, with enthusiasm, but with decent courtesy and no more than reasonable indignation? I, for one, was far from foreseeing this result so lately as two months ago, when the completed play was in my hands. It had reached me, and I had read it, in driblets; and even under these unfavourable conditions I thought it one of the most fascinating things Ibsen had ever done. But as sheet after sheet arrived, and on glancing down the pages I saw nothing but "SOLNESS—HILDA—SOLNESS—HILDA" repeated to infinity—when I came to such lines as "What's all this nonsense you're talking about the crack in the chimney?" and Mrs Solness's threnody over her "nine lovely dolls" (the most beautiful touch in the whole poem, by-the-way)—my imagination shrank from picturing the reception of such a play in an English theatre. When I learned that Miss Elizabeth Robins intended to produce it, I almost besought her to hold her hand. I told her that she was courting certain disaster, and a disaster which would affect not only her own fortunes, but

---

* Performed at the Trafalgar Square Theatre on the afternoons from February 20 to February 24, and from February 27 to March 3. Reproduced at the Vaudeville (evening) March 6—March 25.

those of the whole progressive movement. It would throw things back, I urged, by several years, and undo much of what she herself and other artists had done for the emancipation of the stage. It seemed to me that this was a play of which the critics could sincerely allege what they had deceived themselves into asserting of *A Doll's House* and *Hedda Gabler*—to wit, that it bored them. Nora and Hedda, I am convinced, do not really bore any one of average intelligence. They affect many people more or less unpleasantly, and this unpleasant sensation they describe, in a rough-and-ready fashion, as boredom, whereas in reality it is something entirely different. But *The Master Builder*, I feared, would really and seriously bore as well as bewilder the average audience; and as the progressive movement is, in my conception, nothing but a campaign *against* boredom in the theatre, I would fain, had it been in my power, have kept the play off the stage altogether. The event of this week has proved that Miss Robins was right and I wrong. I did not foresee the intense vitality of her Hilda, which enchained every eye and every mind throughout the longest scenes; I did not foresee the mingled power and discretion of Mr Herbert Waring, who attacked the most dangerous passages with unfailing firmness of grip; and least of all did I foresee the aforesaid open-mindedness on the part of the audience, the evident sincerity of their desire to place themselves at the right point of view. What one chiefly felt, oddly enough, was not that they laughed in the wrong places, but that they sometimes did not laugh, or laughed in a wrong spirit, in the right places. The doll speech was the one point where laughter was very distinctly out of place, and there it was quite inevitable, and by no means so hostile in tone as one had anticipated.* When the play was

---

* The following letter explains itself :—

" *To the Editor of 'The Westminster Gazette.'*

"SIR,—As nothing in *The Master Builder* has exercised the minds of the critics and the public so much as Mrs Solness's 'nine lovely dolls,' you will perhaps allow me to put on record a little incident connected with them which strikes me as curious. At a recent first-night, I happened to be seated just behind a well-known critic. He turned round to me, and said, ' I want you to tell me what is *your* theory of those "nine lovely dolls." Of course one can see that they're entirely symbolical.' ' I'm not so sure of that,' I replied, remembering a Norwegian cousin of my own who treasured a favourite doll until she was nearer thirty than twenty, and may do so, for aught I know, to this day. 'They, of course, "symbolise" the unsatisfied passion of motherhood in Mrs Solness's heart ; but I have very little doubt that Ibsen makes use of this "symbol" because he has observed a similar case, or cases, in real life.' 'What !' cried the critic. ' He has seen a grown-up, a middle-aged, woman continuing to "live with" her dolls !' I was about to say that it did not seem to me so very improbable, when a lady who was seated next me, a total stranger to both of us, leant forward and said, 'Excuse my interrupting you, but it may perhaps interest you to know that *I have three dolls to which I am deeply attached !*' I will not be so rude as to conjecture this

produced in Berlin, this passage (which contains the whole key to Mrs Solness's character, and initiates a totally new phase of feeling in Hilda) was carefully excised! None the less—or all the more—the production failed. In London, not a single word was "cut" that had any special value or intention in it; and anti-Ibsenites joined with Ibsenites in applauding, if not the play, at least the artistic courage and skill of its interpreters. Moral : In dealing with Ibsen, the path of daring is the path of safety.

One critic—certainly not the least able of those who have dealt with the production—alleges as a defect in the play that "the most practised playgoer would fail to make a correct forecast from scene to scene of the workings of its cloudy and word-laden plot." This hasty postulate that the dramatist's invention ought never to outrun that of the "practised

---

lady's age ; but we may be sure that a *very* young woman would not have had the courage to make such an avowal. Does it not seem that Ibsen knows a thing or two about human nature— English as well as Norwegian—which we dramatic critics, though bound by our calling to be subtle psychologists, have not yet fathomed ?—I am, Sir, your obedient servant,

"WILLIAM ARCHER.

" *March* 6."

In the course of a curious little correspondence which followed, one or two other instances of the same nature were brought to light. It appears, by the way, that Her Majesty the Queen is one of the ladies who have treasured their "lovely dolls." A book has been written about the royal *Dukkehjem*.

playgoer," forecasting on the spur of the moment,
is surely not one that the critic would stand to at his
leisure. And, apparently because the thoughts and
actions of the characters baffle his previsions, this
writer joins in the general cry of "Mad, mad, mad!"
But *are* Solness, Mrs Solness, and Hilda so very mad
as all that? The poet obviously does not present
Solness and his wife as persons of perfectly normal
mind; and, unless he alone is to be denied a right
which all other dramatists have exercised from time
immemorial, we cannot complain of his choosing
subjects from the sphere of mental pathology. But
if they are madder than he intends—if he has failed
to realise how far their thoughts and actions depart
from the normal standard—then he has clearly
committed an artistic error, and the excuse of
"symbolism" will avail him nothing. But, again I
ask, *are* they so very mad? Need we go so far as
Norway to find men who feel themselves goaded as
though by a demon—or, in Ibsen's phrase, a troll—to
pursue success at any price, to the destruction of their
competitors, to the ruin of their own domestic
happiness? And is it so inconceivable, is it so
insane, that such men should bitterly resent the
action of the very forces which they are powerless
to resist, and to which they owe their outward
"happiness"? Again, are there no women abroad in
our everyday world who suffer from the warping, the

stunting, of their most potent instincts ? Are there no
women who feel the small sorrows of life even more
than the great, and mourn less for a child whom they
believe to be in heaven than for some dumb pet or
inanimate plaything, the loss of which they cannot
openly bewail for fear of unsympathetic ridicule ?
Solness's conscience, Mrs Solness's heart, are both of
them " sickly "; but I fail to see that their sickli-
ness is either acute enough or uncommon enough to
rank as insanity. As for Hilda, the trouble with her
is surely that she is so radiantly, unscrupulously,
immorally sane. Her relation to Solness rests, no
doubt, upon an occult basis ; but hypnotic influence
is a postulate to which no one can well deny imaginative, if not absolute, assent ; and there is not the
least reason for considering hypnotic sensibility a
symptom of madness. Her descent upon Solness is
not the action of an ordinary, everyday young lady ;
but, even disregarding the element of hypnotism, is
there anything inconceivable, anything insane in it ?
The whole conception of the character is poetical—
granted ; but to what a pass has criticism come if all
that transcends the most ordinary everyday probability
is to be denounced as insane! I shall be told, no
doubt, that there is no more magic virtue in the word
" poetic " than in the words " symbolic " or " allegoric,"
and that a dramatist cannot escape from the laws of
his craft by calling his extravagances " poetic." But

that is precisely where I venture to join issue with the great body of the critics.   I say that a dramatist has a perfect right to produce a great poem even under the guise of a prose play.   It is obvious that he thereby exposes himself to misunderstanding, and I don't say that he has any great right to complain if his critics fail, at first glance, to find the right point of view.   But if *The Master Builder* has anything like the vitality it seems to me to possess, the time will come when many who can now see nothing but madness in it will readjust their mental attitude and find in it, not certainly a realistic play, but a noble and intensely dramatic poem.

XI.

"THE STRIKE AT ARLINGFORD."

1st March.

In dealing with Mr George Moore's first play * (not, let us hope, his last), I propose to ignore altogether the somewhat ludicrous circumstances of its origin. Mr George R. Sims has done exceedingly well in contributing £100 to the exchequer of the Independent Theatre; but there was not the slightest reason for giving his timely donation the form of a challenge to Mr George Moore.   Mr Sims, as I understand the matter, felt that the Independent

---

* Opera Comique, February 21.

Theatre was of small practical service so long as it
confined its attention entirely to works of foreign
origin. This was a plausible, one may almost say
an incontrovertible, opinion ; and Mr Sims could
not have backed it in a more generous and effective
fashion than by offering to contribute handsomely
towards the expense of producing an original English
play. But there was no reason whatsoever why he
should have challenged Mr Moore to write that
play. Mr Moore happened to be, at the time of
the challenge, concerned in the management of the
enterprise, but that fact laid him under no obligation to prove his skill as a playwright. It is not a
manager's business to write plays, but to select and
stage them. Mr Moore's success or failure could
prove nothing more than the success or failure of
any other writer, either for or against the usefulness
of the Independent Theatre. Mr Sims might as
well have challenged Sir Augustus Harris to compose
a grand opera. The challenge no doubt pricked the
lagging sides of Mr Moore's intent, and in so far it
did good service ; but it proceeded none the less
on a false logical basis. Therefore, as aforesaid, I
shall not waste time in considering whether Mr
Moore's play is sufficiently "unconventional" to
fulfil the conditions of the wager. Its unconventionality has, of course, been denied on all hands
— that was inevitable under the circumstances.

There never was a play in this world in which, with
a little ill-will, a hostile critic could not discover
conventionality. What we have really to inquire is
whether Mr Moore's work is intelligent and interesting enough to justify the existence of the Independent Theatre as a mechanism for its production
—whether, in other words, the subscribers to that
institution got their money's worth last Tuesday
evening? I hold emphatically that they did. *The
Strike at Arlingford*, like *Widowers' Houses*, is a very
remarkable dramatic experiment. It cannot fail to
entertain and interest one or two select audiences,
but it is not entirely suited (though much more nearly
so than Mr Shaw's play) to the ordinary commercial
stage. Who can doubt that it is in the highest
degree desirable that we should possess a mechanism
for the production of such works? Mr Sims, I am
sure, cannot but feel that his £100 has been well
expended in supporting and consolidating such an
institution.

Wager or no wager, then, what of the play? I
propose to speak my mind with great, I may almost
say with unusual, frankness, because it seems to me
that the majority of my colleagues have most unjustly
apportioned, as between author and actors, the responsibility for the comparative failure of the first
night. *The Strike at Arlingford* is, to my thinking,
a play with an excellent motive, worked out with an

occasional uncertainty of touch, but on the whole
very ably—and ruined, defaced, massacred by the
most unfortunate acting conceivable. I hasten to
make an exception in favour of Mr Charles Fulton,
who, admirably made up, played like the intelligent,
capable actor he always is. Miss Elsie Chester, too,
showed some ability, but was physically unsuited to
the character assigned her. The main fault lay with
Mr Bernard Gould and Miss Florence West. Miss
West lacked subtlety, seductiveness, distinction; Mr
Gould lacked—well, except a romantic, Vandyke-like
head and face, he lacked everything, everything. I
have no doubt that he was hampered on the night
of the first performance by natural and temporary
nervousness. No one would have been more willing
than I to make allowance for Mr Gould, if other
critics, recognising the inadequacy of his performance, had on that ground made allowance for Mr
Moore. But the assertion that the play was bad
and the acting good is too monstrous a perversion
of the truth to be allowed to pass without emphatic
protest. The whole performance suffered from a
total lack of grip. It never for a moment seized
or held the audience. Not one of the lines at
which the somewhat captious gallery jeered but
could easily have been saved by actors of authority
and tact. Even *Widowers' Houses* was less fatally
misrepresented.

Until I have had an opportunity of either reading
the play or seeing it more adequately acted, I can
form but an imperfect and provisional estimate of its
merits and defects.*   The subject is certainly admirable—none the less so because it can be stated in
half-a-dozen lines.   What can be more truly dramatic
than the dilemma in which John Reid is placed?
He is convinced — sincerely and profoundly convinced—that the continuance of the strike is hopeless and, for the workers, suicidal ; yet his conviction
so obviously runs parallel, as it were, with his re-
awakened passion for Lady Anne, that he feels
himself a traitor in yielding to it, and knows that
when the facts come out he will be so regarded by
all the world, and will probably pay the penalty with
his life.   If this is not a dramatic, a tragic, conjuncture, I know not where to look for one.   It
has the large simplicity of really great drama, and
Mr Moore, in conceiving it, has shown the truest
instinct for the art he is for the first time essaying.

* The play has since been published (by Mr Walter Scott),
but, to my regret, I find nothing very definite to add to this
qualified and hesitating judgment.   It would be easy to point
out faults of detail, but they are neither numerous nor important
enough to account for the comparatively feeble hold which the
play takes upon our imagination and our sympathies.   To say
that it is deficient in "dramatic fibre" is simply to confess one's
inability to formulate any definite or helpful criticism.   But,
whatever its faults, they certainly ought not to deter Mr Moore
from perfecting his unmistakable gifts in the direction of drama.

There are certainly weak points in the working out of
the theme—who ever wrote a perfect play at his first
attempt?—but along with the weak points there are
many touches which seem to me to show a genuine
sense of scenic effect. I am credibly assured that
Mr Moore's sociology is all wrong, that he has con-
founded socialism with trades-unionism, muddled up
two different classes of capitalists, and thereby earned
the pronounced disesteem of the Fabian Society.
Even in my ignorance, I was not without an inkling
that something was amiss. To the veriest outsider
the business of "looking into the books" is unconvincing, and—I may be wrong—but I should think
a rise of twenty per cent. at a single jump must be a
somewhat exceptional demand. All this, however,
matters comparatively little. It would be better, of
course, that the sociology should be correct as well;
but if the human nature is correct that is the main
point. There is, at a low estimate, ten times more
flesh and blood in Mr Moore's play than in a certain
entertaining production of unimpeachable Fabianism
but doubtful humanity, which has already been more
than once alluded to in this article.

XII.

"ALEXANDRA"—"THE IRONMASTER."

8th March.

MR and Mrs Charrington have opened their new

enterprise at the Royalty Theatre—an enterprise which ought to command the sympathy of all who believe that dramatic art is not necessarily a mere profit-grinding machine—with an adaptation from the German of Richard Voss, entitled *Alexandra*.* The adaptor's name is unknown to me—it is a secret which has been better kept than most theatrical secrets—but I am sure he ought not to have been an adaptor, but a translator.   Mr Charrington will doubtless remind me that when I read the German play some months ago, I said it was a play rather for adaptation than translation.   Well, I was mistaken—or rather I expressed my meaning imperfectly.   I meant that the play was not one of those great and, so to speak, inevitable works of art in which any alteration means deformation.   There are writers whose very mistakes, if we may call them so, are more interesting than the happiest inspirations of lesser men—writers whose works appeal to us, not as mere additions to the common stock of dramatic material, but as manifestations of their own individual spirit.   We want to hear what these writers wrote, be it good, bad, or indifferent, and do not care in the least to know what this or that theatrical craftsman, be he never so judicious, thinks that they might, could, would, or should have written.   But Richard Voss, with all

* March 4—March 11.

his talent, is certainly not one of these master-spirits.
He invents characters and situations which have a
particular value for a particular public, and may, without irreverence or loss, be modified in order to suit
the requirements, to appeal to the sympathies, to
come home to the comprehension, of a different
public. *Alexandra*—this is what I meant—might
with advantage have been rewritten with a view to
relieving the high pressure of German sentiment,
which is a trifle exhausting to our more ironic, or, if
you prefer it, more frivolous, habit of mind. I did
not for a moment mean that a play so inherently,
essentially German should be violently uprooted from
its native soil and transplanted to England. That is
the very thing the adaptor has done. He has followed
his original very closely, doing nothing to Anglicise
the tone of sentiment; but he has Anglicised the
names of the characters, and so given us the trouble
of, as it were, retranslating the play into German, if
we are to accept it for a moment as a possible picture
of life. We feel from first to last that these are not
English men and women, that things do not happen
in this way either at Bradley's Hotel, Sackville Street,
or at Knowlesford Abbey, Cumberland. We must
mentally transport Bradley's Hotel to Unter den
Linden, and Knowlesford Abbey to Thuringia or
Franconia, before we can give even provisional cre-
dence to the events and emotions depicted. It is a

pity that we should be put to this trouble ; but when once the retransference is effected, the drama is un-deniably interesting, were it only for the sake of Miss Achurch's original and striking performance of the heroine.

Richard Voss is a dramatist who deals in emotions *en gros*, not *en détail*. The great elemental passions are his theme, and that, too, in their elemental sim-plicity. He knows nothing and cares nothing about their modifications, their ramifications, their perver-sions. His psychology is of quite primitive orthodoxy ; heterodoxy he dreams not of, and he is no more capable of paradox than the Great Pyramid of turn-ing a somersault. In a word, his art is devoid of the two main factors of the higher modern drama—analysis and irony. He presents us with a passion, takes its nature and quality for granted as things of common knowledge, and shows us its workings under a given set of circumstances. In *Alexandra*, the two passions chiefly involved are revenge and maternal love, both presented on a heroic, an ideal scale. Now the passion of revenge, as I have before stated more than once—notably, I remember, with reference to *Esther Sandraz*—is one that interests me but moderately. It is, to my thinking, something of an anachronism. Far be it from me to deny that malice, hatred, spite, and the spirit of retaliation are, and will be until the millennium, among the most active

forces in human nature. But most people, I think,
are coming to recognise that life is too short for
deliberate, elaborate, cold-drawn revenge. They will
hit back when they conveniently can ; they will
cherish for half a lifetime a passive, an obstructive,
ill-will ; they will even wait patiently for years for
an opportunity of " getting their knife into " an enemy.
But they have grown chary of " cutting off their nose
to spite their face " ; they will very rarely sacrifice
their own comfort in life to the mere joy of protracted,
elaborate reprisals. Vitriol and the revolver—an outburst of rage, culminating in a " short, sharp shock "
—these belong, if you will, to modern life. But long-
drawn, unhasting, unresting machination, with no end
in view beyond an ultimate unmasking, a turning of
the tables—in a word, a strong situation—this, I take
it, belongs, if not exclusively to the stage, at least to
a phase of existence more leisurely than ours. If Dr
Voss had shown Alexandra's thirst for revenge to be
nothing but lingering love in disguise, and prevented
by pride from throwing off its mask, I should have
felt her to be more human. Perhaps this, or something like this, may have been his intention ; but in
that case he has failed to make it clear. So far as I
can gather the process of emotion in the third and
fourth acts, Alexandra's vengefulness, perfectly genuine
in the beginning, weakens and falters in presence of
Lady Knowlesford's kindness and sincere desire to

do justice; then, on Eric's return, the old love flares up again all of a sudden; and finally, the inhumanity of Alexandra's earlier feeling is punished by her falling a victim herself to the revelation with which she had intended to crush Eric. We have here, as you see, a strong drama of an old-fashioned and somewhat crude pattern. It is saved from commonplaceness chiefly by a certain largeness and simplicity of hand-ling, an absence of tricky or mechanical sensation, and, in the dialogue, a peculiar combination of vigour with sobriety.

The whole performance was taken, it seemed to me, in an unnecessarily low and monotonous key. There was an artistic idea in this, but it was carried too far. At the risk of seeming to call for staginess, I would counsel Mr Charrington to make his company "play up" a little more, and get a greater crispness and brilliancy of effect out of the chief situations and the more important lines. Under-emphasis is as injudicious, if not as offensive, as over-emphasis. Miss Achurch, in the part of Alexandra, once more proved that in inborn capacity for dramatic expression she is inferior to no actress now on the stage. Beauty and mobility of face, dignity of carriage, strength and suppleness of plastik, sincerity and intensity of emotion —all these qualities she possesses in an extraordinary degree. What she chiefly lacks is *ear*. She does not hear her own voice. She does not know when her tones are (as they often are) convincingly natural and true, and when, on the other hand, they are false, artificial, and mannered. In some characters, too, she lacks artistic self-restraint ; but of that defect there is no trace in Alexandra. On the contrary, it is throughout a study, and a very able one, in repressed emotion ; and the morbid, unnatural tension of the character rendered the unnatural pitch of voice, where it came in, less regrettable than usual. It may even be said to have contributed to the peculiar, weird effect produced by the performance as a whole. Nothing, however, can justify Miss Achurch's habit of occasionally neglecting all natural punctuation or phrasing, and running totally unconnected clauses and sentences into one : for example, " Have-you-always-had-peace-aha-there's-Anthony-I-want-to-see-him." This is a very common, and, to the non-professional mind, a totally incomprehensible mannerism. Even if it were effective, which it isn't, an artist like Miss Achurch should be above such irrational effects of mere peculiarity. Mrs Theodore Wright played the blind mother with that tender and dignified simplicity which is her chief quality, and Mr Herbert Flemming, as her son, was manly and sincere, if not quite the romantic hero of Voss's imagination. Mr Charrington threw a great deal of conviction and intensity into the part of the half-witted Anthony Watt ; but is it necessary that he should be quite so

crazy as the English adaptor and actor make him?
In the original, so far as I remember it, he is not
mad at all, except with repressed passion and hatred ;
and this has at least the advantage of making him
conceivable as a gentleman's servant.   Mr Maurice
was good as the Socialist Q.C., and the performance
went well as a whole.   The mounting was excellent,
considering the small size of the stage, the last scene
in particular being of unusual beauty.   Its snow-
white decoration formed a perfect background for
Alexandra's magnificent costume, to the description
of which my masculine vocabulary is pitifully inadequate.   Miss Achurch's appearance, no less than
her acting in this scene, will long be remembered by
all who saw it.

One cannot with impunity play so shallow and
empty a character as Claire in *The Ironmaster** for
untold hundreds of nights on both sides of the world.
The part never was worthy of Mrs Kendal's talent,
and her performance of it is not now even what it
once was.   It has become deplorably mechanical.
And what a play !   And what a pity to see so excellent a comedian as Mr Kendal throwing himself
away upon such poor and vulgar French heroics !
The revival produced a quite depressing effect on
the first night ; but I daresay there are plenty of

* Avenue Theatre, March 2—April 14.

simple-minded playgoers in London for whom the sentiment and distinction of M. Ohnet have not yet lost their charm.

XIII.

"THE AMAZONS"—"A DOLL'S HOUSE."

15th March.

AN amateur elocutionist of my acquaintance once gave a public reading at which he impersonated Horatius, Mary Queen of Scots, and other worthies, in a pair of white cotton gloves several sizes too large for him, the superfluous finger-tips waving in the wind like the flags that so distracted Master Builder Solness. At the close of the entertainment, the reciter executed a rapid flank movement, stationed himself at the one door of exit from the hall, and insisted on shaking hands with each member of the audience as he or she passed out, and asking : "Have you enjoyed yourself ?" If Mr Pinero had administered this interrogatory to us as we left the Court Theatre after *The Amazons*,* I am sure we could all have answered in the affirmative with perfect sincerity ; but there the conversation would have been apt to flag. I know few plays—certainly none of Mr Pinero's —that call for so little comment. It is vivacious and amusing, it whiles away the evening pleasantly

---

* March 7—July 8.

enough,—and there is practically no more to be said.
Further remark must be entirely negative. It is easy
to point out several things which Mr Pinero has *not*
done. He has not adhered to his old farce-formula
of dignity in difficulties ; it was probably wise to give
us a change. He has not put himself to any expense
of invention, but has produced as plotless and situa-
tionless a play as is humanly possible. That would
be, to my thinking, a merit in a comedy of observation and character ; and even in *The Amazons* it cannot be called a defect, since plot or no plot, situation
or no situation, the play fulfils its purpose of keeping
us amused. Furthermore, Mr Pinero has made no
attempt to play the moralist or the satirist—"contrari-
wise," as Tweedledee would say. He has sedulously
avoided all criticism of life. It must have cost him
no small pains to treat such a subject without con-
veying so much as a hint of his own feeling as to
what is compendiously denominated "the woman
question." All we can possibly learn from *The
Amazons* is that, whatever the cut of their nether
garments, men are men and girls are girls—a proposi-
tion which even that Penthesilea among the Amazons,
the authoress of *The Heavenly Twins*, is not understood to controvert. The same moral is conveyed
by the legend of Achilles in Scyros, by *As You Like
It, Charley's Aunt*, and other classics. Here again
I sincerely applaud Mr Pinero's discretion. Stage

satire is fated to be reactionary, and most people are probably as sick as I am of the stock pleasantries on female emancipation. Mr Pinero's former treatment of the theme on the same boards—in *The Weaker Sex*—was not one of his stronger efforts. Lastly—to come to an end of negations—he has not striven after any great novelty or originality of comic "business." The topics of his humour are sufficiently familiar : boastful cowardice (in two editions), the Frenchman who has shot a fox, and who expresses enthusiasm by crying "Splendid, magnificent, pretty good!" the fierce bull, the carelessly-pointed gun, torn garments, blackened eyes, stumbling over furniture in a dark room, kissing the chambermaid, the interrupted orgie, and so forth. "Why grumble," you ask, "so long as these things make us laugh?" But do we really laugh at these things? If they were not served up with a plentiful seasoning of Mr Pinero's peculiar and original fantasy, should we not find them dismal in the extreme? It is all a question of proportion. A certain quantity of genuine Pinero will serve to float, as it were, a certain bulk of inert matter from the common stock of farce. In *The Amazons* this proportion is nicely observed. But Mr Pinero would do well to take note, I think, that a very little more of the latter element, and a very little less of the former, might easily have led to disaster.

But when all is said and done, *The Amazons* re-

mains a harmlessly-amusing play, such as only Mr
Pinero could have written. It is very hard to note
the limitations of a work of art without appearing to
complain of them ; but that was really not at all my
purpose. I would particularly disclaim any ironic
sub-intention in the remark that the play presents no
criticism of life. An author has a perfect right to indulge, if he pleases, in mere graceful, purposeless
fooling, without a shade of serious meaning to it.
Farce is, in my estimation, an admirable and valuable
art-form, simply because it admits of every gradation
of thoughtfulness or thoughtlessness—it may be pregnant with observation and meaning, or empty of the
smallest intention or pretension, beyond that of filling
up an idle hour with irresponsible laughter. Mr
Pinero has set himself the latter task, and has succeeded. We are his debtors for two good hours of
refreshing merriment ; it is rank ingratitude to complain because we do not carry away any new knowledge of life or food for reflection. As well call a
man a niggard entertainer because, though he gives
us an excellent dinner, there is nothing on the table
which we can conveniently pocket, and live on for the
next week or so.

The play is capitally acted by one of the good-all-
round companies which Mr Pinero has the knack of
organising. Mr Fred Kerr is excellent in a part
which fits him like a glove. Mr Weedon Grossmith

and Mr Elliott are very amusing ; and Mr Beauchamp makes the most of a small part. Nothing could be better than Miss Rose Leclerq's performance of the Spartan mother of "the boys"; and these young gentlemen are represented with grace, humour, and delicacy, by Miss Lily Hanbury, Miss Ellaline Terriss, and Miss Pattie Browne.

Though we all know—or, if we don't, it is not for lack of reiterated assurances on the point — that "Ibsen is played out," that "the craze" or "the cult" has "come to an end," that "the public will not have Ibsen at any price," * and so forth, it somehow or other happens that two plays of Ibsen's are being performed simultaneously at two West End theatres every evening of this week. It is true that both *A Doll's House* at the Royalty and *The Master Builder* at the Vaudeville, are serving, more or less, as stop-gaps ; but managers do not even stop gaps with plays in which there is no attraction, which "the public will not have at any price." *A Doll's House* drew a large audience last Saturday afternoon,† and

---

* After the first performance of *A Doll's House* in 1889 it was confidently announced that "the Ibsen bubble had burst," that we had heard the last of Ibsen ; and the same assurance has been repeated with no less conviction after every Ibsen production. See an article by the present writer, entitled "The Mausoleum of Ibsen," in *The Fortnightly Review* for July 1893.

† March 11. It was placed in the evening bill, March 13, and ran until March 25 (afternoon).

went very well.   Miss Achurch's Nora is greatly improved—as compared, I mean, not with the first
Nora of the Novelty Theatre,* but with the second
Nora of the Avenue.   This third Nora is much like
the first, and, if not so evenly excellent, is instinct
with life and full of beautiful and moving touches.
Miss Carlotta Addison made a very pleasant Mrs
Linden, and Mr W. R. Staveley, though suffering
from insufficient preparation, seemed to have by no
means a bad idea of the part of Dr Rank.   Mr Charrington and Mr Herbert Flemming resumed their
former parts of Helmer and Krogstad.

XIV.

" MAN AND WOMAN."

29th March.

THE American public seems to be blessed with a
robust appetite.   " Make the gruel thick and slab "
is certainly the motto on which Messrs De Mille
and Belasco have acted in compounding their four-
act drama *Man and Woman*,† produced on Satur-

---

* Where the play was produced for the first time in England,
June 7 to June 29, 1889, Miss Achurch playing Nora; Mr
Herbert Waring, Helmer; Mr Charrington, Rank; and Mr
Royce Carleton, Krogstad.   It was revived at the Avenue on the
return of Miss Achurch from Australia, April 19, 1892.

† March 5—April 22.

day night, under Miss Amy Roselle's management, at the Opera Comique. They have not—
they do not seek to have—"a light hand" either
in pathos or in humour, which they serve up in
alternate layers of somewhat stodgy quality. Their
humour, to tell the truth, is very ineffectual, and
ought to be reduced within the narrowest possible
limits. The serious interest of the play, on the other
hand, is really strong, and is, in the third act, worked
up to a scene of great and sustained power, which
ought to become popular. Its elements are commonplace enough, but they are combined with skill and
originality into a singularly telling series of situations.
The fourth act, re-written by Mr Malcolm Watson, is
so much less pompous than the rest that one feels it
would be judicious, even now, to let Mr Watson
"work over" the other acts, and especially re-write the
Autobiography of Governor Rodman, of Arizona,
which is intolerably orotund. The cast is large, and
on the whole efficient. Miss Amy Roselle showed
great strength and sincerity in the part of the heroine ;
Mr Arthur Elwood was quite admirable as a financial
magnate ; Mr W. T. Lovell played a wrongfully
accused cashier with spirit and discretion ; and Messrs
Henry Neville, Arthur Dacre, Charles Fulton, and
Sant Matthews were all good in their several ways.
The comic business was in the hands of Mr Sam
Sothern and Mr Herbert Standing ; and Miss Eva

Moore and Miss Lena Ashwell were pleasant in subordinate parts.

XV.

"THE BABBLE SHOP."

5th April.

I DON'T think even George Eliot would accuse Mr Edward Rose of "debasing the moral currency" in parodying *The Bauble Shop*. Produced at the Trafalgar Square Theatre on Thursday evening, his travesty, *The Babble Shop*,* was received with shouts of laughter. It suffers a little, perhaps, from a lack of fundamental idea, but it is full of ingenious and witty details, and passes its allotted hour merrily enough. Mr Arthur Playfair, as Lord Wyndhamere, is, of course, the life and soul of the performance. His mimicry is perfect, down to the minutest touch, and is sustained to the end with remarkable success. I confess to an unholy passion for good mimicry. "Sir," said Dr Johnson, "it is not a talent, but a vice"; to which I can only reply, like Leech's cabman, that "I wishes I 'ad 'arf" of Mr Playfair's vice. Almost as good, in a smaller way, as Mr Playfair's Wyndhamere, was Mr J. Willes's imitation of Mr W. H. Day in the character of "Caleb Plummer (gone wrong)." Mr

* March 30—April 15.

Garden's Stodge, M.P., was amusing, and Mr Cyril
Maude's Old Sarum, though not very happy as
mimicry, was a clever piece of burlesque acting. The
ladies of the cast have small opportunities—too small,
I think. The part of the phonographic doll ought
certainly to be developed.

XVI.

"THE BLACK DOMINO"—"UNCLE JOHN"— "CLEVER ALICE."

12th April.

WE "indolent reviewers," on sitting down to write for
the five-hundredth time the regulation platitudes about
such plays as *The Black Domino* * and *Uncle John*,†
are apt to feel a pang of self-pity, and to rebel against
the hard fate which allots such mechanical and soul-
less tasks to men of our fine and penetrating genius.
A little reflection should convince us of the unreason-
ableness, nay, the impiety, of such a feeling. A bene-
ficent Providence, as we all ought to know, has so
ordered this world that whenever we find our own lot
unhappy, we need only look around to see some one
still more miserable ; whereupon the well-ordered
mind takes comfort, and, like Peer Gynt when the

---

* Adelphi, April 1—May 27.
† Vaudeville, April 3—April 22.

yacht blew up, enjoys a sense of special favour and protection. For my part, I am proud to say, my days are " bound each to each by natural piety." If it irks me a little to give serious thought to this play or that, I have only to reflect, " What if you had not merely to write *about* it, but to *write* it ! " and I can once more gaze serenely upon the best of all possible worlds. Just imagine the life of men like Messrs Sims, Buchanan, and Raleigh—men of intelligence, wit, humour, and one of them, at any rate, a man of true poetic and literary faculty. Think of such men getting up in the morning and looking forward to their day's labour ! Hear Mr Sims, for instance : " What is my tale of work to-day ? " he says : " Shall I do the scene between the villain and the comic money-lender ? Or is it to be the villain making love to the heroine and luring the hero on to forgery ? Or shall I try, for a change, the reprobate father, who has 'gone a mucker' over the St Leger, blandly coercing his daughter into marrying the man she does not love ? No, I'm feeling too hipped for sentiment —I'll tackle the funny scene between Miss Jecks and Mr Dale, and I'll land the comic money-lender in a fancy dress at Bow Street." Take Mr Buchanan, again, and conceive his feelings at the prospect of bringing the adventuress back to her father's lowly cot beside the church porch, at the very moment when the man who has deserted her is leading his

aristocratic and virtuous bride to the altar! Fancy
him diverting his mind from soaring meditations on
world-historic themes in order to write up the adventuress's malignity at the masquerade ball, or her
penitence over a flower-stall in Covent Garden! As
for Mr Raleigh, that embodiment of ironic common-
sense, it almost brings the tears to my eyes as I
think of him saying to himself over his matutinal
coffee: "How *am* I to give a middle-aged York-
shire manufacturer the smallest conceivable reason
for paying clandestine but strictly honourable visits
to his butler's daughter? And is it possible to get
even a Vaudeville audience to believe that any hero
and heroine out of Bedlam would act as ours must
if we are to get a third act out of our subject?"
How utterly and dismally stale and childish it must
all be to these martyrs to popular amusement! Can
we not hear them asking themselves at each scene, at
each line, "How often have I written all this before?
How often have other men written it before I was
born? And will others, again, go on writing it
when I am dead, 'over again, and over again, and
over again for ever'?" The reason why such plays
are always produced in collaboration is obvious
enough. One man, settling himself down solemnly
to plod over the old, old road, would inevitably go
melancholy mad. Two, on the other hand, can
beguile the way with jape and jest, quillet and

quiddity. Even melodramatising has its humorous side, and two can appreciate it together. The smile of the solitary augur must be a mournful grimace; but when two can enjoy the joke in common, when the twinkle in one eye is sympathetically reflected in another, the sense of human companionship must be inexpressibly soothing. It is said, I hope with truth, that the pecuniary rewards of such toil are princely. There are some people who would not undertake the labour of a hodman even at the salary of a prince; but that, I admit, is probably because they could not. No doubt, if I had it in me, I should convert myself into an automatic machine with the inscription, "Put a thousand-pound note in the slot, take out the melodrama, and replace the drawer." But as my internal works are not adapted for such an industry, I am under no temptation to essay it.

A. B. W., I see, is concerned as to the immorality of *The Black Domino*, and thinks he descries in it a serious danger to the stage. Perhaps he is right. For my part, I have given up trying to understand the incoherent jumble of irrationalities which passes for a moral code with the Censor, the main body of the critics, and the great public. They draw such a zigzag and elusive line, that one never knows whether one is on the side of the devils or of the angels, and by-and-by one ceases to care. It is certain that the man who thrashes the villain in *The Black Domino*, and who may therefore be presumed to stand for the hero, is an abject and contemptible criminal and cur; but I am not at all sure that the snivelling and vicious hero of melodrama is one whit more harmful than the swaggering and virtuous ditto, and I am quite sure that to me he is less offensive. The radical falsity of this whole class of plays is in its very essence immoral; but Lord Dashwood has at least this advantage over the intolerable "bounders" who have preceded him, that he is not held up as a model for imitation. On the other hand, I unreservedly believe with A. B. W. that melodrama has of recent years done actual and wanton mischief in pandering to the popular mania for the Turf, and feeding its devotees upon ideals of life and conduct about on a par with those of the gallant sportsman * whose premature decease we have lately had to lament. It is certain that in the majority of recent dramas of this order, and not at one theatre alone, the yahoo and the demirep have been treated, not merely with indulgence, but with an admiring sympathy which is a strange and scarcely an exhilarating sign of the times. The practical harm lies, I think, not in the occasional choice of a forger and

---

* Mr George Alexander Baird, better known as "Mr Abington," or "The Squire," died March 19, 1893.

wastrel for a hero, but in the general baseness of the ideals presented. To quote (from *Punch*) one of the profoundest truths ever uttered in jest, modern melodrama is "worse than wicked, it is vulgar."

The acting, both at the Adelphi and the Vaudeville, is good of its kind. Mr Glenney and Mr Abingdon are excellently fitted in the parts of hero and villain at the Adelphi; but I own it jars upon my sense of fair play that Captain Greville should be thrashed by Lord Dashwood every evening of the week. Why not let them take night and night about, to thrash and to be thrashed? Miss Evelyn Millard and Mrs Patrick Campbell seemed to me rather too subdued in style for so large a house, but Mrs Campbell played with an effectively undulant and Bernhardtesque languor. Miss Bessie Hatton threw her valuable earnestness into the part of the adventuress's sister; and the comic business was "safe," as the saying goes, "in the hands of" Mr Arthur Williams, Mr Welton Dale, and Miss Clara Jecks. No less safe was Uncle John, at the Vaudeville, in the hands of Mr Charles Groves, who played the part with excellent humour and feeling. Miss Norreys was good as the sentimental heroine, and Miss Annie Hughes, as the comic heroine, did charmingly the little she had to do. Mr Reeves Smith and Mr Lawrance D'Orsay contributed clever character-sketches.

A somewhat old-fashioned but pleasant and entertaining comedy is *Clever Alice*,* adapted by Mr Brandon Thomas from Willbrandt's *Die Maler.* The idea
is charming, but it is rather conventionally worked
out. The astonishing ease, for example, with which
Gerard Douglas falls out of and into love, is of the
stage, stagey, and destroys any impression of reality
the play might otherwise have produced. It seemed
to me, too, that the adaptor had not been very
successful in his studio talk. Much of it did not get
over the footlights at all, and much of what did
sounded rather unconvincing. The charm of the
production naturally lay in Miss Achurch's Clever
Alice. Never, certainly, did an actress enter into a
character in a more uncompromisingly artistic spirit.
Her first make-up amounted to a positive disguise,
such as not many fair ladies would have consented to
assume throughout an act and a half, however striking
might be the ultimate effect of contrast to be obtained.
Her playing, too, was instinct with the spirit of
genuine character-comedy. When the contrast at last
came, its effect was to my thinking somewhat dis-
counted by a maladroitness on the part of the
German author. The change from the "grey moth"
into the butterfly would have been much more telling
without the fancy dress. It struck me as simply

---

* Royalty, April 6—April 22 (?).

G

the substitution of one disguise for another, not as a revelation of the real woman, at the magic touch of love.   Miss Achurch's acting, however, was admirable throughout, though the author had failed to give her the chances in the latter half of the play which might have been extracted from the theme.   Miss Gertrude Kingston was excellent as the heartless woman of the world, and Mrs Theodore Wright made the most of an insignificant part.   Mr Charrington played the artist hero soberly and not ineffectively, wisely eschewing all attempt at the romantic and picturesque ; Mr Herbert Flemming was made up to perfection, and did all that his opportunities permitted ; and Mr Edmund Maurice (a capital character-actor) and Mr John Carter were genuinely amusing in parts of some importance.

XVII.

" THE SILVER SHELL "—" MOROCCO BOUND."

19th April.

SATURDAY night at the Avenue Theatre inspired me with grave doubts as to the propriety of all the fuss we are making over the late Christopher Columbus. *Was* he such a benefactor to humanity ?   Would not he have done better to have let America alone, and lived upon his *talents de société* in the egg-balancing line ?   As they say in the Columbian language,

"Have we any use for America, anyway?" I certainly cannot help conceiving a grudge against the
irrepressible Christopher when I see the effect his
precious discovery has had upon the art of Mrs
Kendal. It has broadened and hardened her style
almost beyond recognition, robbing it of naturalness,
of spontaneity, of charm. She remains an accomplished actress, one who knows her business to perfection; but, alas! the word "business" is a fatally
just one in this context. The habit of driving home
her effects in vast theatres populated with playgoers
who like their art on the vast American scale, has
converted her from a delightful comedian, a mistress
of unforced humour and pathos, into a powerful
melodramatic actress, impressive at her best moments,
stagey—there is no other word for it—at her worst.
Her delivery of the words "Sophia, Prrrincess Karatoff!" in the last act of *The Silver Shell* * was like
a breath from "the palmy days" wafted by some
phonographic miracle across our namby-pamby end
of the century. I begin to see a second great career
opening out before Mrs Kendal. She has all the
makings of a fine tragic actress. If we are to have a
Lady Macbeth, a Volumnia, a Constance, in the present generation, Mrs Kendal is the woman. Having
been our Mrs Jordan, why should she not become

---

* April 15—June 3.

our Mrs Siddons? But meanwhile the transition
stage is somewhat trying. Tragedy in (more or less)
modern dress, and speaking very third-rate modern
prose, is not tragedy but melodrama. I insert the
above qualifying parenthesis as I think of the cloak
which Mrs Kendal manipulates so magnificently in
the fourth act of *The Silver Shell*. It was the pall of
tragedy without the sceptre. Not otherwise must
Clytemnestra have handled her draperies. And this
general effect of emphasis and sublimity, which would
have been very much in place in a drama "presenting Thebes, or Pelops' line, Or the tale of Troy
divine," was a little out of keeping with the modern,
even the melodramatic, surroundings. One felt that,
Nihilist or no, the chivalrous Sir Richard Stanhope
was undertaking rather "a handful." It was like
going bail for the good behaviour of Medea or Lu-
crezia Borgia. "Sophia, Prrrincess Karatoff," seemed
the sort of woman who was bound to blow-up somebody, and one had a horrible presentiment that, if it
was not the Czar, it would certainly be the Baronet.
For my part, I felt quite a glow of admiration for his
intrepidity.

On the credit side of the Columbus account, however, we must place the fact that if he had not discovered America, there would have been no Henry
J. W. Dam—and that would have been a pity. Mr
Dam is an amusing playwright, who, I fancy, has a

career before him in the line of romantic melodrama.
He starts with one priceless gift—that fine contempt
for prosaic probability or consistency, without which
the great effects of this sort of work are not to be attained. We have had many exhilarating romances of
despotism and dynamite on the stage, but none
quainter than *The Silver Shell*. The one rule of
Russian policy upon which all our dramatists are
agreed is faithfully observed by Mr Dam—to wit, that
the public functionaries of that empire never by any
chance function in Russia, but spend their time,
generally in full uniform, between Paris and Monte
Carlo. Mr Dam is rather vague as to Prince Karatoff's actual position. We learn that he is "the
butcher of the Czar," but that can scarcely be his
official style and title. Anyhow, he seems to carry
the knout in his pocket, and to order people off to
Siberia as freely as the Queen in *Alice in Wonderland*
ordered them to execution. One gathers, in short,
that he is Prime Minister and Chief of Police in one ;
yet his appearance is so unfamiliar to his countrymen
that he can venture into a conclave of Nihilists, un-
disguised, without the least fear of being recognised.
The machinery of the French police, moreover, is absolutely at his disposal. Talk about an *entente cor-
diale !*—why, General Prince Karatoff (of course in full
uniform) lords it in Paris as though he were in War-
saw. There is some slight mention of extradition

formalities, but they are evidently the merest farce. Prefects of police tremble at the General's nod, and the whole force is at his beck and call; yet he must needs employ an English comic detective at £15 a week, to—well, to provide the comic relief—I could not discover that he did anything else. But the mysteries of the play do not end with General Prince Karatoff. Why does Katharine Vail, at the end of the second act, decline to tell Sir Richard that the photograph which so disturbs her is that of her late husband? Why is she so desperately anxious to keep the Prince from knowing of his grandson's existence? Why is she at one moment eager to burn the papers on which, it appears, her child's name and inheritance depend, and at the next no less eager to convince the General of what she has all through the play been struggling to conceal from him? What instinct has impelled Sir Richard to draw up a paper assigning to himself the guardianship of Katharine's child before (so far as we can see) he knew of, or suspected, the existence of any such child? To some, at any rate, of these questions, Mr Dam is doubtless prepared with an answer; but the fact remains that he has not succeeded in making the motives and actions of his characters in the least degree plausible. I doubt, indeed, whether he has tried to do so; there was not the smallest reason why he should. Give your average audience a situation, and it does not dream of

inquiring into its why and wherefore. In his third
act especially, Mr Dam has devised a series of exceedingly effective and even novel situations. This
act, as a whole, is an excellent piece of drama of its
class, and quite worth seeing, when you have nothing
better to do. It will make the success of the play,
and, indeed, it deserves to. Mr Kendal is excellent
as the "butcher of the Czar," and another noteworthy piece of acting is Mr C. P. Huntley's impersonation of the benevolent old maker of infernal
machines. His account of his labours and disap-
pointments is by far the best piece of writing in the
play, and Mr Huntley does full justice to it.*

----

* I quote from the *Daily News* of November 20 the
following curious paragraph :—"New York, as our readers
have heard, has not taken kindly to *The Second Mrs Tanqueray*, and Mrs Kendal, in the part of Paula, is acknowledged to have sacrificed something of the popularity which
she has enjoyed among American audiences. On the other
hand, Mr H. J. W. Dam's play of Russian life, which under
the title of *The Silver Shell* was brought out by Mr and
Mrs Kendal at the Avenue Theatre in London, with no
very marked success, seems to have proved much more to the
taste of New York playgoers. The judicious critic of the *Spirit
of the Times* says : 'We can understand and sympathise with a
mistake which was based upon the idea of giving New York the
very latest London sensation, and we are especially proud of the
promptitude with which the mistake was corrected as soon as it
was discovered. Mrs Tanqueray shall now be forgiven and
forgotten, and Mr and Mrs Kendal re-established in the affection
as well as the admiration of the public.'" It appears, however,

When about nine-tenths of the dialogue is cut out (as I daresay it has been ere now), *Morocco Bound*,* at the Shaftesbury, ought to be a very amusing entertainment. Mr " Adrian Ross " is, next to Mr Gilbert, our smartest writer of comic lyrics, and some of the songs in the new " musical farce " are really capital bits of rhyming. Mr Osmond Carr, too, has the knack of turning-out music which catches the ear of the unmusical, of whom I am one. This may seem a left-handed compliment ; but as the great majority of any given audience are probably as incompetent to criticise as I, they may also be no less disposed to enjoy, uncritically, Mr Carr's lively rhythms. The vocal talent of the company is not of the most distinguished. With the exception of Miss Violet Cameron, not one of the artists engaged even professes, so far as I know, to be much of a singer. But Mr Danby and Mr Shine, both excellent comedians in their way, keep the fun afoot with unflagging spirit, and Miss Letty Lind's dancing is as charming as ever. The mechanically restless stage-management of the chorus in the first act seemed to me foolish and irritating.

---

that though the American press in general agreed with the *Spirit of the Times* in considering *The Second Mrs Tanqueray* a thing scarcely to be forgiven, the American public flocked eagerly to witness the reprehensible performance.

* April 13—still running.

XVIII.

"A WOMAN OF NO IMPORTANCE"— LYCEUM REVIVALS.

26th April.

THERE is no such thing as "absolute pitch" in criticism; the intervals are everything. In other words, the critic is bound to deal in odious comparisons; it is one of the painful necessities of his calling. He must clearly indicate the plane, so to speak, on which, in his judgment, any given work of art is to be taken; and the value of his terms, whether of praise or blame, must then be estimated in relation to that plane. Well, the one essential fact about Mr Oscar Wilde's dramatic work is that it must be taken on the very highest plane of modern English drama, and furthermore, that it stands alone on that plane. In intellectual calibre, artistic competence—ay, and in dramatic instinct to boot—Mr Wilde has no rival among his fellow-workers for the stage. He is a thinker and a writer; they are more or less able, thoughtful, original playwrights. This statement may seem needlessly emphatic, and even offensive; but it is necessary that it should be made if we are to preserve any sense of proportion in criticism. I am far from exalting either *Lady Windermere's Fan* or *A Woman of No Importance* * to

* Haymarket, April 19—August 16, with a break of three nights, when *An Enemy of the People* was performed.

the rank of a masterpiece; but while we carp at this point and cavil at that, it behoves us to remember and to avow that we are dealing with works of an altogether higher order than others which we may very likely have praised with much less reserve.

Pray do not suppose that I am merely dazzled by Mr Wilde's pyrotechnic wit. That is one of the defects of his qualities, and a defect, I am sure, that he will one day conquer, when he begins to take himself seriously as a dramatic artist. At present, he approaches his calling as cynically as Mr George R. Sims; only it is for the higher intellects, and not the lower, among the play-going public, that Mr Wilde shows his polite contempt. He regards prose drama (so he has somewhere stated) as the lowest of the arts; and acting on this principle — the falsity of which he will discover as soon as a truly inspiring subject occurs to him—he amuses himself by lying on his back and blowing soap-bubbles for half an evening, and then pretending, during the other half, to interest himself in some story of the simple affections such as audiences, he knows, regard as dramatic. Most of the soap bubbles are exceedingly pretty, and he throws them off with astonishing ease and rapidity—

> "One *mot* doth tread upon another's heels,
> So fast they follow "—

but it becomes fatiguing, in the long run, to have the whole air a-shimmer, as it were, with iridescent films.

Mr Wilde will one day be more sparing in the quantity and more fastidious as to the quality of his wit, and will cease to act up to Lord Illingworth's motto that "nothing succeeds like excess." It is not his wit, then, and still less his knack of paradox-twisting, that makes me claim for him a place apart among living English dramatists. It is the keenness of his intellect, the individuality of his point of view, the excellence of his verbal style, and, above all, the genuinely dramatic quality of his inspirations. I do not hesitate to call the scene between Lord Illingworth and Mrs Arbuthnot at the end of the second act of this play the most virile and intelligent—yes, I mean it, the most intelligent—piece of English dramatic writing of our day. It is the work of a man who knows life, and knows how to transfer it to the stage. There is no situation-hunting, no posturing. The interest of the scene arises from emotion based upon thought, thought thrilled with emotion. There is nothing conventional in it, nothing insincere. In a word, it is a piece of adult art. True, it is by far the best scene in the play, the only one in which Mr Wilde does perfect justice to his talent. But there are many details of similar, though perhaps not equal, value scattered throughout. How fine and simple in its invention, for instance, is the scene in which the mother tells her son the story of Lord Illingworth's treachery, only to hear him defend the libertine on the ground that no "nice girl" would have let herself be entrapped! This exquisite touch of ironic pathos is worth half a hundred "thrilling tableaux," like that which follows almost immediately upon it.

For it is not to be denied that in his effort to be human—I would say "to be popular," did I not fear some subtle and terrible vengeance on the part of the outraged author—Mr Wilde has become more than a little conventional. How different is the "He is your father!" tableau at the end of Act III from the strong and simple conclusion of Act II — how different, and how inferior! It would be a just retribution if Mr Wilde were presently to be confronted with this tableau, in all the horrors of chromo-lithography, on every hoarding in London, with the legend, "Stay, Gerald! He is your father!" in crinkly letters in the corner. Then, indeed, would expatriation—or worse—be the only resource of his conscience-stricken soul. His choice would lie between Paris and prussic acid. The conventional element seems to me to come in with the character of Mrs Arbuthnot. Why does Mr Wilde make her such a terribly emphatic personage? Do ladies in her (certainly undesirable) position brood so incessantly upon their misfortune? I have no positive evidence to go upon, but I see no reason why Mrs Arbuthnot should not take a more common-sense view of the situation. That she should resent Lord

Illingworth's conduct I quite understand, and I
applaud the natural and dignified revenge she takes
in declining to marry him. But why all this agony?
Why all this hatred? Why can "no anodyne give
her sleep, no poppies forgetfulness"? With all respect
for Mrs Arbuthnot, this is mere empty phrase-making.
I am sure she has slept very well, say, six nights out
of the seven, during these twenty years; or, if not,
she has suffered from a stubborn determination to
be unhappy, for which Lord Illingworth can scarcely
be blamed. After all, what material has she out of
which to spin twenty years of unceasing misery?
She is—somehow or other—in easy circumstances;
she has a model son to satisfy both her affections
and her vanity; it does not even appear that she
is subjected to any social slights or annoyances.
A good many women have led fairly contented lives
under far more trying conditions. Perhaps Mr Wilde
would have us believe that she suffers from mild
religious mania—that it is the gnawing thought of
her unpardonable "sin" that nor poppy nor man-
dragora can soothe. But she herself admits that
she does not repent the "sin" that has given her
a son to love. Well then, what is all this melodrama about? Does not Mrs Arbuthnot sacrifice
our interest, if not our sympathy, by her determination "in obstinate condolement to persever"?
May we not pardonably weary a little (to adapt

Lord Illingworth's saying) of "the Unreasonable eternally lamenting the Unalterable"?   Mrs Arbuthnot is
simply a woman who has been through a very painful
experience, who has suffered a crushing disappointment
in the revelation of the unworthiness of the man she
loved, but for whom life, after all, has turned out
not so very intolerably.   That is the rational view
of her situation; and she herself might quite well
take that view without the sacrifice of one scene
or speech of any real value.   The masterly scene at
the end of the second act would remain practically
intact, and so would the scene between mother and
son in the third act; for the complacent cruelty of
Gerald's commentary on her story could not but
cause a bitter pang to any mother.   It is only in
the fourth act that any really important alteration
would be necessary, and there it could only be for
the better.   The young man's crude sense of the
need for some immediate and heroic action is admirably conceived, and entirely right; but how much
better, how much truer, how much newer, would the
scene be if the mother met his Quixotism with sad,
half-smiling dignity and wisdom, instead of with
passionate outcries of unreasoning horror!   There is
a total lack of irony, or, in other words, of common-
sense, in this portion of the play.   Heroics respond
to heroics, until we feel inclined to beg both mother
and son (and daughter-in-law, too, for that matter)

to come down from their stilts and look at things
a little rationally. Even Mr Wilde's writing suffers.
We are treated to such noble phrases as "I am not
worthy or of her or of you," and it would surprise
no one if Master Gerald were to drop into blank verse
in a friendly way. How much more telling, too,
would the scene between Mrs Arbuthnot and Lord
Illingworth become if she took the situation more
ironically and less tragically, if she answered the
man of the world in the tone of a woman of the
world! How much more complete, for one thing,
would be his humiliation! As it is, the vehemence
of her hatred can only minister to his vanity. From
the point of view of vanity, to be hated for twenty
years is just as good as to be loved. It is indifference
that stings. It was all very well, in the second act,
for Mrs Arbuthnot to be vehement in her protest
against the father's annexation of the son; in the
fourth act, when that danger is past, a tone of calm
superiority would be ten times as effective. In short,
the play would have been a much more accomplished
work of art if the character of Mrs Arbuthnot had
been pitched in another key. And I am not without a suspicion that Mr Wilde's original design was
something like what I have indicated. The last
word spoken, "A man of no importance" (which was
doubtless the first word conceived) seems to belong
to the woman I imagine rather than to the one who

actually speaks it.   I think, too, that the concluding
situation would be more effective if some more definite indication of the unspeakable cad who lurks
beneath Lord Illingworth's polished surface were
vouchsafed us earlier in the play.   True, his conduct
towards the fair American was sufficiently objectionable ; but I fear I, for my part, did not quite seriously
believe in it, taking it rather as a mere *ficelle*, and
not a very ingenious one, leading up to the startling
picture-poster at the end of the third act.

Except in one scene, Mr Tree's acting was altogether admirable—thoughtful in intention, masterly
in execution.   The one scene excepted was the opening of the third 'act, in which this nineteenth-century
Lord Chesterfield served out his moral maxims to
his son with a curiously sententious monotony.   Mrs
Bernard Beere looked magnificent in her black robe
and Magdalen-red hair, and played the perpetual
penitent with great force and sincerity—but I think
she would have played the other Mrs Arbuthnot still
better.   Mrs Tree was charming as a heartless woman
of the world ; nothing could have been better than
Miss Le Thiere's rendering of a masterful matron ;
and Miss Rose Leclercq will doubtless make more
of the excellently-drawn character assigned to her
when she overcomes the nervousness which, on the
first night, rendered her almost inarticulate.   As the
young lovers, Mr Fred Terry and Miss Neilson (both

valuable artists in parts that suit them) were distinctly out of place.   A much less practised actor than Mr Terry would have made a far better Gerald, if he could have brought to the part the ingenuous boyishness in which reside its meaning and its charm.   When one sees two parts so miscast, one begins to wonder whether we have retained the disadvantages of the stock-company system, while sacrificing its advantages.

In this play, as in *Lady Windermere's Fan*, among many showy sayings, there is one really luminous and profound.   "Thought is in its essence destructive," says Lord Illingworth.   "Nothing survives being thought of."   Nothing—not even *A Woman of No Importance ;* but then it is so very, very much better worth thinking of than the average play.*

The Saturday night revivals of *Louis XI.* and *The Lyons Mail*, at the Lyceum, afford the rising generation an opportunity of seeing Mr Irving in two, or rather three, of his most memorable impersonations.   His Dubosc has lost none of its grotesque ferocity, his Lesurques none of its pathetic, open-

---

* This article (here reprinted verbatim) has been represented in more than one quarter as grossly and excessively eulogistic. *Is* it so?   It does not read to me like unmixed praise.   There is one sentence in the first paragraph which I would not have written a month later ; but it must be remembered that Mr Pinero still held *The Second Mrs Tanqueray* "up his sleeve." *See* Article XXIV.

minded dignity. I cannot reconcile myself to the needless sacrifice of all verisimilitude in the "business" at the end of the first act; and, in the second, the way in which Lesurques paws his father about shows some lack of consideration for the old gentleman's wounded shoulder. But, take it all in all, Mr Irving's performance is a very fine thing of its kind, and he does well not to suffer it to drop out of recollection.

XIX.

"ALAN'S WIFE." *

Westminster Gazette, 6th May.

IT is right that I should confess my complicity before the fact in the dramatic crime committed by a person or persons unknown at the Independent Theatre last week. I was not only a consenting party—I positively instigated the deed. The history is this: More than two years ago, Miss Elizabeth Robins lent me a Swedish magazine containing a short story named *Befriad*, by a writer of whom I had never heard, named Elin Ameen. I read the story; and then, in some grisly midnight hour no doubt, when my good angel was off duty, the unhallowed thought occurred

---

* *Alan's Wife* was performed twice (Friday evening, April 28, and Tuesday afternoon, May 2) at Terry's Theatre, the home, for the nonce, of the Independent Theatre Society. Some portions of this article are embodied in my introduction to the published play (Henry & Co.).

to me, "Surely there is a play in it!" I took a
fellow-critic apart one day, and in dreadful secrecy
unveiled to him the horrid design. He said it was
intolerable and beyond the limits of art, and that he,
for one, should certainly cry out, "Non, non! Pas
cela! Je ne veux pas! C'est lâche!"* That decided
me; I was overmastered by a fiendish, not to say a
Fat-Boyish, longing to make my fellow-critic's flesh
creep, and I determined that the deed should be done.
So I went forthwith to Miss Robins, told her how the
story seemed to me to shape itself into three scenes,
and mentioned two clever and ambitious young
dramatists to one or other of whom I advised her to
suggest the theme. Then, for a long time, I heard
and thought nothing more of the matter, until one day
Miss Robins informed me that she had acted on my
advice, and that the play was written. She also broke
to me the news that, except as regards the division
into three scenes, my scheme had been entirely thrown
overboard. I had proposed to follow quite faithfully
the lines of the original, which, by the way, was published long before Mr Hardy's *Tess*,† and contains the

---

* M. Jules Lemaître on the torture-scene in Sardou's *La
Tosca.*

† I do not for a moment suggest that Mr Hardy had ever
heard of the Swedish story, but merely wish to point out that
those critics are mistaken who assumed that the baptism scene
was suggested by *Tess of the D'Urbervilles.*

baptism-scene in full. Most of all, I had insisted on
the expediency of keeping the scene in Sweden, on
the ground that impressions of horror are apt to vary
inversely as the square of the distance. But the
incidents were just as natural in England as anywhere
else, and I soon recognised that the author had taken
the wiser as well as the bolder part in placing his
scene in our own North Country. In several other
particulars—especially in the ingenious substitution of
a "little minister" for the doctor of the story and of
my plan—the author had, I was bound to admit, been
most happily inspired. Whether for good or ill, then,
I am in no way responsible for the details of con-
struction, and still less for the dialogue of the play ;
but for the bare fact of its existence I am solely to
blame.

And, like Jean Creyke, I am quite impenitent.
Alan's Wife (it ought simply to have been called
Lovingkindness) is to my mind intensely moving—
harrowing, if you will—from the theatrical point of
view ; and there can be no doubt, surely, that it is
interesting from the literary point of view, since it
opens up afresh the eternally fascinating question of the
conditions and limitations of tragic art. Let me try
to discover some of the reasons (obscure enough even
to myself) why the representation of so distressing an
episode should produce in me sensations which must
presumably be classed as pleasant, in so far as I am

willing, and even eager, to have them repeated from time to time.

First, to remove a misconception. A good deal has been said by the critics about "puerperal mania," studies in insanity, and so forth. Of course this is partly their fun; but some of them appear seriously to believe that we are intended to regard Jean Creyke as insane. Nothing, I am sure, could be further from the intention of either Swedish authoress or English author. Every stage in the process of thought and feeling that leads Jean up to her terrible deed is as clear as daylight. This facile verdict of insanity is worthy only of a coroner's jury, not of a critical College of Justice. Immediately a cry of horror is raised: "What! she is not insane! Then we are asked to applaud her action, and to admit that all deformed children ought to be smothered!" Surely not. Since when have we been expected to approve every sane action that is presented on the stage? There is a vast space of intermediate ground between a criminal lunatic and an ideal heroine held up for imitation; and to cover that space at one leap is surely to beat the record in ratiocinative athletics. Jean Creyke, certainly, is neither lunatic nor heroine. She is a terribly afflicted woman, that is all; and she acts as, somewhere or other in the world, some similarly tortured creature is doubtless acting at the very moment when I write these words. Doubtless, too, there are

thousands of other women bearing even greater bur-
dens with stupid resignation or with cheerful fortitude.
All three phases—the rebellious, the callous, and the
stoical—are in themselves equally interesting, but the
rebellious phase happens to be by far the most dramatic. It is not in the least necessary that we should
either approve or condemn Jean's action. To my
thinking, the great tragic value of the theme lies in the
fact that we can do neither with a whole heart. If
you want to know my own private sentiment on the
subject (though that is quite beside the artistic question), I think with Jean that she must die, that life is
and ought to be impossible to her after such an act,
but that hers is rather a case for the lethal chamber
which Mr George R. Sims was commending the other
day than for the common gallows. But there is not
the slightest reason why one's own particular judgment
of the case of conscience should affect one's estimate
of the work of art. Our appreciation of the *Choëphori*
does not depend (does it?) upon our approval or disapproval of Orestes' matricide. Is it not one of the
great tragedies of the world precisely because we can
neither freely applaud nor utterly condemn the hero?
Well, *Alan's Wife* is a little tragedy, not a great one;
but Jean Creyke has this in common with Orestes,
that she is placed in one of those agonising dilemmas
where it seems equally impossible, equally inhuman,
to act or to refrain. If she were insane, the ethical

problem would vanish, and we should have nothing but a study in mental pathology. I don't say that that might not have its interest, but it is not the interest at which the author has aimed.

Now what are, to me, the elements of attraction in this admittedly painful work? Why do I care to see a crude horror enacted before my eyes, unmitigated even by the graces of poetry? Well, certainly, the play is not in verse, but it does not follow that it is devoid of literary charm. On the contrary, it is admirably written, with rare simplicity and directness of style. I own it strikes me as strange that any one with an atom of critical faculty should fail to recognise the spirit and truth of the character-sketches in the first act, and the exquisite tenderness of the scene between mother and daughter, or should allow even the fiercest moral and æsthetic indignation to render him obtuse to the beauty and eloquence, with little or no rhetorical inflation, of the writing in the second act. The horror, in a word, is *not* crudely served up; simply, if you will, but crudely, no! The merits of the writing, however, are obviously not the sole attraction of the thing, and even the excellence of the acting does not complete the explanation. Much less harrowing themes afford opportunity for equally good writing and acting. There is evidently some sort of satisfaction in the contemplation of the facts themselves, in their crudity, if you like to

put it so.   Where, then, does this satisfaction come
in ?

It has sometimes occurred to me that an element
of superstition enters into our taste for tragedy.   Is it
not possible that, in a vague, inarticulate way, our forefathers may have regarded the mimic presentation of
misfortune as a sort of prophylactic against the real
thing, averting or attenuating it as cow-pox does small-
pox?   Thus stated, of course, the idea is preposterous ;
but others quite as childish have been among the most
potent of human motives, and have sunk into the
very texture of our minds.   Be this as it may, tragedy
is, and will always be, a gymnastic of the emotions, a
painless experiment in pain ; and this, I take it, is
very much what Aristotle meant by his famous, though
elusive, definition.   By a sympathetic study of the
emotions of others, we learn the better to understand,
and possibly to govern, our own.   "But here you go
discussing tragedy," the other side may object, "while
we deny that *Alan's Wife* is a tragedy at all.   Even
in tragedy there must be a note of consolation, of
moral elevation, of what the Germans call reconciliation."   It may be so, though I think it would puzzle
our theorists to discover the note of consolation and
reconciliation in, say, *Hamlet* or *Othello*.   I admit,
in any case, that there is no consolation, no encourage-
ment, in *Alan's Wife*, save only the supreme consolation that " The rest is silence."   But—here we come to

what I take to be the kernel of the matter—do we not
find a peculiar and instinctive satisfaction in now and
again facing fairly and squarely the very grimmest facts
of life? Have we not a certain sense—an illusion, if
you will—of added human dignity when, renouncing
the "consolations" of stereotyped sophistry, we have
recognised and made up our minds to the immitigable
cruelty of "the bludgeonings of chance"? In wit-
nessing such a play as *Alan's Wife*, do we not seem
to be looking life straight in the eyes, and saying,
"There, you great bully! We know you! We are
not taken in by your cajoleries! Now go ahead and
do your worst!" That this is a rational or admirable
attitude of mind I am far from asserting; it may even
be called a sort of cheap posturing, as of Ajax defying
a stage thunderbolt; but I own to taking a certain
foolish pleasure in it. And, however childish this
attitude of mine may be, it behoves even the wisest
of us to adopt *some* attitude towards the sheer horrors
of life. Philosophy cannot simply ignore them, and
art, to my thinking, is conterminous with philosophy
—in other words, nothing human is alien to it. Why,
then, should we despise and reject a play which brings
us face to face with one of the darkest problems of
existence—the problem of undeserved, fortuitous, purposeless suffering—and treats it delicately, tenderly,
humanely, without any of that savage and cynical
pessimism which pervades the works of the Théâtre

Libre playwrights? It will, of course, be represented that because I praise *Alan's Wife* I want to see the drama entirely given over to gloom and horror. That is mere nonsense. Such works should be exceptional in art, as such miseries are exceptional in life. Only I decline to exclude from the province of art any work which speaks from heart and brain to heart and brain, in however agonising accents.

XX.

"ADRIENNE LECOUVREUR"—"JEALOUS IN HONOUR."

3rd May.

THOUGH *Adrienne Lecouvreur* * has come to an untimely end at the Royalty, I must put on record my admiration for the remarkable power displayed by Miss Janet Achurch in the death scene. I am not sure that this is the highest form of art—indeed, it seems to me open to the objection of mere sensationalism which is wrongly alleged against *Alan's Wife*. But it is a sensationalism which has been to some extent hallowed by the practice of many great actresses, and certain it is that none of them, within my recollection, has died more thrillingly than Miss Achurch. There was an indisputable fascination in the scene.

---

* April 26. It ran only a few nights.

Jealous in Honour,* by Mr "Basil Broke," produced last Thursday afternoon at the Garrick, proved to be a well-written and competent drawing-room drama, not quite strong enough, perhaps, to be largely attractive. The author is at his best in the more serious scenes ; comedy is not his strong point. The piece was excellently played by Miss Kate Rorke, Mr Gilbert Hare, Mr Bernard Gould, Mr Sant Matthews, and Mr Edmund Maurice.

XXI.

" FORBIDDEN FRUIT "—" DIPLUNACY."

10*th May.*

Forbidden Fruit,† one of the oldest and not one of the best of errant-husband farces, may make an acceptable enough stop-gap at the Vaudeville, where it is played with a great deal of spirit, and with quite as much finish as it requires. Messrs Charles Groves and Lionel Rignold are really amusing, and Miss Lottie Venne and Miss Norreys make the most of their not very abundant opportunities.

At the Trafalgar Square, on Saturday night, I was able to see only one act and what they call in Scotland "a bittock" of *Mamzelle Nitouche*, which seemed to go excellently with the audience, Miss Yohe's

---

* April 27.   † May 6—July 8.

curious, rather metallic, personality suiting the leading part better than it might some others. Mr Burnand's *Diplunacy*,* unfortunately, fell very flat—unfortunately, I say, for if the dialogue had been audible, I fancy we should have found it ingenious and amusing. The trouble was that the mimic actors bore but the faintest resemblance to the actors mimicked Mr Arthur Playfair now and then caught Mr Forbes Robertson's voice fairly enough, but his appearance and attitudes were grotesque without being amusing. Mr Wyatt was only fitfully like Mr Bancroft, and Mr Cairns James was not even fitfully like Mr Hare. By far the best piece of mimicry was Miss Elsie Chester's clever reproduction of Lady Monckton's gestures and attitudes.

XXII.

"THE GREAT UNPAID."

17th May.

WHEN one has recorded the first-night success of *The Great Unpaid* † at the Comedy Theatre, and has given the actors the praise which they amply deserve, there is really nothing more to be said. Mr W. H. Vernon bore the whole weight of the farce on his shoulders—no trifling burden—and played like the sterling comedian he is. Mr Cyril Maude, Mr Gar-

---

* May 6—June 9. † May 9—May 20.

diner, and Mr De Lange were excellent, and Mr H.
V. Esmond showed a genuine gift of eccentric
comedy such as one had not hitherto suspected in
him. The female parts are unimportant, but Miss
M. A. Victor made the most of her opportunities.
As for the play*—well, there are evidently people who
find entertainment in it, and they have a right to
their taste. " For want of decency is want of sense,"
wrote Roscommon two centuries ago ; but in the case
of adaptations of French farce the sense is apt to
depart with the *in*decency. *The Great Unpaid* is
absolutely incoherent, and bears no sort of resemblance to human life in England, France, or anywhere
else ; but if the audience and the Censor are happy,
who am I that I should complain ?

XXIII.

ELEANORA DUSE†—" THE SECOND MRS TANQUERAY."

31st May.

CRITICISM, like charity, should begin at home, so I

---

* An adaptation by Mr Fred Horner of Bisson's *La Famille
Pont-Biquet.*

† Signora Duse made her first appearance on May 24, as
Marguerite Gautier in *La Dame aux Camélias* (called on the
playbills *Camille,* from a mistaken notion on the part of the
management that the play was familiar to English audiences
under that name). *Fédora* was produced May 26 ; *Cavalleria*

must reserve for Mr Pinero's new play as much space
as possible.   Let me only say, then, of Signora Duse,
that she is without exception the most absorbingly
interesting actress I ever saw.   Her personality and
her art are magnetic in the highest degree, enchaining
the attention even when, as in *Fedora*, the whole
effect does not quite satisfy the judgment.   Moreover, she is an entirely distinguished artist.   Her
shrinking from everything that is cheap and vulgar,
mechanical and tricky, amounts to a fault, a mannerism.   She will often sacrifice an effect simply because
it is an obvious and easy one ; for after the third and
fifth acts of *La Dame aux Camélias* it is hard to
imagine that any effect is beyond her power.   These
are only first impressions, and must be taken for
what they are worth.   Next week I hope to return
to the subject with fuller knowledge and with more
space at my command.   In the meantime I can only
advise every one who cares for great acting to go and
see this fascinating artist.   Her Marguerite Gautier
will always remain one of the landmarks of my theatrical experience.

Well now, Mr Pinero and Mr Alexander, whatever
your box-office returns may say—and I have little

Rusticana, and *La Locandiera*, May 30; *A Doll's House*, June 9;
Antony and Cleopatra, June 19 ; and *Divorçons*, June 30.   Each
of these plays was repeated several times, *La Dame aux Camélias*
more frequently than the rest.

doubt that they will emphatically approve your action*
—don't you feel that you have done a fine thing, a
thing really worth doing, worth suffering for if need
be, a thing that enhances your self-respect, and makes
you realise that "a man's a man for a' that," and not
the slave of a booking-sheet? Of course you are not
going to suffer for it, even in pocket. To dare greatly
is to succeed; it is the man who dares feebly that
pays for his feebleness. I think it very probable,
however, that *The Second Mrs Tanqueray* will not
run as long as *Charley's Aunt*, and will not show,
on the whole, as heavy a balance of profit as *Liberty
Hall*. Perhaps it will not pay you more than a fair
day's wage for a fair day's work, and I know that is
not considered enough by the punters round the
theatrical roulette table. But you are no common
gamblers; you could not have done this at all if you
had not done it for the pleasure of the thing—that
is to say, in the only true artistic spirit. And in this
world nothing is to be had for nothing: artistic
pleasure must be paid for like any other. It is
possible that *The Second Mrs Tanqueray* may bring
in only (say) five per cent. on the time and money
invested, whereas a piece of screaming buffoonery or

---

* They did. *The Second Mrs Tanqueray* ran from May 27 to
July 28, was reproduced after the provincial tour of the company, November 11, and is still running.

trivial sentimentality might have brought in fifteen. But, frankly, isn't the pure joy of effort and triumph cheap at the money? Isn't the trumpery, facile, fifteen-per-cent. success dear in comparison? Now that the thing is done—and not in a tentative, apologetic, afternoon fashion, but with straightforward courage and confidence—don't you feel that if art is not virile it is childish, and that virile art alone is really worth living for? I am no despiser of childish art, so long as there are brains in it, and I am far from urging that the stage should show us nothing but Second Mrs Tanquerays. I have not, thank goodness, outgrown my taste for lollipops, if only they be delicately flavoured, and not too heavily "loaded" with plaster-of-Paris; but one cannot eat nothing but candy, year out year in, and yet preserve one's self-respect and one's digestion.

I wonder if Mr Pinero himself quite realises what an immeasurable advance he has made in *The Second Mrs Tanqueray* on all his former works? He has written a play which Dumas might sign without a blush, and created a character very much better worthy of the art of Eleanora Duse than that paltry Fédora whom she played-with rather than played the other night. It is not merely the seriousness of the subject that distinguishes this play from its predecessors. The subject of *The Profligate*, indeed, was equally serious, and even more largely important. It is the astonishing advance in philosophical insight and technical skill which places the new play in a new category. Technically, the work is as nearly as possible perfect. How masterly, for example, is the exposition—clear, simple, natural, profoundly interesting! There is plenty of wit in it, without a trace of that elaborate conceit-hunting which has hitherto spoiled so much of Mr Pinero's best work. When I remember the first act of *The Profligate*, with the long arm of coincidence dropping Janet Preece in the office of Messrs Cheal and Murray, and with Hugh Murray's metaphor of the wild oats, I can scarcely believe it to be the work of the same man. It is true that we raved over *The Profligate* in its day, and Mr Pinero, remembering this, may be inclined to discount, a little sardonically, our praise of *The Second Mrs Tanqueray*. But there is no real inconsistency. Those of us who kept our heads—as I trust I did— raved with reservations. We did not declare *The Profligate* a positively good play, but only an immensely better and more interesting play than any we were in the habit of seeing. It contained, moreover, one situation which was, and remains, incomparable in its kind. It would have been high-and-mighty criticism indeed which should have failed to recognise these merits, amid all the logical inconsequences and technical defects of the play. But here the case is totally different. Here we have a

positively good play.   Here, without raving, we can
praise almost without reservation.   I do not mean
that the thing is a consummate masterpiece, and that
dramatic art can no further go.   There is plenty of
room for Mr Pinero and others to write profounder,
more beautiful, more moving plays.   Mr Pinero has
not done everything ; but what he *has* done he has
done thoroughly well.   The play suggests reflections,
artistic and philosophical, enough to fill ten times the
space at my command ; but they would take the form
of discursive commentary rather than of cavil and
censure.   If I had the wit, I should like to write
such a preface to *Mrs Tanqueray* as Dumas is in
the habit of prefixing to his own plays, not criticising,
in the narrow sense of the word, but explaining and
expanding them.   The limitations of *Mrs Tanqueray*
are really the limitations of the dramatic form.   To
say that Mr Pinero has not entirely overcome them
is merely to say that he has not achieved a miracle
reserved for the very greatest artists in their very
happiest inspirations.   That is a totally different thing
from saying, as in the case of *The Profligate*, "This
is false ; that is feeble ; here is an inconsistency,
there an impossibility."   There is no illogical com-
promise in *Mrs Tanqueray*, nothing impossible, nothing flagrantly improbable.   There is one coincidence—the fact that the man who falls in love with
the step-daughter happens to be an old lover of the

step-mother's—but there is nothing really unlikely in this, and it would be the merest pedantry to insist that the dramatist should altogether eliminate chance from human affairs. For the rest, the whole course of the drama is smooth, natural, life-like. There is no great situation, as in *The Profligate*, but there are a hundred dramatic moments worth all the attitudinising situations ever conceived. In brief, the play is modern and masterly. Painful, yes—to me, I own, it is far more painful than certain works which Mr Pinero and those who think with him would not touch with the tongs. Why? Well, I think it is because there is a certain aridity in its painfulness —it feels gritty to the mental palate. Mr Pinero is a poet in his fantastic moods, with the Dickens stop on ; but in *Mrs Tanqueray* he writes the sternest of prose. Frankly, it is not a play I hanker after seeing again. I want to read it, to study it—but, with Mrs Patrick Campbell in the title part, though, or because, her performance is almost perfect in its realism, the sensation it gave one could not at any point be described as pleasure. It interests and absorbs one ; it satisfies the intelligence more completely than any other modern English play ; but it is not in the least moving. Not once during the whole evening were the tears anywhere near my eyes. Yes, once—when Mr Pinero came before the curtain, and the house rose at him. Then I felt a thrill of

genuine emotion to think that here at last, in spite
of all the depressing and stunting influences of our
English theatrical world, was a man who had had
the will and the talent to emancipate himself and
give the artist within him free play—to take care of
his soul, and let his pocket, for the nonce, take care
of itself.

Some critics objected to Mr Pinero's *Lady Bountiful* that it was rather a novel than a play ; whereupon
I argued that this was, in itself, no valid objection,
the real trouble being that the novel was a poor and
commonplace one. It is the highest praise, then,
that I can find for *Mrs Tanqueray* to say that its
four scenes are like the crucial, the culminating,
chapters of a singularly powerful and original novel.
In the fact that we would fain see the intermediate
chapters written and the characters of Tanqueray
and Paula worked out in greater detail, we touch
one of the aforesaid limitations of the dramatic form.
Tanqueray in particular remains decidedly vague.
What there is of him is excellent, but we want a
good deal more. We want to understand more fully
the conditions of his case. His conduct towards
Paula is clearly the resultant of two factors, affec-
tionate pity (or, in more general terms, philanthropy),
and physical passion ; but we want to know more
clearly in what proportions these factors are operative.
Neither his temperament nor his culture is very clearly

indicated. Paula, again, is drawn with an admirably bold and certain touch in all that we actually see of her; but, without overstepping the limits of the dramatic form, it might surely have been possible to give us a somewhat clearer view of her antecedents. I do not mean of her life as "Mrs Jarman" or "Mrs Dartrey" (that we can take on trust), but of her parentage, her girlhood, her education, of the instincts and influences that have made her what she is. She talks now and again like a woman of intelligence, and even of culture, and she acts like a perverse child, so utterly incapable of self-restraint as to fly in the face of her own ambitions and interests at every second word. I do not say that this is inconsistent; on the contrary, I believe it to be absolutely true to nature; but I think a little retrospective analysis, so to speak, might have shown the underlying harmony of certain superficial discords. As the character developed in the second act, I felt for some time as though Mr Pinero had repeated the mistake he made in *The Profligate*, and failed to present a fairly typical case. Just as Dunstan Renshaw was not the ordinary loose liver, but a peculiarly heartless seducer, so it seemed to me that Paula was not the ordinary upper-class courtesan, but simply a woman of diabolical temper, with whom life would have been impossible even if she had been chaste as the icicle that hangs on Dian's temple. But I soon recognised the injustice of this view. In *The Profligate*, Mr Pinero was bound by the conditions of the case to present an average type ; in *The Second Mrs Tanqueray* he was under no such obligation. A vivid and truthful individual character-study was all we had a right to demand of him, and that he gave us. Nor was it the case that, like Mr Shaw in *Widowers' Houses*, he had complicated the problem by unnecessary and irrelevant ill-temper. Paula's irritability, though partly constitutional no doubt, is embittered and rendered morbid by social slights, isolation, idleness, and the frigid politeness of Ellean—in short, it is not only natural, but almost inevitable, and belongs to the very essence of the situation. The indications of generosity and good feeling in the later acts are lightly and skilfully touched in, and the play is nowhere marred by sentimentality. On the side of the woman, as of the man, we miss a clearer definition of the elements which go to make up their relation. How far, in the beginning, is she influenced by love, how far by ambition? Is she capable or incapable of genuine passion for her husband? And are we to understand that the breakdown of the experiment is in some measure due to the perversion of her natural sensibilities by her past life? The physical factor, in short, which in one way or another must enter largely into any such problem, is left very much in the vague ;

but here again the inherent limitations of the dramatic form are largely to blame, to say nothing of the statutory limitation embodied in the Censorship. Finally, I am not quite certain that Paula's suicide, though natural enough and most effectively handled, is absolutely the most artistic close to the play. It would perhaps have been bolder and better simply to have left the thing at a loose end, dropping the curtain upon Mr and Mrs Tanqueray's determination to go abroad and try to make a fresh start, and leaving the spectator to forecast for himself the course of their future life.

In Mrs Patrick Campbell, Mr Alexander has laid his hand upon the very woman for the part of Paula. Her performance was as novel and unconventional as the character itself, and her triumphant success was thoroughly deserved. Never was there a more uncompromisingly artistic piece of acting. It was incarnate reality, the haggard truth.* Mr Alexander

---

* On August 31st, Mr and Mrs Kendal produced *The Second Mrs Tanqueray* at the Opera House, Leicester, for the first time in the provinces. I quote the following paragraph from a notice of this performance, contributed by me to the *Pall Mall Gazette* of September 1st: "What of Mrs Kendal's reading of the part of Paula? It is the work of an accomplished comedian, who has at her command all the resources of her art. Comparisons are odious, and I do not propose to compare Mrs Kendal with Mrs Patrick Campbell, except on one point. She certainly puts a greater depth of feeling into the later acts, and on the whole (I should say) she does rightly; though it was the effort to

himself played Aubrey Tanqueray with his unfailing
tact, elegance, and self-restraint, and Mr Cyril Maude
was exceedingly good in the capital character of
Cayley Drummle.   Miss Maude Millett did not seem
to me quite the Ellean designed by Mr Pinero, but
she played the part pleasantly and intelligently.   Miss
Amy Roselle was good as Mrs Cortelyon ; the Orreyeds

---

render this sincerity of emotion which made the actress so unhappily inaudible.   In the earlier acts Mrs Kendal, no less than
Mrs Campbell, and indeed even more deliberately, emphasises
the comic side of the character.   It is true that audiences, metro-
politan as well as provincial, show an inherent disposition to
laugh at poor Paula where they ought rather to weep.   There
were points last evening at which I felt inclined to use towards
my guffawing neighbours Paula's favourite epithet of 'Beasts !'
But the actress, whether in town or country, is not altogether
blameless in the matter.   Mrs Kendal 'plays for the laugh' so
often that she cannot wonder if the laugh sometimes comes in
where she neither expects nor desires it.   The ideal Paula Tanqueray, to my thinking, should not excite one-fifth part of the
laughter which greeted Mrs Kendal last night, or which used
to greet Mrs Campbell at the St James's.   There were many
speeches, however, which Mrs Kendal spoke altogether admirably—notably her ironic description of her happy days at Higher-
combe in the second act, and some of her phrases of despairing
self-reproach in the last acts.   The performance was altogether
an accomplished and most interesting one, and it is quite possible
that *my* ideal Paula is not the author's ideal.   At the same time
I am not without hope of seeing it some day.   Paula Tanqueray
is evidently a character which will tempt every ambitious actress
for many a year to come ; each one, doubtless, will give us her
individual reading ; and among them I may possibly find my
ideal—a Paula whom we shall feel throughout to be far more
pitiable than laughable."

were amusingly played by Miss Edith Chester and Mr A. Vane-Tempest; and Mr Ben Webster, as Captain Ardale, did well in his one scene.

XXIV.

"MRS TANQUERAY"—AND AFTER?

St James's Gazette, 3rd June.

"AN epoch-making play!" cried a critic, in a fine frenzy of enthusiasm over *The Second Mrs Tanqueray;* and I am in nowise disposed to quarrel with the expression. It behoves us to remember, however, that it is a prophecy, not a statement of fact. No single play, and for that matter no single playwright, can make an epoch. Looking back upon the history of the stage, we note certain plays in which the tendencies of a particular period first made themselves unmistakably felt, and we call them, not very logically, "epoch-making," when in fact they are only "epoch-marking." Such plays are Marlowe's *Tamburlaine, Les Précieuses Ridicules, Die Räuber, Hernani, La Dame aux Camélias,* and even, in a small way, Robertson's *Society.* But it can only be as the harbinger of others that a play deserves to rank as epoch-marking; so that to apply the term to a new work is to rush into the perils of prophecy. It was a hope, not a judgment, that the critic expressed, though a highly favourable judgment was, of course,

implied.   My present purpose is to inquire what
grounds there may be for such a hope.   The epoch,
it is certain, is yet to be made; how are we to set
about making it?

In the first place, what is it that distinguishes *The
Second Mrs Tanqueray* from the plays of the bygone
epoch, if you choose to put it so?   Simply the fact
that in writing it Mr Pinero has thrown to the winds
all extrinsic considerations, compromises, superstitions, and has set himself, for his own personal satisfaction, to do the best work that was in him.   He
has not written-up a part to suit this or that actor-
manager or leading lady; he has not dragged in a
comic under-plot because "the public wants to be
amused"; he has not falsified character and stultified
logic because "people don't like gloomy plays"; he
has not permitted himself all sorts of cheap licenses
because "they do these things on the stage" or "the
perspective of the theatre demands them"; in a word,
he has acted up to his conviction that the drama, even
in England, is not necessarily a craft of base com-
promise, of timorous catering to a vulgar demand,
but may yet become a liberal art, a worthy life-work
for a thinking man.   The result has been a splendid
victory, and the ignominious rout—for the moment,
at any rate—of the superstitions which have weighed
like a nightmare on the English drama.   But it is not
enough to fling up our caps and cry "Huzza!"   We

must take care that the victory prove not barren, and that we hold the ground which the skill and daring of one man has conquered for us.

Of course there went quite as much skill as daring to the making of the play. It shows a profound knowledge of the stage, not merely a knowledge of the trumpery technical half-truths which playwrights and critics have elevated into a system ; and it shows a competent knowledge of men and things, along with a real delicacy of insight into feminine character. But Mr Pinero does not stand alone in the possession of these qualities. We have several dramatic craftsmen of comparable, if not of equal, skill, and two or three whose general outlook upon life is at least as large as his. It is not merely or mainly superior gifts, then, but superior strength of character, which has given this victory to Mr Pinero rather than to Mr Oscar Wilde, Mr Henry Arthur Jones, Mr Grundy, or Mr Carton. Any difference of endowment there may be between him and them is not sufficient to account for the immense difference between *The Second Mrs Tanqueray* and the very best work of any of these writers. It is the attitude of mind in which he approached his task, the artistic ideal he proposed to himself, and his unflinching devotion to that ideal, that have enabled him to produce the one play of what may be called European merit which the modern English stage can as yet boast. It follows, then, that the question whether the play is or is not to mark an epoch depends upon the question whether Mr Pinero's fellow-craftsmen have it in them to imitate his singleness of artistic purpose. He has inserted the thin end of the wedge; but it is not in the nature of things that one man alone should be able to drive it home, or, in other words, to create a worthy dramatic literature. I firmly believe, however, that not only the ambition but the material interests of our other dramatists will prompt them to follow his lead, and that, therefore, we are indeed on the threshold of a new epoch.

We must hope, of course, that new talents will presently come to the front, now that the way has been so far cleared for them. But we will not count these chickens before they are hatched. Let us see, in the meantime, what we may expect from the known forces of the theatrical world.

I have been accused of wantonly overrating Mr Oscar Wilde because I said that his two plays stood alone on the highest plane of modern English drama. That remark, I believe, was absolutely true (so far as there can be any absolute truth in criticism) at the time when it was made, more than a month ago. Now, Mr Pinero's tragedy stands alone on a still higher plane; but *Lady Windermere's Fan* and *A Woman of No Importance* surely rank as far above *The Profligate* and *Lady Bountiful*, *The Dancing Girl*

and *The Crusaders*, as they rank below *The Second
Mrs Tanqueray*. "Mr Wilde's pyrotechnic wit," I
said at the same time, "is one of the defects of his
qualities—a defect which he will one day conquer
when he begins to take himself seriously as a dramatic artist. At present he approaches his calling
cynically;" and I went on to remark that there was
only one scene in his Haymarket play in which he did
his talent full justice. Is this extravagant eulogy?
Is it not precisely because he has taken himself
seriously as a dramatic artist that Mr Pinero has so
far outstripped Mr Wilde in the present instance?
It is none the less true that Mr Wilde is a writer, an
écrivain, of the first rank. He has written things of
the most exquisite quality both in verse and prose
(have you read his delightful fairy-tales?), and in one
or two masterly scenes and a hundred minor touches
he has proved himself possessed of dramatic instinct
in its highest potency. He has certainly the talent,
if he has but the will, the character, to raise his
work to the highest possible plane. Hitherto he has
done little more than trifle gracefully with his art; but
the time for trifling is past.

In *The Bauble Shop*, as it seems to me, Mr Henry
Arthur Jones has trifled somewhat ungracefully with
his art; but this is surely to be regarded as a
momentary aberration. Mr Jones has given proof of
his ambition for better things. His experiment with

The Crusaders, though not entirely fortunate, was exceedingly well meant, and no doubt he will presently vindicate his claim to rank as one of the pioneers of the new movement, if new movement there is to be. Mr Sydney Grundy has for years been afflicted, I take it, with paralysis of artistic ambition. It is assuredly no lack of inborn talent that he suffers from, but lack of will to use it to the best advantage. Let us hope that *The Second Mrs Tanqueray* may reawaken his dormant interest and pride in his art. We have yet to learn whether there is a serious (as opposed to a merely sentimental) side to Mr R. C. Carton's charming talent; but I see no reason why there should not be. He has given us his *Sweet Lavender* in *Liberty Hall*: when may we look for his *Second Mrs Tanqueray*? Then we have Mr J. M. Barrie, Mr Louis N. Parker, Mr Malcolm Watson, Mr George Moore, from all of whom we may hope for worthy work now that the way has been opened for them. I think we may say that the prospects of the new epoch are far from unpromising.

It is a curious little coincidence that the production of *The Second Mrs Tanqueray* should precede by only a single day the commencement of the short series of Ibsen performances at the Opera Comique.* Curious, I say, because these performances practically

---

* *See* next Article.

express the dissatisfaction with the ordinary theatrical
fare of the day which is felt by numbers of men and
women of social and intellectual note.   Their interest
in Ibsen is in most cases critical rather than enthusi-
astic ; but in one way or other (sometimes by repulsion
as much as by attraction) his plays *do* interest them
so much more than any other readily available form
of theatrical entertainment, that they are willing to
incur the trouble of organising and the expense of
subsidising this brief season.   Of course it marks an
unhealthy state of things that the most intelligent
class of theatre-goers should have to look abroad for
plays commensurate with their intelligence ; and if
The Second Mrs Tanqueray be indeed an epoch-
marking work, this state of things will not long endure.
Like Rector Kroll in *Rosmersholm*, " I hear I'm
denounced as a desperate fanatic ; " but there is one
point on which I cordially agree with the rabidest
Anti-Ibsenite, and that is that we have had too much
of Ibsen.   In *The Second Mrs Tanqueray*, Mr Pinero
has done more than all the invectives of all the Old
Critics together to put Ibsen in his place, so to speak.
Far be it from me to compare a piece of good honest
manly prose like *Mrs Tanqueray* with such strange,
and subtle, and fascinating poems as *Rosmersholm*
and *The Master Builder ;* but home-made prose, if
only it be good of its kind, is certainly a more whole-
some and nourishing everyday diet than exotic poetry.

Actors and actresses of high intelligence and poetical feeling will long continue, we may be sure, to find an irresistible attraction in the problems which Ibsen offers them, so that there is little likelihood of his being entirely banished from the English stage—in our time, at any rate. But if a new epoch is really dawning, he will undoubtedly bulk much less largely than he does at present, both on the stage and in critical discussion. So soon as our own drama achieves intellectual virility, Ibsen will be no more to us than a foreign dramatist ought to be to a nation whose native art is adequate to its own spiritual needs. Then, too (though this may seem absurdly sanguine), a rational Ibsen-criticism may perhaps be within the bounds of possibility. Certain it is, in any case, that the true policy of the Anti-Ibsenite faction is to take care that the new epoch which *The Second Mrs Tanqueray* is supposed to herald may soon become a living reality.

XXV.

ELEANORA DUSE—IBSEN PERFORMANCES—
THE INDEPENDENT THEATRE—FIVE
ENGLISH PLAYS.

7th June.

I HAVE just had the curiosity to look up Francisque Sarcey's account of Eleanora Duse, whom he saw in Vienna about this time last year, in the character of

Cleopatra—Shakespeare's not Sardou's.   She made
such a furore in the Kaiserstadt that Sarcey had difficulty in procuring a place, and the enthusiasm of the
audience was so great that he suspected the presence
of a claque.   The Viennese, it would seem, were too
polite to interrupt the performances of the Comédie
Française with applause during the progress of the
acts ; but in the case of Duse they forgot their
manners.   Monsieur Sarcey himself was not much im-
pressed.   " Il n'y a pas à dire," he says, " elle n'est
point jolie " ; her voice is not harmonious, but it has
very effective metallic vibrations ; her physiognomy is
of rare mobility, and her mimik curiously expressive ;
but in her explosions of fury and returns of tenderness
there is more of temperament than of art.   " Our
Sarah," he continues, " has a marvellous grace of attitudes and gestures ; she always remains, even in her
most violent transports of passion, her most audacious
escapades, a queen, the Queen of Egypt.   The Duse
has the air of a crowned grisette."   Well, we have not
yet seen her Cleopatra, and Sarcey did not see her
Marguerite or her Mirandolina, so that we are
scarcely on common ground for a discussion of these
judgments.*   It may be curious, however, simply to
pit impression against impression, and leave the

---

* As will be seen in a later article, Signora Duse's Cleopatra
fully explained Monsieur Sarcey's lack of enthusiasm.

reader to pay his money (at the Lyric Theatre) and
take his choice. I should say, then, that in *La Locandiera* (in which, by the way, she makes-up in the
ordinary fashion*) she is precisely "jolie—mais jolie
à croquer"; while in tragic parts she is better than
"jolie," she is "belle," she is beautiful. (Ah! how
much more beautiful is our English word!)   Her
voice has moments of harshness, certainly; but, besides the metallic vibrations which Monsieur Sarcey
notes, it is capable, when the artist so wills it, of the
most exquisite and limpid tenderness, the most penetrating sweetness. Her "rare mobility of feature"
is, oddly enough, what strikes me least about her.
From her Marguerite Gautier and Fédora I brought
away an impression of a certain facial monotony. I
seemed to remember nothing but two great black
eyes gazing, with a sort of pathetic intentness, from
out a pale, sad, nervous countenance. It is clear that
she possesses ample power of facial expression (her
smile is indescribably charming), but in tragedy I
should say that she made comparatively sparing use
of it, playing much more with voice and gesture than
with her features. Her movements, indeed, are
wonderfully varied, unconventional and expressive;
she seems to live all over, in every nerve, and yet she

---

* It was reported that Signora Duse disdained the aid of
"make-up," and so far as her serious characters were concerned
the rumour seems to have been well founded.

has very little of that excessive Southern exuberance of gesture which renders some of her comrades a trifle ludicrous in our Northern eyes. As to her playing with more of temperament than of art, I should be inclined to suggest an amendment, and say that her art is so delicate as to suffer her temperament always to shine through it ; and is not that the highest possible praise ? Since the comparison with Sarah Bernhardt is thrust upon us, I must admit that Duse gives me far more pleasure than Sarah has given me for years past, simply because her art is delicate, noble, and unobtrusive, while Sarah s art has overlaid her native talent until we are too often conscious of nothing but her tricks and processes. It sometimes seems as though Sarah Bernhardt were no longer a real woman, but an exquisitely - contrived automaton, the most wonderful *article de Paris* ever invented, perfect in all its mechanical airs and graces, but devoid alike of genuine feeling and artistic conscience. Of course this is a gross, an ungrateful, exaggeration. Sarah Bernhardt has been, and still is, a great actress, to whom we owe countless artistic pleasures. But there is a noble simplicity, a searching directness, in the art of Eleanora Duse, which certainly comes as a relief after the excessive artifice of Sarah's later manner. One has a sensation of passing out into the fresh air from an alcove redolent of patchouli.

Marguerite Gautier is to my thinking the most

noteworthy thing Signora Duse has as yet done. In
Fédora she seemed to be hampered by anxiety not to
imitate Sarah ; and as there is nothing in the part but
precisely what Sarah put into it, any departure from
the Bernhardt tradition is necessarily a change for the
worse. Her Santuzza in *Cavalleria Rusticana* is a
fine and impressive performance ; but the play is a
sketch, a mere incident, a scenario, rather than a
developed drama. Her Mirandolina again, in Gol-
doni's *La Locandiera*, is one of the gayest and most
vivid pieces of comedy I have ever seen. In the
Italian plays, too, her company shows to some advantage, especially Signor Flavio Ando and Signor
Ettore Mazzanti.

The English theatre, in these days, is cosmopolitan
enough in all conscience. I have to deal in this
article with fifteen plays in all—two French, two
Italian, four Norwegian,* one Dutch, and six English.
Two of the Norwegian dramas—*Hedda Gabler* and
The Master Builder—may be very briefly dismissed,
Mr Lewis Waller's Lövborg and Solness being the

---

* A series of twelve Ibsen performances at the Opera Comique
Theatre was subsidised by a subscription in the nature of an
abonnement, Mrs John Richard Green and Sir Frederick Pollock
acting as trustees of the fund. *Hedda Gabler* was performed on
the afternoons of May 29 and 30, the evenings of June 5 and 6 ;
Rosmersholm on May 31 and June 1 (afternoon), and June 7 and
8 (evening); *The Master Builder* and the fourth act of *Brand* on
June 2 and 3 (afternoon), and June 9 and 10 (evening).

only new features of much importance in the two
revivals. His Lövborg seemed to me excellent, except
for a slight over-elaboration in the third act ; and he
has every qualification for an admirable Solness, if he
will only throw himself into the part with confidence
and energy. He played it on Friday last under grave
disadvantages, having had very scant time for preparation. Next Friday he will, no doubt, have a
firmer grip of it. The novelties of the past week at
the Opera Comique were *Rosmersholm* and the fourth
act of *Brand*. When one has been present at the
rehearsals of a play, one stands too near it to judge
quite confidently of the merits of the acting ; but
there is no reason why I should not express the great
personal pleasure given me by the performance of
Rosmersholm. Mr Lewis Waller's personality is not,
at first sight, particularly suited to the gentle, dreamy,
irresolute Rosmer ; but he subdued it in the most
artistic spirit, and achieved a genuine character-creation. Rebecca West seems to me the largest, finest,
most poetical thing Miss Elizabeth Robins has as yet
done. The part is not a showy one, like Hedda and
Hilda, but it is far more difficult than either, and
Miss Robins's mastery of it is, to my thinking, almost
complete. There are passages in her Hedda and her
Hilda which I have never liked, and to which repetition does not reconcile me ; but in her Rebecca,
though there may be room here and there for elabora-

tion, there is nothing that seems to me other than right. In any case, whatever faults of detail we may find in her performances, there can be no doubt that the actress who, in one week, can play three such overwhelming parts, and can so absolutely differentiate and individualise them, possesses an astonishing breadth of intellectual sympathy and versatility of executive power. Altogether admirable, too, was Mr Bernard Gould's Ulric Brendel. He presented the "damaged archangel" (there is really a touch of Coleridge in Brendel, though he is even more "damaged" than poor S. T. C.) with singular breadth and vividness of touch, and just the right quality of posing picturesqueness. Mr Athol Forde repeated the part of Kroll, in which he made a deserved success two years ago. Mr Scott Buist's Mortensgaard was a capital bit of character, and Miss Frances Ivor, as Madame Helseth, rendered most valuable assistance. As to the fourth act of *Brand*, I really cannot form anything approaching an independent opinion. I have known it, wellnigh by heart, for twenty years, and the very thought of it has always been enough to bring the tears to my eyes. If only it were written in Greek instead of Norwegian, Agnes's soliloquy,

> " With its droppings of warm tears,
>   And its touches of things common,
>   Till they rise to touch the spheres,"

would assuredly take rank among the world's master-

pieces of pathos.   Of course it loses infinitely in
translation — that the accomplished translator, Pro-
fessor C. H. Herford, would, I am sure, be the first to
admit—but even in its English guise it never fails to
touch me profoundly.   For my part, I love rhymed
verse on the stage; but to those who love it not, I
cannot pretend to give any rational reasons for my
taste, any more than they, probably, can give rational
reasons for their distaste.   It *is* simply a matter of
taste, and beyond all argument.   Miss Robins's performance of Agnes seemed to me singularly beautiful
and true; but I own that a very inferior actress would
perhaps have moved me scarcely less in the part,
simply because, from old habit, I can no more help
crying over that scene than Diggory could help laughing at Mr Hardcastle's story of the grouse in the gun-
room.*   Mr Bernard Gould has not quite the

* I leave this misquotation from Goldsmith uncorrected in
the text, in order that I may have the pleasure of quoting the
correction which it elicited from Mr W. Moy Thomas in the
Graphic for June 10th :—" There seems some reason to fear that
the habit of extravagant adulation of foreign playwrights may
lead to the neglect of the study of our standard dramatists.   A
prominent Ibsen-idolater, for example, assures us this week that
for twenty years past he has been no more able to help crying at
the thought of the fourth act of Ibsen's *Brand* than Diggory
could help laughing at Mr Hardcastle's story of 'the grouse in
the gun-room.'   By a curious coincidence, twenty years was
exactly the time that Diggory had been affected in the laughing
way ; but this writer ought to have known that the allusion in

requisite authority for Brand, but he spoke his lines
admirably, and Miss Frances Ivor made a picturesque
Gipsy Woman.

"Josine Holland's" three-act play, *Leida*, translated by Mr A. T. de Mattos, and produced on
Friday last by the Independent Theatre Society,* is a
curious and interesting dramatic character-study.   It
smacks a little, at first, of Buckstonian farce of the
Good for Nothing order, but it presently takes a
more serious turn and becomes genuinely dramatic.
For my part, I hold with Mr Pinero that "of all
forms of innocence, ignorance is the least admirable,"
and consequently studies of that form of innocence,
as in M. Jules Lemaître's *Mariage Blanc*, always
give me a sense of discomfort.   But *Leida* is much
less unpleasant than *Mariage Blanc*, and much more
genuinely human.   The first act seemed inordinately
long, because no hint was given of any sort of dramatic action.   It is one thing to dispense with intri-
cacies of plot, and quite another to omit everything
that can arouse any sort of interest or expectation on
the part of the audience.   Miss Martha Conyngham,
a young American actress, played Leida with a great

Goldsmith's text was not to 'the grouse' but to 'ould Grouse.'
Light was thrown long ago upon the passage by the discovery
that 'Grouse' used to be a common name in Goldsmith's native
country for a sporting dog."

   * At the Comedy Theatre, June 2.

deal of somewhat uncouth, unrestrained ability.   She has evidently plenty of intelligence and dramatic instinct.   Mr Basset Roe showed ease and vivacity in the part of a good-humoured libertine, and Miss Henrietta Cowen was good as a cantankerous old maid— the very antithesis of the part she plays so charmingly in *Hedda Gabler*.   Mr H. M. Paull's one-act play, *At a Health Resort*, showed a distinct cleverness which somehow fell short of genuine dramatic inspiration.   There was nothing to which one could definitely take exception, unless it were one or two speeches in which the brutal puritanism of the Pharisee was laid on a little too thickly ; but on the other hand, there was nothing that very forcibly arrested the attention or stirred the sympathies.   It must be remembered, however; that Mr Paull received no assistance from his actors.

Mr Charrington should, I think, rearrange the order of his five plays at Terry's Theatre,* putting *Bud and Blossom* first, *Becky Sharp* second, and then introducing " half-price at 9.30," for those who wish to see the remainder of the programme, to wit, *An Interlude*, *The Three Wayfarers*, and *Foreign Policy*. In *Bud and Blossom*, an " up-to-date farce," Lady Colin Campbell has evidently been animated by a somewhat cynical contempt for the intelligence of the

---

* June 3—June 9.

British Public. But since the reception of *The Second Mrs Tanqueray* by the said British Public, cynical contempt for it is no longer "up to date." What we have now to do is to give the British Public a chance, and when Lady Colin Campbell brings her wit and penetration to bear upon a serious study of the world she knows so well, I am sure the British Public will bear no malice on account of *Bud and Blossom.* As a good Thackerayan, on the other hand, I shall certainly bear the blackest malice against Mr J. M. Barrie, for at least a week to come, for making a stupid and vulgar farce out of the conclusion of *Vanity Fair*, and persuading Miss Achurch that in order to embody Becky Sharp it is sufficient to redden her nose and indulge in "comic business" with a brandy bottle. *An Interlude*, by Mrs W. K. Clifford and Mr Walter H. Pollock, is at least interesting in its unconventionality. It presents a situation which ought to be worked out more fully—why should not the authors do so yet?—but, even as it is, it serves to impart an agreeable dash of bitterness to the bill of fare. It is the caviare, the olive of the entertainment, and would serve as an appetiser to the half-price audience. It gave Miss Achurch an opportunity for a very subtle and effective piece of acting. Mr Thomas Hardy's "legendary trifle," *The Three Wayfarers*, is the work of a poet and artist, and is highly dramatic in the widest and only true sense of the word—for what can be undramatic that exhibits human character and emotion in dialogue in such a way as to interest a theatrical audience? It is a strange and somewhat " creepy " fantasy, a thing to be seen and to be remembered. The speech of the younger brother, by the way, is an error, and ought to be corrected. Mr Herbert Waring was good as the fugitive, and Mr Charrington's performance of the Hangman was to my thinking almost the best thing he has ever done—full of a grim originality and power. Dr Conan Doyle's *Foreign Policy* is a very brightly written comedietta, well worth seeing. In it Miss Achurch does a good piece of character-acting as a middle-aged woman, but her grey wig is by no means a success. Mr Charrington appears as a gouty diplomatist, and Mr Edmond Maurice's sketch of a fashionable physician once more proves his remarkable skill in representing comic character with a slight dash of caricature.

XXVI.

" A Doll's House "—" A Scrap of Paper."

14th June.

It is pleasant—and in things of art it is sometimes possible—to be on with the new love without feeling the least necessity or temptation to be off with the

old. Some of my most esteemed colleagues have, I
think, been curiously unjust to Signora Duse's Nora.*
It gave me very great pleasure ; it seemed to me, on
the whole, a wonderfully impressive and beautiful
performance ; and yet it has not made me abate one
jot of my admiration for our English Nora, the Nora
of Miss Janet Achurch. I make no apology for thus
plunging head-foremost into comparison. Where
comparison is to the advantage of both parties it
ceases to be odious. Physically, Signora Duse comes
very near the ideal of the character. Other critics,
with keener eyes or more powerful opera-glasses
(which they would do well to leave at home), found
her old-looking and unattractive ; to me it seemed
that in the first act she " put on beauty like a garment," or rather the precise quality of sparkling prettiness which the character demands. Her opening
scenes, up to Krogstad's entrance, struck me as the
very perfection of natural acting, her gaiety being
spontaneous, effervescent, iridescent, so to speak,
without being in the least overdone. Nora, it must
be remembered, is not a child in years—we may
safely take her to be six- or seven-and-twenty—nor is
she the brainless butterfly of anti-Ibsenite legend.
She is a brave little woman who has fought a hard
fight against illness and poverty, has made a cosy,

---

* 9th June.

cheerful home for her husband without letting that
superior being dream of the struggle it has cost her,
and has remained through it all, if not "felice," at
least "allegra." If she were really and essentially
the empty-headed doll we hear so much about, the
whole point of the play would be gone ; so that there
is not the least reason why we should demand from
the actress a waxen, flaxen prettiness, on which experience has left no traces. The critics, in fact, sub-
limely unconscious of the way in which they thereby
drive home the poet's irony, fall into the very same
misunderstanding of Nora's character which makes
Helmer a bye-word for masculine stupidity, and are
no less flabbergasted than he when the doll puts off
her masquerade dress and turns out to be a woman
after all. And if Nora is not really childish, still less
is she "neurotic." That word is as comfortable as
Mesopotamia to critics who cannot understand Ibsen,
and yet want to appear abreast of the age. Because
Ibsen has drawn two neurotic women—Ellida and
Hedda Gabler—they conclude that they are safe in
applying the term to all his creations ; whereas the
physical characteristic of Nora, Mrs Alving, Rebecca
West, and Hilda Wangel, is, in fact, robust and even
radiant health. One may pretty safely conjecture,
indeed, that so sensitive an artist as Signora Duse is
personally far more "neurotic" than Nora ; and it is
precisely a proof of her art that in the first act she

produces an impression of absolutely fresh and whole-
some vitality.   It is true that in the later acts Nora
is wrought up to a high pitch of nervous tension,
such as the circumstances of the case would naturally
produce in the healthiest woman ; but what sort of
criticism must we call it which confounds nervousness arising from momentary terror and suspense with
constitutional or chronic neurosis ?

It was in the first scene with Krogstad that I
began to be conscious of the fault, or at any rate the
peculiarity, which renders Signora Duse's Nora less
consummate than in the opening scenes it promised
to be, and on the whole less satisfying than Miss
Achurch's.   In her dread of becoming melodramatic,
the Italian actress neglects to be legitimately dramatic, and omits or slurs effects which the poet evidently intended.   For example, she declines to give
the slightest start when Krogstad points out the remarkable circumstance that her father endorsed her
note of hand "three days after his death."   Now
this is mere pedantry.   Up to that moment Nora has
been quite unconscious of her blunder ; she could not
but give some sign of surprise on being confronted
with it.   Again, Helmer's use of the word "crime"
produces no special effect upon her, and she does
nothing to bring out the tragic irony which she
feels in his remark, "It gives me a positive sense of
physical discomfort to come in contact with such

people." Still, her first act is on the whole delightful ; it is in the second that Miss Achurch, simply by
reason of her faithful and sympathetic study of the
poet's intentions, has a marked advantage. Signora
Duse begins by altogether omitting the very important scene with the nurse. Then she makes a
number of quite purposeless cuts in the scene with
Rank, ignores the stage directions, and fails to mark
what may be called the rhythm of the scene, or to
contrast the gloom of the opening passage with the
hectic gaiety of the middle portion and the serious
dignity of the close. In short, she paints the whole
scene in one colour instead of in the three shades
which the poet very clearly indicates. Still more astonishing is it to find her cutting out the conclusion
of the scene with Krogstad, in which she is mustering
up her courage for suicide. There cannot be the
smallest doubt that the effects of horror and despair
which belong to this scene, and which Miss Achurch
made so memorable, are well within Signora Duse's
range. It is probably because she feels them to be
cheap and easy that she neglects them. But this, I
say again, is pedantry. It is true that the effects are
not of the very highest order ; but if a scene is to be
played at all, it should be played in the key in which
it is written. On the other hand, one can scarcely
quarrel with Signora Duse's almost total omission of
the tarantella. This is Ibsen's last concession to the

old technique, and the effect is always in the inverse
ratio of the effort. It generally wins applause simply
as a dance, but as drama it invariably misses fire.
One can readily forgive Signora Duse for feeling it to
be beneath her dignity.

Her third act is altogether masterly, though here,
again, the sentiment of the scene with Rank is destroyed by foolish excisions. I now understand what
those critics mean who claim for Signora Duse a
wonderful variety of facial expression. Her features
have no great instantaneous mobility, if I may so
phrase it. Her expression does not, as a rule, alter
very greatly from moment to moment ; but for each
large phase of feeling she has a totally different countenance. Her Nora, for example, has four distinct
faces. In the first act, up to the scene with Krogstad, her expression sparkles with cloudless gaiety ;
in the second act her face is harassed, overstrained,
tense with anxiety ; at the opening of the third act
she has grown old, haggard, almost deathlike ; while
in the concluding scene intellectual animation and
indignation have to some extent rejuvenated her, and
fashioned a countenance entirely different from the
other three. I have seldom seen anything ghastlier
than her hollow-eyed, ashen face, in the first half of
this act, contrasted with her Capri costume. One
felt that Helmer must indeed have drunk an incredible quantity of champagne not to see that the

shadow of death lay over this woman. Her open-mouthed, stony astonishment, where he turns upon her and upbraids her, was as daring as it was impressive. Her concluding scene again (in which, by the bye, scarcely a word was cut out), conflicted with all my prejudices as to the tone in which it ought to be taken, and flew in the face of the poet's explicit directions. But it was so brilliant, so vivid, so true in its own way, that it conquered all objection. It was Ibsen's last scene translated into Italian, not merely in words, but in tone and temperament. The melancholy dignity, the subdued intensity of feeling, which made Miss Achurch's performance (at its best) the perfection of poetic acting, would have been impossible to Signora Duse. Methods of expression which are true and natural in the Teuton would be false and unnatural in the Latin ; so that here, for once, it cannot be denied that there was some justification for overriding the poet's directions. For once, and for once only. If Signora Duse wishes to number Nora among her perfect successes, she will reconsider her whole second act, restore the text, and make Ibsen her stage-manager, instead of Signor Flavio Ando. No one who has ever had to do with staging a play of Ibsen's, can doubt that any essential departure from the " business " he prescribes, is a departure for the worse.

In *A Scrap of Paper** at the Avenue Theatre, it is delightful to find Mrs Kendal quite her old self again. Her Susan Hartley is by far the best thing she has done since her return from America, and remains, what it always was, one of the most accomplished pieces of comedy of our generation. Colonel Blake too is one of Mr Kendal's best parts, and the play is probably the cleverest and most amusing of its class. In sum, a very pleasant entertainment.

XXVII.

" AN ENEMY OF THE PEOPLE "—THE COMÉDIE FRANÇAISE.

21st June.

THE success of *An Enemy of the People*† at the Haymarket is to me, personally, a very keen satisfaction, though not precisely for what I may call the orthodox reasons. Several of my friends have congratulated me, as a notorious "Ibsenite," on the fact that Ibsen has at last received the sanction, not to say the consecration, of acceptance at the hands of an actor-manager. I hope Mr Beerbohm Tree will not think me churlish if I confess that for this I care

---

* June 5—June 23.

† First performed June 14 (afternoon). Repeated June 21 and 28 (afternoon), and July 20, 21, 22 (evenings), and July 22 (afternoon).

not a jot. I greatly admire and appreciate Mr Tree's
courage in flying in the face of probably the most
obstinate and rancorous prejudice recorded in the
history of the stage ; but it is Mr Tree himself, and
not Ibsen, who is to be congratulated on this act of
daring. Ibsen has not suffered one whit for lack of
actor-manager patronage. In pocket, yes, possibly ;
if he had been "taken up" from the first by one or
two actor-managers, his pecuniary profits from England might perhaps have been greater. But as he is
understood to be fairly well off, and as no farthing
of any such profits comes to me, I am naturally not
much troubled about that aspect of the matter.
Artistically, it has been a distinct gain to Ibsen to
be left alone by the managers. From what I have
seen and heard of Ibsen performances abroad, I do
not hesitate to say that, take it all round, his plays
have nowhere been better acted, or (except by the
press) more intelligently received, than in England.
And why? Because they have been left to seek out
their elective affinities ; because they have not been
treated as mechanical matters of business and routine,
but studied and staged by artists with special intellectual and technical qualifications for their work. Even
the most "frumious" anti-Ibsenite will admit that,
except in one or two trivial instances, the productions
have been as well prepared, as smooth, as adequate,
as they could possibly have been in any actor-

managed theatre. The performance of *An Enemy of the People* at the Haymarket was incomparably the roughest and "fluffiest" we have yet seen. Never has the voice of the prompter been heard in the land with such painful frequency and distinctness. This was the result, I fancy, of over-rehearsal rather than of under-rehearsal; but, whatever the reason, the fact remains that the first actor-manager performance of Ibsen, despite the excellent talents employed, was distinctly below the level of the so-called "scratch" performances to which we have been accustomed. As to the treatment of the text, I cannot speak with certainty until I know how much was deliberately omitted and how much merely forgotten. The play is undeniably one which will bear free "cutting," for there is no reason in the world why local details, incomprehensible to an English audience, should be suffered to bore them and distract their attention from the wide and permanent interests of the action. When the company know their parts, I believe that all that is really essential will be found to have been retained; but whatever it may become at subsequent performances, it was a monstrously mutilated text to which we listened on Wednesday last. Well then, if I do not regard the Haymarket performance as either a "moral victory" or an artistic triumph, where does the aforesaid "keen satisfaction" come in? Simply in the fact that, with all its shortcomings, the performance vindicated Ibsen's claim to rank not only as a great dramatist but as a skilful playwright. *An Enemy of the People* is, in the best, the only true, sense of the word, a well-made play. It is, and it was felt to be, the work of a man who knows the stage as well as he knows the human heart.

Mr Sydney Grundy, a man who also knows the stage, has expressed in no doubtful terms his contempt for the stupidity of the criticism which has nothing but contempt for Ibsen ;* but even he, I think (if it was not he I beg his pardon), has rejected as utterly undramatic the fourth act—the meeting scene—in *An Enemy of the People.* Well now, no one who was present at the Haymarket can doubt that this scene was *the* success of the play, the one which most interested and moved the audience. And why? Simply because Ibsen knows his business well enough to be able to transcend with success the pettifogging rules of constructive orthodoxy. As for the rest of the play, it might have been constructed by Scribe himself so far as neatness is concerned, though Scribe, of course, would have developed the

---

* In the second of two letters to the *Era* (17th January 1891) entitled "Personal Animosity," Mr Grundy wrote :—". . . It was my desire to avoid mentioning English plays that caused me to instance Ibsen—not that I am an Ibsenite. I do not even like Ibsen. But when I see a little boy scribbling rude words on the pedestal of a Colossus, I cannot help boxing his ears."

intrigue so as to crush out the character. When the company is thoroughly at home in the play, it will certainly be one of the most entertaining entertainments on the stage. I am sure that, if properly worked, there is even "money in it." For my own part, I hold it of more importance that a play should have poetry in it; but there is no harm in its having both.

Mr Tree gives us the appearance of Stockmann to perfection, and has also caught with fine sympathy the hot-headed geniality of the man. He is the only *genial* character Ibsen has ever drawn; in his mingling of idealism with humour he suggests Don Quixote and Sancho rolled into one. What Mr Tree has not as yet quite seized is the bustling loquacity, the eager effervescence, of Stockmann's sanguine, expansive nature. He is too emphatic, too pontifical, above all too *slow*. He has not " le diable au corps." He is too apt to rely for his effects upon solemn pauses, and to import into the vivid, ebullient Stockmann the aristocratic languor of Lord Illingworth and the dreaminess of Hamlet. Stockmann ought to be, as "Spectator" happily puts it, an "agreeable rattle." If Mr Tree recognised this, he would never dream of cutting such delightfully characteristic little touches as his whisper after he has sent one of his boys for the cigar-box : "I believe he cribs one now and again, but I pretend not to notice." The pre-

vailing deliberation was particularly notable in the
fourth act.   I sat on thorns during the Doctor's speech
—I wanted to shout, "Go on! Go on! Don't let the
thing down!"   Compared with that which Ibsen
designed, Mr Tree's delivery was as a fitful breeze to
a tornado.   Even so, the effect was great; if the
scene were properly worked up it would be overwhelming, like that of Antony's oration in the
Meiningen *Julius Cæsar*.   There was a monotony
and a lack of gradation in the utterances of the crowd
which might easily be remedied; and the drunken
man should not be allowed to circulate with the
regularity of a postman on his rounds.   Mr Tree's
last act is probably his best; but when he has
announced that "the strongest man is he who stands
most alone," why does he proceed to build himself
inextricably into a pyramid of other people?   This is
certainly not suiting the action to the word.   On the
whole, Mr Tree's performance is as yet but a rough
sketch of Stockmann; but it is a sketch which gives
every promise of developing into a brilliant portrait.
Mr Kemble is excellent as the Burgomaster, and Mrs
Wright is charming as Mrs Stockmann.   Miss Hanbury makes quite an ideal Petra, Mr Welch a good
Hovstad, and Mr Allen a capital Morten Kiil, if only
he would slightly moderate his chuckle.   Mr Robson's Aslaksen is extremely, and in itself quite
legitimately, funny; but Mr Tree is inclined to make

illegitimate capital out of the contrast between his
stature and Mr Robson's, going out of his way to
emphasise it, especially in the second act.   This is
cheap and inartistic ; and so are some other merely
farcical touches introduced from time to time.   By
the way, it is a great mistake to make the Burgomaster in the second act call his brother "an enemy
of the people."   As well represent Lord Salisbury
using "aristocrat" as a term of reproach.   Peter
Stockmann cares nothing about the people ; what he
says is "an enemy of *Society*."

We critics are greatly the gainers by the extraordinary energy displayed by the Comédie Française
in changing their programme every evening.*   It
gives us an opportunity of passing a whole dramatic
literature under review.   The past week alone has
been a liberal education, and I, for one, have availed
myself of it with gratitude.   But I doubt whether the
general public or the treasury of the theatre finds
equal advantage in the arrangement.   Of course the
comedians of Molière were bound to open with
Molière and Racine ; but *Andromaque* or *Britannicus*

---

* The visit of the Comédie Française to Drury Lane began
on Monday, June 12, and ended on Wednesday, July 12.   The
original intention of changing the bill at every performance, and
playing no piece more than once, was very soon abandoned.
Nevertheless, thirty-two plays were presented during the month.
I have not thought it necessary to give the precise date of each
performance noticed.

would have been far less lugubrious than *Les
Plaideurs ;* and as for Coquelin cadet's Argan in
Le Malade Imaginaire, its mechanical clowning is
distinctly unworthy of Molière and of the company.
How different was Thiron's reading of the part !
The *Cérémonie* was the most interesting feature of the
first night.   It was like the Apotheosis of Tradition,
and had a dignity and impressiveness of its own amid
all its gigantic buffoonery.   Then came *Un Père
Prodigue*, which I am delighted to have seen, since
even the weaker plays of a man like Dumas are
always worthy of study.   Moreover, it showed us our
old friend Febvre in one of his happiest characters
(what on earth tempts him to retire in the maturity
of his powers ?), and introduced us, in Mme. de
Marsy, to a very able actress who seems to occupy
the place left vacant by Sophie Croizette.   But, from
the business point of view, how much better it would
have been to have skipped *Un Père Prodigue* altogether, played *Denise* on Tuesday, and then repeated
it on Thursday !   *Denise* is an infinitely stronger,
more interesting, more modern and human play,
and it is acted to perfection by Got, Worms, Silvain,
and Baillet, and by Mesdames Bartet, Pierson,
Muller, and Pauline Granger.   The cast does not
even lose greatly by the substitution of Silvain for
Coquelin in the part of the monogamous Thouvenin.
Coquelin's mordant delivery, of course, is beyond

imitation ; but he was not "the man of the part" and Silvain is.   On the whole, the piece is as well played as *The Second Mrs Tanqueray* (no better), and is almost as interesting.   If, now, it had been produced on Tuesday night and announced for repetition on Thursday or Friday, the critics would have told the public that it was a thing not to be missed, and there would have been a crowded house for its second performance.   As it is, the critics cannot possibly be expected to give adequate attention to performances which they have merely to record as things past and done with—" sans lendemain," as Sarcey would say— and which can therefore have but a meagre interest for their readers. Richepin's *Par le Glaive*, pro- duced on Wednesday, suggested an opera without the music, and, like Arcedeckne at Thackeray's lecture, I missed the "pianner."   It is a robustious production, the work of a lyrist rather than a true dramatist ; for fine alexandrines do not make fine plays.   The character-drawing is entirely superficial, the plot is anything but clear, and even the situations are not very firmly handled.   I, personally, am charmed to have seen it, but I feel that the Comédie Française are putting themselves about too much for my education.   They certainly put themselves about enormously in *Par le Glaive*.   Such bellowing as Paul Mounet's I don't remember to have heard except at Buffalo Bill's Wild West Show.   It is good bellow-

ing, not at all unpleasant ; for Mounet has a fine voice
and knows how to use it ; but really his Conrad le
Loup ought rather to have been called Conrad le
Taureau. Even Mounet-Sully, it seemed to me, gave
us too much, from time to time, of his lovely voice ;
but it is always a pleasure to listen to him.   Mesdames Bartet and Dudlay were both admirable.   In
Les Effrontés we had a good specimen of Augier's
sane and robust, but somewhat bourgeois, talent ;
while in *Le Gendre de M. Poirier* we found the same
talent with an added touch of grace and humour,
doubtless due to his collaborator, the author of *Mlle.
de la Seiglière.*   Got's Giboyer is a brilliant piece of
comedy, though the type is not now very recognisable ;
and his Poirier remains one of the masterpieces of
contemporary French acting, a veritable incarnation.
Madame Jane Hading's personality struck me as
rather too showy for Augier's Marquise d'Auberives.
Beauty is always a good fault ; but Madame Hading's
beauty seemed too Olympian for the play and its period.

I have no space for more than a passing mention
of the Independent Theatre performance of *A Blot
in the 'Scutcheon,** in which Mr Louis Calvert played
Tresham with intelligence and power, while Miss
May Harvey, as Mildred, seemed to possess genuine
talent as well as great personal charm.

---

* Opera Comique, June 15.

XXVIII.

" ANTONY AND CLEOPATRA "—THE COMÉDIE FRANÇAISE.

28th June.

IT is said that Signora Duse understands no English ;
and this fact, if fact it be, is the explanation and
excuse of her Cleopatra. If she could read Shakespeare's *Antony and Cleopatra*,* she would either
drop the part altogether from her repertory or act
it very differently. She would realise that the play
is not a badly-constructed domestic drama in out-
landish costumes, but a glorious love-poem, portray-
ing and celebrating that all-absorbing passion for
which the world is well lost. Shakespeare and
Wagner, like the gods of old, have translated two
pairs of lovers to the firmament of the ideal, where
they blaze, as constellations, for ever. Three pairs
for that matter, for we must not forget Romeo and
Juliet ; but they are the types of first love, youthful, fanciful, exquisite : while Antony and Cleopatra,
like Tristan and Isolde, are the titanic embodiments
of adult passion. The idealisation which Wagner
effected with the help of music, Shakespeare achieved
by means of poetry alone. *Antony and Cleopatra*
is a poem or it is nothing ; whereas in the Italian
version it is only a spasmodic series of scenes in

---

* June 19.

more or less unnatural prose. I am not sufficiently
familiar with Italian verse to know whether the
whole text was entirely and intentionally unmetrical;
but, certainly, my ear could catch no trace of rhythm
or cadence. The result was a complete confutation
of those intransigeant theorists who pretend to find
satisfaction in prose translations of verse and to scorn
all metrical translations. There are some poems,
it is true, that can only be translated in prose,
but there are others that must be rendered in verse
or not at all; and to this class belong dramatic
poems almost without exception. If they cannot be
reproduced in fairly adequate verse, they cannot
be reproduced at all—on the stage. Who wants to
hear a "crib" recited or a libretto acted without
the music? Those who can affect to find anything
like keen satisfaction in poetry prosaised must be
singularly inaccessible to the supreme pleasure which
poetry in its natural state, so to speak, is capable
of giving. Take, for instance, Cleopatra's great
outburst:

> "I dreamt, there was an emperor Antony:
> O, such another sleep, that I might see
> But such another man ! . . .
> His face was as the heavens, and therein stuck
> A sun and moon, which kept their course, and lighted
> The little O, the earth. . . .
> His legs bestrid the ocean; his rear'd arm
> Crested the world; his voice was propertied
> As all the tuned spheres, and that to friends;

But when he meant to quail and shake the orb,
He was as rattling thunder.   For his bounty,
There was no winter in 't ; an autumn 't was,
That grew the more by reaping : his delights
Were dolphin-like ; they showed his back above
The element they liv'd in : in his livery
Walked crowns and crownlets ; realms and islands were
As plates dropped from his pocket. . . .
Think you there was, or might be, such a man
As this I dreamt of ? "

The whole beauty, meaning, and justification of
these hyperboles lies in the movement, the harmony,
the lyric impetus of the verse.   Translate them into
prose and they become merely grotesque.   The
difference is as great as between a Bacchante in
dithyrambic rapture and a skeleton rattling his dry
bones.   If we cannot have the Bacchante, at least
spare us the skeleton.   For Italians, perhaps, who
do not know English, the dry bones may be better
than nothing.   But we, who have the great harmonies
in our ears, how can we have ears for anything else ?

" Show me, my women, like a queen ; go fetch
My best attires ; I am again for Cydnus,
To meet Mark Antony. . . .
Give me my robe, put on my crown ; I have
Immortal longings in me ; now no more
The juice of Egypt's grape shall moist this lip. . . .
I am fire and air ; my other elements
I give to baser life.   So ; have you done ?
Come, then, and take the last warmth of my lips.
Farewell, kind Charmian ; Iras, long farewell. . .
Dost thou not see my baby at my breast
That sucks the nurse asleep——"

I declare it gives me more pleasure, more emotion,
to repeat these lines in my own mind than to see
Signora Duse's Cleopatra from beginning to end.

For, along with the poetry, the elevation, the
idealism of the part, she entirely misses its passion.
Pity that so richly gifted an artist should be mastered
every now and then by what one can only describe
as a perverse spirit of paradox. Her Cleopatra is
a paradox incarnate, a contradiction in terms; for
cold fire is not more inconceivable than a passion-
less Cleopatra. There is nothing in the least volup-
tuous, sensuous, languorous about her performance.
Her very embraces are chilly, and she kisses like a
canary-bird. One does not see what attraction the
part can have for her, if she declines to throw herself
into it more fully than this. There were moments,
of course, in which we recognised the accomplished
actress, the mistress of her art. The Messenger-
scene was fine and daring, and there were touches
of beautiful sincerity in the last act. But even where
she was good, she was good in the abstract, as it
were—she sometimes played like a great artist, never
like a great Cleopatra. We can, of course, like
Mercutio, conceive "Cleopatra a gipsy," alluring
her lovers rather by a sort of intellectual sprightli-
ness than by a splendid harmony of spirit and flesh.
But I am very much mistaken if this be the Cleopatra of history; and assuredly it is not the Cleopatra

of the world's imagination, to whom Shakespeare gave immortal form and voice. Signora Duse's Cleopatra is never for an instant that incarnation of love and luxury, of all that is superb and seductive in womanhood, which has haunted the minds of men for nineteen centuries. She is simply a bright little woman, like her Nora or her Mirandolina. She is not Cleopatra, but Cleopatrina, Cleopatrinetta.

The excellent and very disinterested advice which I tendered last week to the management of the Comédie Française was, it appears, unnecessary. Even as I wrote, the programme was being modified, and both *Denise* and *Les Effrontés* have been, and are again to be, repeated. For the rest, we have had *Le Demi-Monde*, which I was constrained to sacrifice to *Antony and Cleopatra* (I can scarcely call it a case of "The Half-World Well Lost"); *Henri Trois et sa Cour*, a piece of more historical than actual interest; *Mlle. de la Seiglière*, one of the few genuine comedies in existence, deflecting neither on the side of farce nor of drama; *Adrienne Lecouvreur*, another piece which ought to be kept under a glass case in a historical museum; and, above all, we have had *Francillon*, which I take leave to consider Dumas's masterpiece, and one of the wittiest and most entertaining plays ever written. It, too, must certainly be repeated, and when it is, I adjure you to go and see it. The performance,

if not better than that of *Denise*, is at least more
satisfactory; for there is an inherent artificiality in
Francillon which accords with the artificial method
of the company.   *Denise*, in spite of Thouvenin,
is real and moving, and we now and then feel the
want of a somewhat less highly-polished realism than
that of Worms and Madame Bartet; but *Francillon* is
so patently an exercise in dramatic logic (an incomparably brilliant exercise), that all we demand is a
performance of perfect finish and style.   Madame
Bartet is beyond all praise; Baillet, though not as
good as Febvre, is more than passable; and Worms,
in his original part of Stanislas, shows himself a
versatile as well as an impressive actor, though I
don't know that he is quite so thoroughly the man
of the part as Le Bargy, whom I saw play it in
Paris some time ago.   The only dull moments in
the play are those devoted to the chatter of Annette,
one of Dumas's most intolerable *jeunes filles*.   Perhaps
I ought to mention that it is not an entertainment
for a young ladies' boarding-school.   Indeed, if
consistency were to be looked for in these matters,
some of our critical " myrmidons of morality " ought
to be denouncing the laxity of the Censor and
threatening prosecutions under Lord Campbell's Act.
"The conversation that goes on in your drawing-
room," says Stanislas to Francillon, " would not be
tolerated by Rosalie Michon "—and we can quite

believe it, without accusing Mademoiselle Michon of any exaggerated affectation of prudery. And if you ask me whether, apart from its excessive frankness of speech, the general effect of the play can be described as moral, I fear I cannot very confidently reassure you. Here, as elsewhere, Dumas preaches a morality as stern as that of Mr W. T. Stead; but here, as elsewhere, he treats vice as the normal and natural condition of man, and virtue as a pious opinion, to be commended in a spirit of humorous paradox. His recipe for social salvation is about as practical as the famous cure for toothache: Fill your mouth with cold water and sit on the hob till it boils; and he is perfectly aware of its futility. Therefore the general impression we carry away is, that vice is exceedingly amusing and virtue exceedingly unattainable; which is not, perhaps, a doctrine that makes point-blank for righteousness. Dumas, indeed, affords from first to last an extreme instance of the radical contrast between the French and English methods of envisaging moral questions. We, in England, always assume virtue to be the rule, vice the exception, while in France they start from the contrary hypothesis. Whatever be the facts of the case, ours is certainly, from the point of view of the conventional moralist, the wiser and safer plan.

I am delighted to see that *Œdipe Roi* is to be given this week; but what has become of Corneille

and Racine? If Monsieur Claretie has been advised
to suppress classic tragedy altogether, I think he
has been ill-advised. We are not so utterly illiterate
as all that.*

XXIX.

" ŒDIPE ROI "—DALY'S THEATRE—" DIVORÇONS "— " A WOMAN'S REVENGE."

5*th July.*

IF I had been obliged to select one play from the
repertory of the Comédie Française, and to see it
only, I should without a moment's hesitation have
chosen *Œdipe Roi*. And I should have chosen
rightly. The immediate pleasure of seeing the great
tragedy roll majestically along was as keen as it was
rare ; and the reflections excited by the performance
were so innumerable that I want to write a book
about it instead of a paragraph. There is no play in
the world so brimming with historical, technical, and
ethical interest. A complete analysis and criticism of
it—involving, of course, a comparison and contrast
between it and the masterpieces of the modern stage
—might be to the Drama what Lessing's *Laokoön* is
to the plastic arts. Nay, it ought to be a great deal
more, for it would practically amount to a history of
the evolution of dramatic forms. Ah ! what a book I

---

* It was entirely suppressed.

see in my mind's eye !—a very miracle of acumen and
erudition ! The worst of it is that the acumen and
erudition are also in my mind's eye, not in my mind ;
so the book, like Ulric Brendel's, must remain un-
written — known and appreciated by myself alone.
For the general public, of course, *Œdipus Tyrannus*
cannot have the absorbing interest it has, or ought to
have, for specialists, so that I was not surprised to see
a comparatively, though not an exceedingly, meagre
house. But I should at least have expected all the
specialists—to wit, the dramatic critics—to be at their
posts on so rare an occasion as the production in
London of a tragedy of Sophocles. They may have
been present — from where I sat I could see but
a small portion of the house—but, if so, their raptures
must have struck most of them speechless, for I
searched the morning papers in vain for a notice
of the event.   Several of them contained careful
appreciations of a play named *Fireworks ;* but of
the *Œdipus Tyrannus* never a word ! Perhaps the
original Greek sings so sweetly in the ears of the
critics, that they shrink from listening to the worthy
Jules Lacroix's alexandrines ; but, in that case, I
beg to assure them, they neglect an opportunity.
However familiar we may be with it in the study,
there is always something to be learnt from seeing a
play on the stage ; and Sophocles in French is much
nearer the real thing than Sophocles in Greek, as

recited from time to time at the universities. All the
rule-of-thumb scansion in the world can never restore
to us the true rhythmic movement of the iambic line,
any more than the untrained voice of a callow under-
graduate, bow-wowing his lines with all the vowels
transmuted into English, can reproduce the splendid
resonance of tone which rang through the vast
theatres of Athens and Syracuse. Now in the French
performance we at least have rhythm and melody,
though not *the* rhythm and melody, and we have
certainly all the sonority that is necessary or desirable
in our smaller and roofed-in theatres. Moreover, we
have the solemn dignity of carriage which belongs to
the drama of gods and heroes. The actors do not,
indeed, wear the cothurnus, but their performance is
" cothurnate " none the less. In a word, we have as
near an approach as is conceivable, under modern
conditions, to the tragedy of the ancients ; and I
should have thought that, as a mere item of news,
that would be at least as interesting, even to the man
in the street, as—well, as *Fireworks*. But no, " the
oracles are dumb ; " and, to tell the truth, this silence
of theirs seems to me eloquent.

Yes ! it is an experience, which I, for my part,
would not willingly miss, to listen to a drama twenty-
three centuries old, and to thrill with the same sense
of tragic irony, to feel one's heart-strings gripped with
the same pity and terror, which moved the Athenian

populace in the Theatre of Dionysus, at the other end
of history. For it is an intensely moving story this
of the downfall of King Œdipus. The man who can
criticise the conduct of the plot as Corneille and
Voltaire did (so I read in Jules Lemaître) must be
strangely lacking in historic sense. Lemaître himself
seems to me to treat it rather too much as if it were
a play of Sardou's. To be sure, Œdipus ought, if he
had been strictly reasonable, to have baffled the
oracle by refraining from killing any gentleman, and
from marrying any lady, whom he did not know
to be younger than himself. But an oracle is not to
be trifled with in that way. The very awe of the
thing resides in the feeling that the powers who predict know how to accomplish their prediction, even
by blinding the reason of their victims. That would
not be a good plea for Sardou, but it was perfectly
good for Sophocles and his audience ; and the whole
fun of the thing, if I may phrase it so, is to put ourselves in the place of the Athenians. Then, again,
Monsieur Lemaître confesses that Œdipus's great
" pathos-scene " (technically so called) at the end of
the play bored him " horribly " ; and adds that, if
every one were sincere, every one would say the same
thing. Such an assertion, of course, silences all
argument ; I can only affirm, with all the sincerity of
which I am capable, that the scene moved me very
deeply. "The sin is in the will, not in the material

act," says Monsieur Lemaître. Why, certainly ; we
say so, we think so, and some of us, now-a-days, have
even succeeded (more or less) in *feeling* so as well.
But if that truth has even now entered but imperfectly
into the world's consciousness, how much further was
the world of B.C. 440 from any effective realisation of
it ! And how much further still the primitive
Hellenes, among whom the folk-tale of Œdipus took
its rise ! No doubt Sophocles, as Monsieur Lemaître
states, realised the truth as we do ; but is it a dramatist's business always to make his characters act
by the light of pure reason ? The question is not
whether Œdipus *ought* to have "taken on" as he did
about the little accidents of his manslaughter and
marriage, but whether he *would* have done so.
Monsieur Lemaître must surely be aware that, even
in this rationalistic, Herbert-Spencerian age, thousands
of men are worrying themselves into strait-waistcoats
or Salvation jerseys, if not into their coffins, over
"sins" for which they are no more morally responsible than was Œdipus for his parricide and incest.
And shall we refuse him and them our pity ? That
would be Pharisaic rationalism with a vengeance.

Mounet Sully's declamation, or rather intonation,
of his verses seemed to me absolutely what the play
and part demanded. His habit of marking both the
cæsura and the end of the line by a sort of prolonged
or sustained roar on the vowel of the last syllable is,

as a rule, apt to become monotonous; but I don't think it is possible, in antique tragedy, to emphasise too much the rhythm of the lines. His appearance was superb, and his intense earnestness gave the whole thing an air of living reality, so that we never for a moment felt the performance to be a mere academic revival of a curiosity of literature. It was a hundred times as real, as vital, as *Par le Glaive* or *Henri III. et sa Cour.* Paul Mounet made a magnificent Tiresias, and Albert Lambert fils was excellent as the old Shepherd. Madame Lerou's Jocaste, too, seemed to me profoundly and memorably tragic. Her last exit is a piece of incomparable stagecraft on the part of the despised Sophocles—despised of the morning press. If there is anything more impressive and even appalling in drama, I should like to hear of it. The appearance of Œdipus in the last scene, with his empty eye-sockets yet streaming blood, was undeniably hideous; but for my part I am never so much "mis dedans," as Sarcey phrases it, in the theatre, as to forget that red paint is, after all, only red paint. My experience last Thursday night, rather to my own surprise, was a curious proof of this. In real life I am horribly sensitive to anything wrong with the eye of another person. I will go a mile out of my way to avoid seeing a bleared eye, and the merest glimpse of inflamed lids or a bloodshot eyeball will make my own eyes smart and water. Consequently, I rather

expected that the gory orbits of Œdipus would cause
me sensible discomfort; but no! I felt none whatever. If some one had told me, for example, that the
paint had got into the actor's eyes, and that he was
really suffering, I should have been in a sympathetic
agony; but as it was, my nerves were unmoved. On
the other hand, it was acutely painful to me to think
of the tortures which poor "A. B. W." must be
enduring. I expected every moment to see him
carried out in a swoon. But he, too, stuck to his
post like a Trojan—or an Athenian. He does not
even, in his criticism of the play, express a desire to
"take Sophocles by the throat," though his sins were
certainly much more scarlet than those of the author
of *Alan's Wife*, to whom Mr Walkley, not satisfied
with the critical lash, proposed to apply the
garotte.

Mr Augustin Daly has built a really beautiful and
commodious theatre in Cranbourne Street. The
decoration of the auditorium seems to me singularly
original and effective, and the entrance hall and foyer
are roomy, airy, and well-designed. It is a welcome
addition to our list of playhouses, the more so as it is
intended to serve as a permanent home for the most
brilliant comedienne of our time and language. Miss
Rehan's Katherine * is as vivid and daring and irre-

* *The Taming of the Shrew*, June 27—July 10.

sistible as ever. It struck me that at one or two
points she slightly overdid the deliberation of her
contemptuous iambics, but it may have been a mere
fancy on my part. On the other hand, it was no
fancy, but a fact, to which Mr Daly's attention ought
to be drawn, that, even apart from the loss of Mr
Drew, his company is quite the weakest he has as yet
presented to us. It would be affectation, and even
ingratitude, to pretend that Mr Drew is not greatly
missed. Mr George Clarke, who takes his place as
Petruchio, is a "responsible" actor who knows his
business, but he has neither the lightness nor the iron
firmness of his predecessor in the part. But even if
Mr Clarke left nothing at all to be desired, the company as a whole would still be a comparatively weak
one. The Tranio, the Lucentio, and the Bianca are
by no means up to the former mark. There is even
something a trifle amateurish about this little group.
The Latin lesson, in particular, goes for little or nothing. Then, again, Mr Daly and his stage-manager
should be advised that a recall in the middle of a
scene is a thing not tolerated on the English stage.
It is excusable, perhaps, in "the expansive emotion
incident to" the opening night of a new theatre; but,
whatever the occasion, the actors should, in their own
interest, disregard the clamours of indiscreet friends.
The stage can only suffer, as a whole, from practices
that wantonly destroy its illusion.

Signora Duse accepted a recall in the middle of
the second act of *Divorçons !* * It was, of course, no
less inartistic in her than in Miss Rehan ; but she
had the excuse of precedent on the Italian stage,
which has been ruined by opera. Her Cyprienne is
one of her most brilliant and charming performances.
The second act in especial is the perfection of comedy,
buoyant, sparkling, irresistible. Her diction is as
consummate as Céline Chaumont's, and she has the
advantage of being a real, credible, fascinating woman,
instead of a croaking incarnation of Parisian *gaminerie*.
In the third act she does not "give herself away"
quite enough to carry out the author's intention. It
is impossible for an actress who declines to overstep
the limits of absolute refinement to embody to perfection the titubant Cyprienne of the supper scene.
But I, for one, shall never quarrel with a little over-
refinement. In the part of Des Prunelles, Signor
Flavio Ando proved himself, as his tragic acting led
us to expect, an excellent comedian.

I was detained elsewhere during the greater part of
Saturday evening, and consequently arrived at the
Adelphi just in time for the murder in Mr Pettitt's
new drama, *A Woman's Revenge*.† I found the

---

* June 30.

† July 1—still running. With the exception of *A Life of
Pleasure*, at Drury Lane, this was Mr Pettitt's last play. He
died December 24, aged 45.

audience profoundly absorbed in Mr Pettitt's beautifully symmetrical fable, in which the hero and heroine,
villain and villainess, seem to dance a sort of quadrille
of cross-purposes.   The trial scene of the last act is
remarkably well put on the stage, and, up to a certain
point, is not without an air of verisimilitude.   Why it
should be allowed to break down at that point I cannot understand—why the case for the prosecution
should be smashed up by a set of unsupported assertions on the part of the prisoner's counsel, who
happens also to be her husband.   For the first time
in my life, I wanted an Adelphi drama to be ten
minutes longer.   I wanted evidence to be called as
to the identity of the fifty-pound note, and I am sure
the audience, who were intensely interested in the
mimic murder-trial, would have been only too glad
to see the thing rationally instead of ridiculously
wound up.   I gathered that the piece had been
throughout a genuine Adelphi success.   It was acted
in genuine Adelphi fashion by Mr Charles Warner,
Miss Elizabeth Robins, Mr Herbert Flemming, Miss
Gertrude Kingston, Mr Cartwright, Mr Arthur
Williams, and Miss Fanny Brough.

XXX.

THE FRENCH PLAYS—" THE HUNCHBACK "—
" JERRY-BUILDER SOLNESS."

19th July.

THE Comédie Française has departed, and has left,
if not precisely an aching void in our hearts, at any
rate a store of pleasant memories. (The aching void,
one fears, must be in somebody's pocket—not that
of the British playgoer.) Of the recent performances,
the most interesting have been Mounet Sully's Hamlet, and Madame Dudlay's rendering of the title part
in Parodi's *La Reine Juana*. Monsieur Sarcey, who
has been imparting a good deal of surprising intelligence to the readers of the *Temps*, informed them
the other day that one of the chief objects of the
American managers who financed the season at Drury
Lane was to " boom " Mounet Sully with a view to a
projected tour through the States, and that the tra-
gedian's illness greatly disconcerted their plans. If
this is the case—I put it hypothetically, for Monsieur
Sarcey does not seem to have been uniformly fortunate in his sources of information—the managers
must be congratulated on having made a conclusive,
if costly, experiment. Mounet Sully, with all his
merits (and I, for my part, am profoundly grateful for
Œdipus), is not an artist to be " boomed " in English-

speaking countries.   He is a fine romantic actor, profoundly interesting, both in his qualities and his defects, to students of the stage ; but he is not, like Salvini, or Sarah Bernhardt, or Eleanora Duse, what may be called a cosmopolitan genius.   Even if there were less mannerism, less rodomontade, in his art, the plays in which he shines are clearly not for all markets.   To audiences who do not know French, or know it imperfectly, nothing can be more monotonous, more soporific, than a long tirade of alexandrines, with its perpetual systole and diastole, as of a force-pump.   I am not pleading the cause of my personal taste or distaste.   Personally, I am a fanatic for rhythm, for poetry ; and though I don't profess to understand the principles of French versification, the sonorous roll of a tirade, delivered in Mounet Sully's magnificent voice, gives me very real and even intense pleasure.   My chief regret in connection with the Drury Lane season is that we have had nothing of either Corneille or Racine.   But what proportion of any given American audience could be expected to share this fanaticism ?   And to audiences which do not comprehend or care for the alexandrine, what would Mounet Sully be but a weariness of the flesh ? He is the embodied spirit of the alexandrine ; in it he lives and moves and has his being.   Among a people which would hear in his rhetoric nothing but an interminable see-saw, a meaningless alternation of pianos and fortissimos, he would be a veritable " vox clamantis in eremo."

What was once alleged of another Hamlet may much more justly be said of Mounet Sully's—it is " funny without being vulgar."   There are fine moments in it, ingenious pieces of " business," touches of pathos and of power—it may even be said to be elaborated throughout with intelligent enthusiasm— but to our Teutonic eyes this spasmodic and eruptive ultra-Gallic Hamlet is, if the truth must be told, hope- lessly grotesque.   When Mounet Sully sets himself to assume a dejected 'haviour of the visage, he can look liker a dying duck in a thunderstorm than any other mortal man ; his rapid strut is often indescribably comic ; and he is so " jumpy " in his sanest moments that, when he assumes madness, he has to go to almost farcical extremes in order to mark the differ- ence.   Hamlet may or may not be Germany, but assuredly he is not France ; and Mounet Sully, as Tennyson said of Hugo, is " French of the French." Fechter I never saw ; but if he was, as he seems to have been, a good Hamlet, there must surely have been a German strain in his composition.   His name, indeed, suggests it.

Even the French are not proof against the afore- said soporific influence of the alexandrine.   During the fourth act of *La Reine Juana* I saw Monsieur Sarcey—but soft ! I scorn to tell tales out of school ;

and besides, I bethink me of a proverb about dwellers
in glass houses.   M. Parodi's play, however, was not
one which tempted me to imitate Monsieur Sarcey's
method of expressing his opinion.   It is a strong,
stirring, genuinely dramatic piece of work, vastly
preferable, except perhaps in point of versification, to
Richepin's *Par le Glaive*.   The political motives, it
is true, are a trifle obscure, especially in the first act ;
but one easily picks up enough to go on with.   I
gathered that Juana was fanatically bent upon Home
Rule for Castile, while her father and son were convinced Unionists, and would have nothing to do with
the dismemberment of the Empire.   That, I take it,
is the gist of the situation ; the details don't much
matter.   The second and third acts are really powerful pieces of drama, and the mad scene of the fourth
act affords a rare opportunity for the actress, of
which Madame Dudlay availed herself with great
originality and daring.   She is an imposing artist of
the Siddonian school.   If she spoke English, one
would like to see her in Lady Macbeth, Constance,
and Volumnia.   Leitner's Charles V. was rather too
dapper to be convincing—though, for aught I know,
Charles may in truth have been dapper, just as
Catherine de Medicis, it would appear, was fat.   Paul
Mounet was impressive as the Marquis de Denia ;
Laugier, a valuable actor, was excellent as the
accommodating physician ; and " la petite Gaudy "

showed really wonderful cleverness as the Infanta Catalina.

As *The Hunchback* * will have strutted its week upon the stage before these lines are published, and will then, let us hope, be heard no more, there is no need to say much about it. I went to Daly's Theatre with an entirely open mind, hoping that, after all, the genius of Miss Rehan might transfigure even Sheridan Knowles, and prepared to enjoy whatever was in the least enjoyable. But no ! the sham Elizabethanism, the stolid, laborious fustian, the pretentious conventionality, the humourless humour of the thing, were as intolerable as ever. Not even Miss Rehan could lend grace or distinction to its incurable mediocrity of invention, thought, and style. There were striking moments in her performance, but even technically it was not one of her best. She seemed to be suffering from nervousness, and the consequent shortness of breath. The sharp and gasping method of inhalation, which in Katharine's outbursts enhanced the effect of fury, became in Julia an almost distressing mannerism. Mr George Clarke was good as Master Walter, and Miss Isabel Irving made an attractive Helen. If ever he should revive the piece (which Heaven forfend !), Mr Daly may be entreated to spare us the horse-play of the comic servants. We go to the

---

* July 11—July 17.

music-halls when we want to see "knock-about artistes." If the audience had hissed the interlude between Fathom and Thomas, my sympathy would have gone with the hissers. It was senseless and irritating.

Mrs Hugh Bell's parody, *Jerry-Builder Solness*,* produced at Mr Grein's "At Home" last week, is a witty and amusing trifle, and the actors entered heartily into the spirit of the thing. Neither Mr Welsh nor Miss Vanbrugh appeared to me to shine in the way of mimicry. Their "business" was good enough, but the voices of Mr Waring and Miss Robins seem to have eluded them, and in mimicry the voice is more than half the battle. Nevertheless the little travesty went very merrily.

XXXI.

"LOVE IN TANDEM."

26th July.

SOME of us—I don't think I was one of the worst— used to reproach Mr Daly for his partiality to German farce. That preference, however, had probably some reason on its side, for his new "eccentric comedy," *Love in Tandem*,† seems to show that French farce

---

* At St George's Hall, July 10, along with *Dante*, by Dr Dobbs and Mr Righton, in which Mr Hermann Vezin and Miss Laura Johnson appeared.

† July 18—August 4.

does not Americanise so well as German. It is only by accepting it as a piece of the wildest unreality that we can avoid finding a distinctly unpleasant flavour in this adaptation of *La Vie à Deux*. In whatever light we look at it, moreover, the play cannot but suggest *Divorçons*, and cannot but suffer by the comparison. Miss Rehan, however, is quite irresistible in the two later acts. Her part gives ample development to the lighter side of her talent, and is at any rate an immense relief after the intolerable Julia. Mr James Lewis is excellent in a small part. Mrs Gilbert, to our great regret, figures practically as a *muta persona ;* and Mr Arthur Bourchier shows a distinct and valuable talent in the direction of light comedy.

XXXII.

"A TRIP TO CHICAGO"—"THE SLEEPWALKER."

16th August.

AFTER all, there is no reason why one should be ashamed to admit and yield to the fascination of the theatre. Even in the wretchedest performance, the man of philosophic mood may feel the pulse of Humanity beating strongly, nay, feverishly. The proscenium-opening, with its sheet of light, so to speak, stretched between the audience and the performers, is like the object-glass of a huge microscope,

through which it is given us to observe some of the
most curious phases and phenomena of human nature.
I do not speak solely, or even primarily, of human
nature as purposely depicted by the dramatists ; the
part they contribute to our entertainment is often
exiguous enough. But when the theatre ceases—or
before it begins—to interest us as art, it interests us
profoundly as life. The wretchedest performance
aforesaid is in itself, quite apart from its dramatic and
mimetic qualities, that ideal of the realists, "une tranche
de la vie." It is only now and then, however, that we
are in the mood to recognise this, and, ceasing to
trouble about art or its absence, can yield ourselves
up to the contemplation of the passing show simply
as a curious little section in the tragicomic pageant
of existence :—

> "While with an eye made quiet with the power
> Of harmony, and the deep power of joy,
> We see into the life of things."

For my part, I own that some of my most delightful
evenings at the theatre have been due to this lazy,
half-philosophic, half - sentimental, non-moral, non-
artistic, sensuously and complacently contemplative
attitude of mind, the crude rhythms of the orchestra
(mark the "power of harmony"!) helping, as the most
rudimentary music will often do, to dispel the mists
of habit and bring us nearer to the apprehension of
the *Ding an sich.* My thanks are due to the Messrs

Gatti and Mr John F. Sheridan for enabling me to
enjoy such an evening at the Vaudeville on the first
night of *A Trip to Chicago*.* There was perhaps a
spice of cynicism, even of misanthropy, in my enjoyment; but what then? One cannot live, intellectually,
on the milk of human kindness alone. The evening
had something of the charm of half-hours with two
of the best authors—to wit, Swift and Voltaire. Is it
not as good as a chapter of *Gulliver* to see a man—
an excellent person, for aught I know, and a model of
the domestic and civic virtues—pass his life in exhibiting himself in petticoats and a bustle, talking
insensate patter in an Irish brogue, retailing "wheezes"
that were hackneyed when Columbus discovered
America, representing human nature, so far as that
comes into the question at all, in its most sordid and
despicable aspects, and finally investing himself in a
white night-cap and dressing-gown in order that he may
knock a door off its hinges, and tumble on the top of
somebody, or be tumbled upon, I really forget which?
Do not think that I am belying my assumption of
passivity and playing the superior person, the moralist,
the critic. I was not a superior person at all—that is
where the interest of the thing comes in for me. The
Widow Murphy amused me very much, and if you
tell me that Mr John F. Sheridan is an excellent

---

* August 5—August 26. Subsequently revived.

comedian, I shall not dispute the assertion. The oddity of the thing lies precisely in the fact that, in the best of all possible worlds, that paragon of animals, man, should take pleasure (as I did) in seeing his own nature thus degraded and vilified, and should remain withal so blithely unconscious of the degradation. But still more interesting from this point of view was the second act of the so-called " Musical Farcical Comedy." Here, in the grounds of the Chicago Exhibition, peopled for the nonce by Watteau shepherds and shepherdesses, attired in aniline hues that would have thrown Watteau into convulsions, there occurs a music-hall entertainment, which does not even pretend to have anything to do with the play, such as it is. A young lady, who has gone through the first act in the character of a pert American girl in an accordion - pleated frock, now comes forward in the costume of a pantomime prince (blue all over), and sings in a high metallic voice "Charles K. Harris's beautiful valse-song (now the rage in America), 'After the Ball.'" Poor child— for she looked little more—what intense eagerness she put into her work! How she strained and struggled to bring home to the audience the rhythm and sentiment of the dismal doggrel which is now the rage in America! No doubt she was as intent on making her success in London as was Eleanora Duse on the first night of her Marguerite Gautier—perhaps a great deal more intent, for that matter. I fancy she made it—I am sure I hope so—and "After the Ball" may presently be the rage in London too.* Then we had two sisters, whom I at first, in my innocence, supposed to be importations from America, but whose accent soon proclaimed them children of the Wild East—of London. They sang in an incredibly acute and scratchy voice—*a* voice, I say, for it sounded like one, and I trust there is not such another in the world—two songs in praise of debauchery, whereof the frank paganism charmed me unspeakably. They were not nervous or intent, these nymphs, but entirely self-satisfied, and at their ease—indeed, if anything, a trifle bored. There was something perfunctory and insincere, it seemed to me, in their expression of instant and constant readiness for "a nice little fuddle and a nice little——" well, the rhyme is obvious, and as the word is, to my thinking, the ugliest in the English language, I shall not print it. I should not be in the least surprised to learn that these Sisters Blank are hard-working, excellent young women, to whom this blatant vulgarity comes all in the way of business, and means nothing whatever. But there we sat, and listened and applauded, as they squeaked their refrains, and tripped to and fro, and kicked and pirouetted; and somehow or other there ran in my

---

* It duly became "the rage."

head all the while that line of Tennyson's, "I, the heir of all the ages, in the foremost files of Time." I looked at the other heirs of the ages around me, and at the two heiresses on the stage, and felt that life was distinctly amusing enough to be worth living. Next came a gentleman who was either an "American Comedian" or a "Grotesque Dancer"—I could not discover which. He was principally remarkable for the elaborate shabbiness and ugliness of his dress and make-up. It was not picturesque, it was not grotesque, it was not in the least indecent : it was only squalid and ugly to the last degree. He did his shuffling neatly enough, introduced a stupid parody of a ballet-dancer, and then was seen no more. Then followed other "turns" which I pass over, noting only the performance of a very stout lady, of a style of beauty to which it may be possible to become reconciled in time, who positively conquered a somewhat recalcitrant audience by the irresistible energy of her determination to succeed. I never saw a more notable instance of the power of will. The audience, not acclimatised at first to her somewhat sultry charms, and finding the song she shouted unutterably stupid, showed a certain disposition to hiss. But she returned to the attack with bent brows and a jaw which bespoke unconquerable volition, and the public yielded with the docility of the Wedding-Guest who "could not choose but hear."

I am quite sure that if this lady—she was called in the programme by an endearing and diminutive nick-name—had happened to fix me personally with her glittering eye, I, too, should have applauded vehemently, lest worse might befall me. Altogether, it was a delightful, memorable evening. I rose as from the perusal of a strange "human document," and left the theatre with a multitude of reflections simmering idly in my brain. The most definite of these, perhaps, was a vague wonder at the marked predilection for sheer hideousness displayed by the mass of the amusement-haunting public. Of course this is no new thing; but it strikes me with fresh wonder every time it is brought home to me. Why is the Cult of the Ugly so rampant in the music-hall? It is very hard to say; for vulgarity seems to be the one great essential of popular amusement, and outward ugliness is not at all essential to vulgarity. No doubt the all-pervading hideousness of such an entertainment as this *Trip to Chicago* must answer to some deep-seated need in human nature; but I search my own consciousness in vain for any rudiment of such a craving.

Unless *Wide Awake* is very unlike the majority of Mr W. S. Gilbert's sketches, there must be an ingenious and humorous idea in it ; but Mr C. H. Abbott, the author of *The Sleepwalker** at the Strand Theatre,

---

* July 25—August 18.

has contrived most successfully to eliminate everything of the sort. The third act may be very funny,
but in the first two I could discover neither felicity
of invention nor humour of dialogue. Thanks to the
exertions of Mr Willie Edouin, Mr Harry Paulton,
Miss Alma Stanley, Miss Clara Jecks, and their
comrades, the farce seemed to please the audience
on the first night. Perhaps I was not in a duly
philosophic frame of mind, else it might have afforded
me no less gratification than did the *Trip to Chicago*.

XXXIII.

" A STRANGE COINCIDENCE."*

13th September.

A SIMILARITY has been pointed out between *The*

---

* I have removed from this article one or two unnecessarily
acrimonious expressions, into which I was betrayed by the belief
that Mr Clement Scott had brought against Mr Pinero an accusation of plagiarism—one may almost say, of habitual literary
dishonesty. Mr Scott has since averred that he had no such
intention, and I have accordingly deleted any remarks of mine
which seemed aggressive in tone, while preserving the body of
the article as a record of a curious and instructive incident. In
order to show that my misunderstanding of Mr Scott's intention
was not quite inexcusable, I quote a few passages from his
original article, which appeared in the *Illustrated London News*
of 19th August. It is headed,

A STRANGE COINCIDENCE ; OR " THE SECOND MRS WIFE,"
and opens with a vivid and romantic account of the way in which
a detailed scenario of Paul Lindau's play came into the writer's

Second Mrs Tanqueray and a drama by the German
playwright, Paul Lindau, entitled *Der Schatten*. Mr
Pinero has publicly stated that, until he read the news-

---

hands. Mr Scott then proceeds to give his peculiar version of
Lindau's plot, repeating no fewer than seven times the phrase
"The Second Mrs Wife," in order to impress upon the reader
the (purely imaginary) coincidence that both plays deal with a
second marriage. He says:—" . . . The husband, so
anxious to rehabilitate in society the lady of questionable reputation, has a sister—not a daughter this time by his first marriage—
but a sister Ada, who lives with him [She doesn't], and is on a
very friendly footing with his wife. While this sister—not
daughter—is away from home, she meets and becomes engaged
to a man of some importance. Why, would you believe it? this
man engaged to the sister—not the daughter—of the hero of the
play, the noble rehabilitating husband, *was the former lover of
the husband's second wife!* Dear me, what a strange coincidence,
is it not? . . . At this point, reading with my cigar still
alight, I threw down the elaborate scenario. Would you believe it? I was transported in imagination to the St James's
Theatre, London. . . . The more I read Paul Lindau, the
German, the more I recalled the masterpiece of the English
Pinero. But to proceed. The young man engaged to Mr
George Alexander's German sister—not his English daughter,
remember—refuses to leave the house just as, strange to say, Mr
Benjamin Webster did in the English masterpiece. [Captain
Ardale, in Mr Pinero's play, does *not* 'refuse to leave the house.']
Edith, or the German 'Second Mrs Wife' . . . is in temperament more like the ruined Denise ; but perhaps this shows
originality, and gives the English play the claim to be called the
finest dramatic work of the century. . . . Pinero's name is
never mentioned in Germany as the author of *Der Schatten.* Or
is the brilliancy of the English idea due to the fact that the ' Second
Mrs Wife's ' old lover, or seducer, is her husband's sister's *fiancé*
and not his daughter's intended husband? These are, no doubt,
fine points of debateable originality which will not escape notice.

paper article in which this discovery was announced, he had never heard, directly or indirectly, of Paul Lindau's play ; so that the resemblance, such as it is, resolves itself into a pure coincidence. My present purpose is to point out that the coincidence is entirely superficial, and that internal evidence alone, without any assurance from Mr Pinero, should have been quite sufficient to prove that the two plays had no connection with each other.

. . . My difficulty is that, when I have adapted Paul Lindau's play, I may be very properly charged with plagiarism by Arthur Wing Pinero. . . . I doubt not that there is a very simple explanation of the mystery. Somebody told somebody else a story. It is ever so. And somebody never tells somebody else that this story is in a play or a novel. These somebodies are so forgetful. Perhaps Pinero's play was written long before Paul Lindau's. I am quite prepared to hear that. . . . There was an explanation ready to hand when some of us actually thought that *The Squire* reminded us of Thomas Hardy's *Far from the Madding Crowd.* Somebody blundered then, if I mistake not, but Hardy's influence still hangs about *The Squire.* It was so foolish—was it not?—to mistake what seemed an innocent fact for a strange coincidence." The reader will scarcely wonder, I think, that I, in common with Mr Pinero and others, mistook this article for a deliberate and elaborate accusation of plagiarism. It was not until October 7th that our error was made manifest by the following letter addressed by Mr Scott to the Editor of the *Illustrated London News :*—"SIR, —I desire to state that in the article written by me, and published in your paper of August 19 last, I did not intend to suggest that Mr Pinero had in any way obtained his plot from Paul Lindau's *Der Schatten*, or had ever heard of that play." There, of course, the matter ends. What Mr Scott *did* "intend to suggest" must for ever remain a mystery.

What is the story of the German play? Edith
Mühlberg, an operetta singer, has for three years been
the mistress of Heinrich, Freiherr von Brücken, a
Government official. Of their own free will they
would never dream of marriage. Nothing is further
from Heinrich's thoughts than Aubrey Tanqueray's
desire (which is the whole basis of the English play),
to attempt the rehabilitation of a "fallen" woman by
means of matrimony and domesticity. Edith is not
at all a "fallen" woman in his eyes. She is a woman
of the highest character, who, on the contrary, has
rehabilitated *him*, having cured him of a passion for
play which threatened to be his ruin. Then an external circumstance occurs to force upon them the
idea of marriage. Heinrich is offered a post of high
advancement in the Service ; but his notorious *liaison*
with Edith stands in the way. Desert her he cannot,
and there is only one alternative : they must marry.
When he proposes this course to her, she declares it
impossible, and, pressed for her reason, confesses that
she had a lover before she knew and loved Heinrich.
This confession has been insisted upon as a point of
resemblance between the two plays. It is, on the
contrary, a point of radical dissimilarity. Paula, in the
English play, makes nothing that can rightly be called a
confession. Tanqueray has never been in ignorance
of the general nature of her history. All she has ever
done is to tell him certain of its details ; what she

does in the first act of the play is to offer him a still more minute account of her adventures, which he refuses to read.   This is not properly a confession at all; and, in any case, Paula's position has nothing in common with that of Edith, who has for years passed for an immaculate woman in her lover's eyes (he says to her, "I have searched the very depths of your heart, and found you pure and noble"), and then confesses to him a single lapse, of which he has previously had no suspicion.   Edith, a woman of a single misfortune, has deceived her lover with regard to it during a communion of years; Paula, a woman of many adventures, has been under no temptation to deceive her lover, to whom the nature of her past life has from the first been a matter of notoriety.   Could two situations be more essentially dissimilar?   They have nothing in common, except the fact that they both deal with the marriage of a "fallen" woman; and that they have in common with scores of other plays.

Well then, we have this "coincidence" that two playwrights, like twenty before them, treat of the marriage of a "fallen" woman.   Both show society turning its back on the wife; but what else could they possibly do?   In this Mr Pinero, like Herr Lindau, has simply "plagiarised" from life.   The playwright who should show society welcoming with open arms a married wanton (without a title) would give incontestible proof of originality; but it would be the originality of a painter who should depict a man with three eyes and magenta hair.

Given, then, the marriage of a "fallen" woman, from which a drama has to be evolved, to what external circumstance does the playwright naturally, inevitably turn to bring about the crisis of his action? Why, to the reappearance of the woman's past in the person either of a former lover, or of a child, or (as in Dumas's *Monsieur Alphonse*) of both. Herr Lindau and Mr Pinero have chosen the former lover, just as Dumas did ten years ago in *Denise*. In Herr Lindau's play, as in Dumas's, the former lover wants to marry the husband's sister; but we do not hear that German critics have accused Herr Lindau of plagiarising from Dumas. Why? Because German critics know that similar causes are apt to produce similar effects, and that playwrights do not take the trouble to steal from each other incidents which are forced upon them, so to speak, by the logic of a situation. It must often happen to a playwright like Dumas, Lindau, or Pinero, that in thinking out the possible developments of a theme, he rejects this one or that because it has already been used, perhaps in one of his own former plays. But to suppose that Mr Pinero should go fumbling around among German plays in search of so obvious and inevitable an idea as this reappearance of the wife's former lover, is to betray a total misconcep-

tion of the way in which such a play fashions itself in
an author's mind.

If there were the slightest importance in these
merely nominal resemblances, it is clear that any one
who was bent on establishing a plausible case of
plagiarism would do much better to accuse Mr Pinero
of borrowing from Dumas than from Lindau. There
is a vague similarity between Marthe and Ellean.
They are both young girls, convent-educated, and
ignorant of life; Marthe quarrels with Denise, Ellean
with Paula; and neither Marthe nor Ellean has anything in common with Lindau's Frau von Loesnitz, a
widow, and a woman of the world. (But, by the bye,
Frau von Loesnitz and Mehringen, like Ellean and
Ardale, met in Paris—a most damning coincidence!
Mr Pinero would clearly never have thought of so
recondite a spot as Paris if Herr Lindau had not suggested it to him.) One could easily go on by the
hour weighing grains and scruples of likeness and un-
likeness between *Denise*, *Der Schatten*, and *The
Second Mrs Tanqueray*; but no occupation could be
more unprofitable. It is only by word-juggling that
we can make out any resemblance at all between the
three plays. The moment we get behind the words
and examine the things, or rather the people, they
represent, it is their total *dis*similarity that strikes us.

In one very important respect, however, *Denise*
and *Der Schatten* are fundamentally alike, while *The

Second Mrs Tanqueray stands in sharp contrast to them. Denise and Edith are ideal characters, models of the sympathetic personage. Each has met with a misfortune in early life, and Edith has, of course, sinned against the conventional code in living with a man who is not her husband; but Edith, no less than Denise, carries with her the unmixed sympathy, if not the unmixed approval, of both author and audience. In brief, they are a pair of heroines in the good old sense of the word. Poor Paula, on the other hand, is not a heroine at all; she is not a sympathetic personage; she is only a character, and an exceedingly faulty character to boot. That is what places Mr Pinero's work in a totally different category from the other two —different, and, to my thinking, distinctly higher. The difference between Denise and Paula is the difference between a rhetorical puppet and a living woman. I do not mean that there are no living women capable of acting, and perhaps even of talking, like Denise; but the playwright's first aim has not been to make her natural, but to make her noble. Everything she does is perfectly magnanimous, perfectly unselfish, perfectly right. There may be, doubtless there are, such women in the world; but it is not because *there are* such women that the author draws Denise, but because he thinks *there ought to be*. She ministers, not to our sense of the real, but to our craving for the ideal. Paula, on the contrary, is nothing if not real. She must stand or fall as a representation of what *is*, for she certainly cannot pass as an embodiment of what ought to be. Her nature presents the flaws, the inequalities, the inconsistencies of average human nature, exaggerated to a morbid degree by her unhappy life-history. And if, as some of us believe, it is a higher and more difficult thing to study a real character than to construct an ideal, it follows that Paula is a higher artistic achievement than Denise.

Be this as it may—be the achievement high or low, the portraiture successful or unsuccessful—who can doubt that the character of Paula is the germ, the nucleus, of the play? To depict this character, and to show the failure of the experiment in rehabilitation, that was the adventure which tempted Mr Pinero, and which finds no precedent either in the German or the French play. He did not cast about for a plot, and fit his character to it; he conceived his character, and the plot, such as it is, grew from it by a sort of natural necessity. Mr Pinero, I am sure, would be the last to claim any great merit of invention in the simple chain of events which constitutes his plot. Its merit lies precisely in its simplicity. The one point in which the events transcend the commonplace is the chance which makes Paula's former lover a suitor for Ellean; and this, as we have seen, is so obvious an expedient

that the difficulty would have been, not to invent it,
but to avoid it. Mr Pinero's ingenuity—and a very
fine ingenuity it is—manifests itself, not in the main
lines of the action, but in what may be called the
minor adjustments. Note, for example, the process
of the scenes in the first act, that masterpiece of
exposition ; did Mr Pinero get this from Herr Lindau
or any one else? Mark, again, the way in which the
character of Ellean, and her whole share in the action,
are deduced, as it were, from the character and
influence of her dead mother. I can think of few
finer instances of what may be called economy of
motive. It is Ellean's resolve to take the veil which
makes Tanqueray consider marriage with Paula
possible. Then, at the last moment, when Tanqueray
can no longer retreat with honour from his engagement, Ellean, in obedience to a dream, returns to the
world and to her father's house. The same influences
of heredity and education account for her antipathy
to Paula ; while the very contrast of character and
history goes a long way to explain Paula's jealous
yearning towards Ellean. Then, again, how natural
and sufficient is the adjustment which accounts for
Ellean's acceptance of a man like Ardale, who has led
"a man's life"! Yes, in the inweaving, the infiltra-
tion of character and action, Mr Pinero displays a
very rare and subtle ingenuity ; and it is not pre-
tended that there is anything in Herr Lindau's play to

suggest either the characters themselves or these felicities of adjustment.

In sum then, there is no real resemblance between the two plays, except in the bare fact that both authors treat of the marriage of a "fallen" woman. From this similarity of theme one or two external and mechanical similarities of detail naturally and almost inevitably result. But the characters, the circumstances, and all those features that constitute the individuality of the two plays, are utterly and fundamentally unlike.

It must be admitted, however, that in the "Strange Coincidence" set forth there was one really strange circumstance. The writer's account of the German play opens as follows: "An officer and Government servant, Freiherr von Brücken, who has been unhappy in his first marriage, determines to marry again;" and, by wittily entitling his article "The Second Mrs Wife," and repeating that phrase again and again throughout, he does his best to drive home this curious similarity, that the husband in both cases should be a widower whose first experiment in matrimony had been a failure. Well, here was an odd sport of chance; for there was nothing in what I have called the logic of the situation to force this previous marriage upon both playwrights. It was by far the strongest point in the accuser's case, and it was natural that he should insist upon it. At least, it would have been natural if the facts had been as represented ; but, unfortunately, they are not. There is not the slightest foundation for the writer's explicit and reiterated statement. Heinrich von Brücken has never been married ; on the contrary, the fact that he is a bachelor is emphasised as strongly as possible. Thus the one "coincidence" worthy of the name resolves itself into—a blunder!

XXXIV.

"THE TEMPTER"—"THE OTHER FELLOW"— "DOLLARS AND SENSE."

27th September.

THE daily papers, morning and evening, of this present Thursday (September 21st) have filled my soul with astonishment and pleasure. I left the Haymarket Theatre last night under the impression that I had assisted at a blank, hopeless fiasco ; that a dramatist who, two years ago, seemed to be steadily advancing towards maturity of thought and workmanship, had made a flagrant and deplorable false step; and that the most intelligent and progressive of our actor-managers had sustained a blow to his prestige, in both capacities, from which it might take him long to recover. That was the melancholy conviction with which I laid me down to rest : imagine my surprise and joy to find on awakening that I had been the victim of a grisly hallucination, that English literature had been enriched by a noble poem (better fitted, possibly, for the study than the stage), that the audience had been enraptured by a masterly piece of acting, and that what I had taken for the conventional applause which is but a polite expression of boredom, was in reality the thunderous utterance of irresistible enthusiasm! My astonishment would have been even greater had I not once before gone through a similar experience—on reading the first-night notices of Mr Irving's revival of *Lear*. This time a very sincere satisfaction mingled with my amazement. The total miscarriage of earnest effort, however mistaken, is always to be regretted. Had *The Tempter* been the doleful failure I thought it, both Mr Jones and Mr Tree might have been forced to fall back upon mere "safe" trivialities, and progress might thus have been sensibly retarded; while on the other hand, I cannot fear that *The Tempter* will be *such* a success* as to tempt them further on this particular line of—advance? I am delighted that the verdict of the first-night jury should have been "Not guilty," for I am convinced that, on calm reflection, their own common-sense will add the rider, "But don't do it again."

Were it not that Mr Jones has so loudly asserted

---

* It ran from September 20 to December 2 (afternoon).

his emancipation from the bonds of the actor-manager, one could almost suspect Mr Tree of having played the Tempter in good earnest, and led him to spoil a simple and beautiful tragic theme by plastering it over with what may literally be called "cheap and nasty" diablerie. It almost seems as though Mr Jones had told Mr Tree the story of his Leon, Isobel, and Avis—a very pretty and very dramatic legend—and had been met by the inquiry, "But where do *I* come in?"* What ruins *The Tempter*, as a work of art, is precisely what ruined *Hypatia*, namely, that the stage is pervaded by a useless, excrescent character, who is always posturing as a consummate wirepuller, when in fact there is no occasion whatever for his interference. In *Hypatia* the superfluousness of Issachar was more or less disguised; indeed, he *had* a certain function to perform, if only he had not been suffered to elbow every one else aside; but in *The Tempter* the Devil has absolutely no necessary connection with the action. It is true that in the third act he plays the part of Iago with tolerable expertness; but a human traitor would have done every whit as well. Sir Gilbert Morbec, for

---

* It is sufficiently obvious, I hope, that this remark is intended merely to throw into relief the "externality" of the character to the action, not to suggest a definite theory as to the genesis of the play. I am assured that, as a matter of fact, Mr Tree had no such influence on Mr Jones's work.

instance, might have been the Iago instead of the mere Roderigo of the story. For the rest, the Devil is nothing but a chorus to the action. And what a chorus! How trivial! How obtrusive! How vulgar! How nauseous! And, withal, how pretentious! And this, mark you, is not *a* devil, but *the* Devil—not a mere understrapper, a camp follower of the host of evil, a sort of cad-demon who has somehow been suffered to go at large in the world, bringing Hell into discredit by his shallow clowning, but, forsooth, the Prince of Darkness himself, the Archfiend, the apostate Angel "that led th' imbattell'd Seraphim to war." "How art thou fallen, O Lucifer, Son of the Morning!" I am, perhaps, as inapt as any man living to be "shocked" by the free handling of "sacred" subjects, but there was one passage in *The Tempter* at which I could almost have found it in my heart to cry out "Blasphemy!" It is where the Devil—since we must call him so—expresses a longing to

> "take on me
> Flesh's (!) soft robe and veins of tingling blood,
> The sluice of tears, the sting and pant of life,
> Labour and hunger, sweat and sleep, hopes, fears,
> Joys, sorrows—*all their great Deliverer*
> *Took on Him when He came to overthrow*
> *My kingdom in this world of mine.*"

There was something inexpressibly offensive to me in hearing this foul-mouthed, tinsel-eyed Flibbertigibbet place himself on an equal footing, as it were, with the Hero of what was, at the least and lowest, a great and strange world-tragedy.

I shall be asked to substantiate my denunciation of this pseudo-Satan. Well, given space, nothing could be easier. The best plan of all would be simply to reprint his whole part, and offer a prize to any one who can discover in his feeble declamations and feebler jocosities a single passage that is not cheaply farcical, pretentiously platitudinous, or impotently revolting. As it is, I must content myself with citing a few of his diabolic pleasantries, selected chiefly from the leering asides which he is never weary of addressing to the audience. " Damn him," says Sir Gilbert of the intrusive stranger, who, overhearing him, remarks to the public, " Damn me ! That's quite superfluous ! That's butter on bacon." " Pray for my soul," says the Earl of Rougemont, whereupon

" *The Devil*: Ay, pray for his soul. The breath that's wasted hereabouts would turn a dozen windmills. But pray away ! Pray away ! "

Again :—

" They whip themselves for my misdeeds. I like
This doctrine of vicarious suffering.

. . . . .

Poor little soul ! It's rather sorry work
Damning such sprats. But I'm a wholesale trader ;
All's fish that swims within my net.

    .   .   .   .   .

Isobel. Perhaps your character will be restored.

Devil. I trust so.   I have many influential
        Friends at Court.   Meantime, I'm cruelly slandered.

                      [Note the verse.]

    . . . But whatsoe'er
    Folk say, I'm not so black as I've been painted.

    .   .   .   .   .

That rogue has caught hypocrisy from his master.   It's very catching here in England !   There must be something in the climate of this favoured isle that suits with it !   When I have time, I'll look me out a pair of very choice hypocrites, and plant them here in England ; they'll breed, they'll breed, and in a few hundred years the country will swarm with them !

    .   .   .   .   .

I'm always meeting folk with good intentions.   Strange that anybody should be damned in a world where everybody has such good intentions !   But the government of this planet is my perpetual riddle.

    .   .   .   .   .   .

    It's time my other dicky-bird were here.
    I hope she won't be long.   My time is precious.
    I wish my clients wouldn't waste it so ;
    They are so inconsid'rate.   And at night,
    When I'm so busy."

This sorry facetiousness, this poor, mechanical, grimacing irony, is the staple of the part.   It is all so old, so commonplace, so easy, so devoid of invention, thought, or skill.   We are not even spared the scene in which the Devil disguises himself as a monk and shrives a penitent ; but never has this mediæval mummery been carried out with less ingenuity or effect.   Then, at intervals, by way of reminding us that he is not a mere Pickle-herring or Merry-Andrew, his Devilship must needs burst forth into language of such sheer, unmitigated, fetid ugliness that I, for my part, decline to smirch my paper with fragments of it. Some of it, indeed, is not spoken, and must be read in the printed book by amateurs of the "curious and disgusting"; but quite enough remains to stain the memory. And yet this is the work of a man who has posed again and again as the champion of sweetness and light in art, who has (quite gratuitously) bidden us flee the dissecting-room and the gutter, and wear "Gargantua's livery," or I know not what frippery of second-hand æstheticism! Why, in the prologue to this very play, does he not adjure us, in would-be Morrisian strains, to turn our backs upon the ugly present, with "its cheap, pert aims," and "waken in long past lovely years"? Well, well; I have long observed that if you want a fine, rank, odoriferous vocabulary, you must go to the professional champions of sweetness and light. I can only imitate the philosophic profundity of Mr Jones's Devil, and say, "It's a queer world!"

How far Mr Tree may be responsible for the very existence of the Tempter I cannot pretend to guess; but he certainly throws himself into the part with a gusto which proves that he accepts it in all good faith. He revels in it, he luxuriates, he spreads himself out, with an infinite, an imposing, a pathetic

self-complacency.   He is here, there, and everywhere, grimacing, posturing, eavesdropping, leering,
fleering, playing clown, harlequin, and policeman all
in one.   He leads his limelight-man such a dance
that I should think that official must find life
scarcely worth living with an actor-manager diabolis-
ing for three hours on end at his own sweet will.
Certain it is that the manipulator of the scarlet and
magenta slides deserves a special "call" before the
curtain, for to him belongs a large share of the credit
of this lurid impersonation.   Frankly now, *is* this
acting?   Is it the composition and assumption of
a character?   I say it is not.   Mr Tree is merely
exhibiting and, as it were, magnifying his own personality in what he considers its most picturesque
and advantageous aspects.   I do not mean that
there is anything particularly fiendish in Mr Tree,
but merely that in this cheap sarcasm and conventional attitudinising he follows the line of least
resistance, and does what is easiest to him.   His
physical labour is severe enough ; indeed, no one
could wish for a more conscientious, hard-working,
eager, emphatic, painstaking fiend ; but of intellectual
or technical labour there is not a trace.   Even the
mechanical tricks, the appearances and disappearances
and changes of dress, are clumsily contrived.   For
ludicrous inadequacy of scenic effect commend me
to the opening of the last act, where the Devil

surveys the City of Canterbury from a "gargoyle" no higher than a common lamp-post, and then descends from that dizzy eminence by means of a slide like a dinner-hoist. Still funnier is the passage where Isobel apostrophises him :

> " Why dost thou look at me
> So mockingly triumphant ; and dost glow
> Resplendent and majestic and enlarged,
> As though some evil spirit in thy breast
> Swelled thee to wear the diadem of darkness ? "

The vision of Mr Tree "glowing resplendent and majestic and enlarged" in an effulgence of red lime-light is the one truly precious memory I have carried away from the performance of last Wednesday.   It is imprinted like a picture on my mind, and I call it "The Apotheosis [if the word may be used in this connection] of the Actor-Manager."   Mr Tree has indeed given us an object-lesson to prove the viciousness of the system which thus permits him to abuse, or rather to disuse, his fine and admirable talent.   One could almost suspect Mr Jones, that erstwhile *malleus* of the actor-managers, of having had a malicious design in luring Mr Tree on to this reduction to absurdity of actor-management. He certainly could have imagined no better way of proving the case he once maintained with such ardour of conviction.

Here, unfortunately, I must break off for to-day

—unfortunately, because in what I have still to say I shall find occasion to qualify very largely the almost unmitigated dispraise conveyed in the above paragraphs. It is to "the Tempter" only that my objections apply; in the conception, and even in the execution, of the love-tragedy on which he is so deplorable an excrescence, there is a great deal to admire and to praise. This side of the matter I shall consider next week.

There is said to be a vast amount of ingenuity in *Champignol malgré lui*, translated by the industrious Mr Horner, and produced at the Court Theatre under the title of *The Other Fellow*.* The ingenuity, I own, escaped me, perhaps because I did not concentrate my attention on the threads of the so-called plot sufficiently to bear in mind who was who, and who was supposed to be who, and who knew him to be who, and who did not, and so forth to infinity. One can understand that in France, where the farce presents a caricature of a known phase of life, it may be amusing enough. Here also it appears to be amusing enough for the Court audience, who laughed consumedly at its extravagances, without pausing to inquire why reservists who have, by hypothesis, gone through two or three years' regular training, should conduct themselves like an awkward squad of the

* September 9—November 15. Transferred to Strand Theatre, November 18—November 25.

rawest recruits. Mr Weedon Grossmith was really funny; so, in their way, were Mr Charles Groves and Mr Brookfield; Miss Aïda Jenoure played brightly and pleasantly, and Miss Pattie Browne displayed an engaging vivacity.

The chief merit of *Dollars and Sense*,* at Daly's Theatre, is that, dating from a period before Miss Rehan became such a very bright particular star, it affords fairly good parts for those delightful comedians Mr James Lewis and Mrs G. H. Gilbert. They are altogether charming as the quaint old Quaker couple Eliphalet and Priscilla Lamb, and for their sakes alone the farce (or is it a comedy?) is worth seeing. Miss Rehan's part is entirely unworthy of her, and I own it is a little painful to me to see so fine an artist making an exhibition of herself in the ugly and brainless tomfoolery of the Jenny O'Jones scene. Still, there are charming touches in her performance of Phronie. Mr Arthur Bourchier, too, shows distinct talent as a light comedian. The minor female parts are filled with a crude amateurishness to which we are quite unaccustomed on this side of the water. Mr Daly must be warned against letting down the average strength of his company, and relying too exclusively upon Miss Rehan's personal popularity.

---

* September 19—October 2,

XXXV.

" THE TEMPTER " AGAIN—" SOWING THE WIND "— " A MODERN DON QUIXOTE."

4th October.

I WAS moved last week to express a tolerably sweeping condemnation of *The Tempter*, and my space, unfortunately, ran out just as I came to the extenuating circumstances.   The truth is that Mr Jones and Mr Tree have failed in what was from the outset a hopeless attempt.   The time is past for the elementary Manicheism on which *The Tempter* is based. One cannot found a philosophic play on so unphilosophic a hypothesis.   Goethe worked-up a mediæval myth into a vast, fantastic miracle-play, of which the Gretchen tragedy was only an episode.   Goethe, moreover, had the advantage of writing when the world was a hundred years younger, and of being Johann Wolfgang Goethe, not Henry Arthur Jones. And with all these points in his favour, even he could not save his Mephistopheles from trembling on the verge of vulgarity.   Take away the wit and charm of the verse, and materialise for the stage the manifestations of diablerie, and Mephistopheles very readily sinks back into the mere puppet-show buffoon he was when the poet found him.   I own that, until *The Tempter* was produced, I could conceive nothing paltrier in its way than Mr Irving's pantomimic demon. The modern mind, in fact, revolts from what may be called "special maleficence," no less than from "special providence." This mechanical opposition of forces involves at once an ethical and a psychological crudity. Not only are we conscious of carrying heaven and hell within us—we feel that there is no bridgeless abyss between them, but that they merge into each other by the finest gradations. The story of passion at war with faith imagined by Mr Jones is a singularly beautiful one, presenting such subtle enigmas of conduct as cannot be solved in rough-and ready terms of "virtue," "vice," "sin," "salvation," "damnation," and so forth. Let me re-tell the story, with such trifling changes as are involved in the elimination of "the Devil" and of the low-comedy pilgrimage.

Prince Leon is bound by child-love, by a family agreement, and by political necessity, to the Lady Avis. Journeying to their marriage, he is supposed to have been drowned at sea, and arrives at her father's castle in the dress of a squire. As he is on the point of revealing himself to his betrothed, he sees in her company her cousin Isobel—a full-blooded, queenly woman beside a shrinking girl—and he determines to wait awhile before making himself known. A rapid passion springs up between the two; but Isobel is half-pledged to the Church, Leon is wholly pledged to Avis. The Prince, if he confesses himself, cannot marry Isobel, and, on the other hand, Isobel cannot marry the low-born groom. As a matter of fact, Isobel has penetrated his disguise (means to this end could very easily be invented); but it is the man she cares for, not the Prince, and she fears to break the charm of their as yet but half-avowed love by even telling him that she knows him. The lovers are tormented in spirit by hearing the lamentations of poor Avis over the bridegroom she supposes drowned—this is a finely imagined scene of Mr Jones's—but faith and friendship are swept away like straws on the tide of their love. Their struggles of conscience only bring them closer together, and at last desire carries all before it. What need is there here for diabolic intervention? Why should not Mr Jones have dramatised once more, in one form or another, the eternal idyll of Paolo and Francesca and the romance of Lancelot:

> " Galeotto fu il libro e chi lo scrisse :
> Quel giorno più non vi leggemmo avante."

Indubitably the best scene in the existing play is the meeting of the lovers on the morrow of their "sin." This is bold, original, human, and "the Devil"—thank Heaven!—has nothing to do with it. But a rejected suitor of Isobel's has surprised their secret (a hundred chances might reveal it to him without Satanic interposition), and proceeds to bruit it abroad, while persuading Isobel that it is her lover himself

who has boasted of his conquest.   In all such lawless
and overhasty passion, defect of knowledge constitutes an element of danger.   Isobel does not know
Leon well enough to repel the calumny with perfect
faith.   She knows only that he has been false to
Avis ; may he not also be false to her ?   Meanwhile
the rejected suitor has been poisoning Leon's mind
against Isobel ; and when, in reproaching him with
his supposed baseness, she betrays the fact that she
knows him to be the Prince, he, also lacking the
knowledge of her nature which comes with long
friendship alone, too readily takes her for a mere
wanton, who has entrapped him from motives of
ambition.   Thus a double misunderstanding poisons
their love, their recriminations become more and
more vehement, and at last, in a frenzy of rage and
shame, and taking counsel with no other devil than
her wounded pride and " love to hatred turned," she
stabs him to the heart.   Is not this a fine, a subtle,
a probable and consistent romantic tragedy ?   It shows
the natural Nemesis of even venial unfaith and of
"rashly importunate" passion.   It possesses what I
conceive to be a great merit in tragic as opposed to
melodramatic themes—that equipoise of good and
evil which tends to mitigate the trenchancy of our
moral judgments.   Our sympathies are evenly distri-
buted, or, rather, are torn two ways.   We pity Avis,
we cannot wholly blame Leon ; for no moral code

makes absolutely binding an engagement contracted in nonage and under external pressure. Thus his fault amounts to insincerity rather than treachery, and we feel that the moral issues of his position are far too complex to be disposed of in a hard-and-fast formula of condemnation. Some people may hold that the effect of this partition or distraction of our sympathies is *im*moral; but these are the morally colour-blind, to whom everything that is not white is black. If art may not deal in half-shades and quarter-shades of conduct—may not show the inadequacy of our off-hand and superficial judgments to the great majority of cases—we had better give up talking of tragedy and comedy, and let melodrama hold the field. The play I have sketched above is not only human but humane. It does better than make for righteousness: it makes against self-righteousness. And observe that, except in a few trifling adjustments, it is Mr Jones's play. "The Tempter" forms no organic part of the structure, but is merely plastered on, as it were, like tawdry stucco ornamentation on a fine building. This "scab," as Mr Jones would call it, I have torn away, and have smoothed the little roughnesses of surface left behind it; but I have invented nothing whatever. Why should not Mr Jones one day or another—there is no hurry—write the tragedy he has so finely conceived? It is no paradox, but a sober truth, that *The Tempter* with the character of the

Tempter omitted might make a noble and moving play.

Before attacking this, or any other, poetical theme, Mr Jones would do well to cultivate correctness and simplicity of diction, and to learn (for, up to a certain point, it *can* be learnt) the art of versification.   Robustiousness is an old vice of his; even in his prose plays he could never resist an opportunity for a good, blusterous, blood-and-thunder rant.   Is it over-sanguine to hope that his experience in *The Tempter* may have a chastening effect upon his style, and open his eyes to the difference between violence and strength ? As for his verses, some of them are good, many of them are bad, and a considerable percentage are not verse at all.   Here is a specimen of his best :

> " Come both with me, and be for ever tossed,
>   *Frustrate and devious, on tormenting winds,*
>   Inseparable, locked from doom to doom
>   In one last timeless, measureless embrace."

This passage shows that Mr Jones had in his mind that fifth canto of the *Inferno* which I have quoted above; and the line italicised is one no poet need blush to own.   In many other passages there is a good deal of spirit and movement; but every now and then we come across such lines as these :

> " Together across outrageous oceans . . ."
> " 'Tis in his keeping.   He shall restore it . . ."
> " Ravish us of this immortal moment . . ."
> " Than the brutes ; false, envious, vicious, greedy . . ."

which are neither good verse nor bad, but mere cacophonies.   In one case Mr Jones has been at curious pains to ruin a line by splitting an infinitive :

"Of stagnant air.   Then to suddenly snatch thee,"

is an outrage on both syntax and prosody ; while

"Of stagnant air.   Then suddenly to snatch thee,"

would be not a bad line at all.   Mr Jones might quite well cultivate his ear, so that such discords should be impossible to him.

In *Sowing the Wind* * Mr Sydney Grundy has done a very clever and very delightful thing.   He has set himself to prove that subject is nothing and treatment everything, and he brings down his curtain upon a triumphant Q.E.D.   He has said to himself (or so it would seem) : " What is the very oldest, tritest, most improbable motive in the whole theatrical lumber-room ?   Whatever it is, I will rummage it out and furbish it up.   Moreover, I will let the audience into the secret from the very outset, telling them frankly that it is all a storm in a tea-cup.   And yet, by dint of sheer brain-power and theatrical expertness, I will keep them laughing and crying—especially crying— through 4—FOUR—acts.   If I don't, may I be—— well, 'greeted with tokens of disapprobation.'"   He has won his wager and been greeted with tokens of

---

* Comedy Theatre, September 30—still running.

lively and well-deserved approbation, in which I very heartily concur. And he played fair—he handicapped himself heroically. There is certainly no theme of hoarier antiquity than that of the stern guardian opposing the marriage of his ward, until he finds that the object of the youth's affections is his own long-lost daughter. To say that it is old because it is the theme of *Sweet Lavender* is like vaunting the antiquity of the Pyramids on the ground that they existed in the days of Napoleon. Why, the theme is as old as Menander at the very least. You remember Mr Kipling's story of the bank clerk who, in a previous existence, had served on board the Carthaginian triremes? Well, Mr Grundy's Rosamund is in very much the same position. She was stolen by a Phenician slave-merchant (Lord Petworth) somewhere about 500 B.C.—I won't swear to a century or two—she was exposed as a singing girl in the slave-market of Athens, and was loved by Annesley, traduced by Cursitor, and recognised by Mr Brabazon (by means of the strawberry-mark on her left arm) just as in Mr Grundy's play. And it is not at all probable that this Athenian incarnation heads the list of her avatars. She is doubtless coeval with the Pyramids, if not with the Himalayas. She came into existence along with the Family. Discover the date of that institution, and you have her exact age.

In one respect alone has Mr Grundy condescended

to simplify his task—in throwing his period back to
the early years of the century. This is a quite legitimate, and indeed very artistic, device. Old-fashioned
dresses and old-fashioned formality of expression
harmonise perfectly with the old-fashioned theme.
And he thus disarms criticism of his criticism of life,
by saying, in effect, "You must not look for the
sentiments of the 'nineties in the atmosphere of the
'twenties." Whether we look for them or not, I think
we find them here and there in the play. Rosamund,
in the famous third act, seems to me curiously pre-
scient of *La Dame aux Camélias*, and I am cerrain
that Maud Fretwell has read *Dodo* as well as *Evelina*.
But to consider so were to consider too curiously.
The play is interesting, moving, amiable, humane,
full of excellent literary and theatrical workmanship.
Personally, I could find it in my heart to dispense
with the fourth act, in which Rosamund's magnanimity becomes the least bit overstrained. But that is
a mere trifle. The essential fact is that the play is by
far the best Mr Grundy has ever done, because in it
he has abandoned ingenuity in favour of simplicity
and nature. It is a delight to welcome him back to
the ranks of our "live" dramatists. I hope he will
print this play.

Miss Emery's Rosamund is simply one of the most
beautiful and moving dramatic creations of our time ;
Mr Brandon Thomas will be admirable as Mr Bra-

bazon when he gets rid of his nervousness ; Mr Cyril
Maude's Mr Watkin is delightful ; Miss Rose Leclercq's
Mrs Fretwell is probably the cleverest thing she has
ever done, a masterpiece of highly-coloured comedy ;
and Mr Sydney Brough, Mr Edmund Maurice, Mr
Ian Robertson, and Miss Annie Hughes are all as
good as need be. Thoroughness is evidently going
to be the motto of Mr Comyns Carr's management.

Of *A Modern Don Quixote* * at the Strand, I need
only say that it has, fortunately, nothing whatever to
do with *Don Quixote*, and that Mr Arthur Roberts'
performance is extravagantly, almost unintermittently,
funny.

XXXVI.

" THE FORESTERS "—" THE TWO JOHNNIES."

11th October.

THE production of *The Foresters*† at Daly's Theatre
awakens one keen regret. Since the late Laureate—
would that we could say the Last of the Laureates !
—was covetous of stage success, why did he not
write a pastoral ballad-opera for Sir Arthur Sullivan
to set to music ? It might have been, in all probability it would have been, a possession for ever to

---

* September 25—October 14.

† October 3—October 21 ; but after October 13 *The Last
Word* alternated with *The Foresters*.

the English-speaking world. I have the greatest
respect for Mr W. S. Gilbert's metrical genius. It
may most be said of him that, if he were the least bit
of a poet, he would be a very great one; but even in
mere rhythms Tennyson was his master. And Sir
Arthur Sullivan's music—if one who scarcely "knows
a symphony from a boiler explosion" may venture an
opinion—has precisely that clearness, fluency, elegance, and (to be quite candid) that superficiality
which harmonises with the Laureate's lighter lyrical
strains. The opera would not, perhaps, have been a
very great work, either dramatically or musically, but
it would have set all Britain, Lesser and Greater,
singing exquisite words to graceful and charming
melodies. The theme of *The Foresters* might have
served as well as another, if only the lyrical portion
had been multiplied by five, and the dialogue—even
what Mr Daly has left of it—divided by three. Even
as it is, the production may most conveniently be
classed and criticised as a ballad-opera in which the
dialogue has, unfortunately, taken rather the upper
hand. It is not very interesting or very dramatic
dialogue, but it contains some pretty passages, such
as only Tennyson could have written, and it has
all a certain delicacy of texture that makes it pleasant to the ear. And we might easily forgive much
feebler dialogue for the sake of the lyrics—of such
stirring rhythms as "Long live Richard, Robin and

Richard," or "Now the king is home again, and never more to roam again," such dainty ditties as "Love flew in at the window," or "The bee buzz'd up in the heat," such popular strains as "There is no land like England," and such an exquisite evensong as this :—

> "To sleep ! to sleep ! The long bright day is done,
> And darkness rises from the fallen sun.
>   To sleep ! to sleep !
> Whate'er thy joys, they vanish with the day ;
> Whate'er thy griefs, in sleep they fade away.
>   To sleep ! to sleep !
> Sleep, mournful heart, and let the past be past !
> Sleep, happy soul ! all life will sleep at last.
>   To sleep ! to sleep !"

If we could analyse the charm of this versicle we should have mastered the secret of poetry. There is not a word in it that a child might not use, not an idea that a child might not understand. The rhythm, the stanza, everything is simplicity itself. Nothing could be easier, one might suppose, than thus to lisp in numbers ; yet hundreds of men, and these not without poetic faculty, have passed their lives in weaving verses, and have produced no lyric like this. It is nothing, and it is everything. It is only a baby's lullaby, yet none but a great poet could have written it.

By all means, then, go and see *The Foresters*. It has delightful moments, and is altogether innocent and graceful. Miss Rehan has seldom looked hand-

somer than in the robes of Maid Marian, and I have
no doubt she brings out all the character there is in
the part. She speaks her lines, whether prose or
verse, with a curious, slow grandiloquence, for which
I do not exactly perceive the reason ; but it is not
ineffective. Unfortunately she is not so careful either
of metre or emphasis as she ought to be. In more
than one place she murdered the verse by inserting
small words not in the poet's text, and she made
several slips of accent, such as this :—" We leave but
happy *memories* to the forest," whereas the emphasis
should clearly be on the "happy." Mr Arthur Bourchier made a somewhat unromantic, but bluff and
business-like, Robin Hood ; if Mr George Clarke
could have taken some four inches from his girth and
added them to his stature, he might, when seen from
behind, have suggested Richard Plantagenet to the
imagination ; and Miss Catherine Lewis was at some
pains to vulgarise the part of Marian's woman, Kate,
mainly by introducing into it an extraordinary gurg-
ling stage laugh, with which she nearly drove us distracted in a farce produced at this theatre some
months ago. Miss Lewis, however, sang the Bee
Song pleasantly enough, and would doubtless be a
capable comedian if she would only consent to be
natural. The mounting was quite adequate, the fairy
scene being very pretty indeed, though the twinkling
of the lights in the branches at last became rather

wearisome. The stage management was conventional and operatic ; but as the piece, I repeat, may best be regarded as a ballad opera, the conventional groupings and gestures did not seem inappropriate.

It is my duty to record that *The Two Johnnies*,* an adaptation by Mr Fred Horner of *Durand et Durand*, was applauded, and not hissed, at the Trafalgar Square Theatre on Thursday evening last. Not having seen the French play, I do not know whether it bore any possible resemblance, however caricatured, to French life ; the English play had certainly no sort of relation to English life, outside Colney Hatch. Its leading character is a publican, who adores barristers, and has a violent contempt for grocers, and who, having married his daughter to a grocer, under the belief that he is a barrister, goes about addressing his son-in-law as " Learned Sir," and presenting him with second-hand wigs and gowns as tokens of reverence. I have often wondered whether the imbecile bourgeois of French farce really exists in France. Labiche, who is my pet literary vice—I read and re-read him when I ought to be devoting my mind to Shakespeare and the musical glasses—Labiche lives upon the vain, pompous, ignorant, contemptible bourgeois, of whom M. Perrichon is the immortal type, and Labiche's humour makes

---

* October 5—October 14.

him (to me) a joy for ever. But I cannot help doubting, at moments, whether he really exists, and whether Labiche and his imitators are not libelling their countrymen. In England, certainly, we have no corresponding type—our imbecility takes other forms. Therefore the lunatic father-in-law of *The Two Johnnies* is like nothing in heaven or earth; but that, as aforesaid, does not diminish the enjoyment of Mr Fred Horner's audience. I told you our imbecility took peculiar forms. The company, including Messrs Lionel Rignold, Charles Glenney, and Frank Wyatt, put plenty of spirit into their work.

XXXVII.

"THE LAST WORD"—"AN AMERICAN BRIDE"— "A GAIETY GIRL."

18th October.

AT last, in *The Last Word*,* we have recovered the Ada Rehan of former years — the fascinating, the irresistible, the infinitely various. Last Friday night was the true "house-warming" of Daly's Theatre. Hitherto it has seemed rather chilly and unhomelike; there has been, to tell the truth, no genuine warmth of spontaneous emotion and enthusiasm to dry the new paint and plaster. On the first night, though we

---

* October 13. (*See* previous article.)

had Miss Rehan's Katherine, some of us, at any rate, were too much occupied in regretting the absence of her heaven-born Petruchio to find a very lively satisfaction in the performance. Then came *The Hunch——*; but no! I will not resurrect that grisly error. *Love in Tandem* was distinctly below the Daly average, both in conception and execution; *Dollars and Sense* exhibited Miss Rehan in a somewhat degrading character; and *The Foresters*—well, it was a pretty curiosity, no more. But *The Last Word*, though not a serious masterpiece, is a curiously human and sympathetic play—we rather undervalued it before — and Miss Rehan's performance of the Baroness is one of the things that make one rejoice to be alive in the 'nineties, and snap one's fingers at the "palmy days." She never played the part better than on Friday. I had begun to fear that her voice was permanently, though ever so little, impaired; but I was totally mistaken; it is as rich, as flexible, as velvety and caressing as ever. The audience was not very large or very much disposed, at the outset, to enthusiasm; but Miss Rehan soon seized them and swept them away in a whirlwind of pleasure and emotion. The performance, as a whole, was very passable, its chief defect being that whereas the Baroness's passion for Harry Rutherell seemed credible enough when Mr John Drew played the part, with Mr Herbert Gresham in the character, her infatuation rather taxed our powers of make-believe.

It is melancholy to reflect that if all the money which is squandered year by year on hopeless and foredoomed theatrical enterprises could be collected and wisely administered, it would serve to endow a National Theatre—ay, and a National Opera to boot. I do not mean all the money that is lost in theatrical speculation—the mere interest on that would richly endow a *Comédie Anglaise*—but simply the money sunk in undertakings which never had the ghost of a chance of succeeding. It is notoriously impossible to predict success, even for the ablest work ; but there are many cases in which failure can be predicted with the utmost certainty. We see every season, whether at matinées or evening performances, at least a score of plays as to whose utter uselessness no competent critic, with the manuscript before him, could possibly have the least doubt. *An American Bride* * is the first predestinate failure of the season 1893–94. We may await the remaining nineteen (if not more) with the utmost confidence. The playwrights, in whom " die Kraft ist schwach, allein die Lust ist gross," are punctual in paying their tribute to the great god Average.

Not that *An American Bride* is the foolishest or

---

* Terry's Theatre, October 11—November 7.

most futile play one has ever come across. On the
contrary, it stands nearer the top than the bottom of
its class. The story is not devoid of common-sense,
though the mental pathology of the last act certainly
strains our credulity ; the dialogue is for the most part
rational enough, and only occasionally inept; the
characters, though lifeless, are not, as a rule, preposterous. Messrs Lawrence Olde and Maurice
Noel, in a word, are by no means the ordinary
matinée imbeciles ; the defect of their play is simply
a total lack of any quality that could possibly
attract people to a theatre. Only that, and nothing
more.

Plays that are in reality a good deal lower in the
intellectual scale than *An American Bride* have been
known to succeed. To say nothing of the ineptitudes
of burlesque and comic opera, it would be easy, without racking one's memory, to name half-a-dozen
abjectly contemptible "farcical comedies" which have
had, or are having, a certain measure of apparent
success. In intention, and even in execution, the
work of Messrs Olde and Noel is distinctly a cut
above these outrages on sense and taste. But that
should have made its failure all the easier to foretell.
The judicious "tipster" would hesitate to declare
even the most imbecile farce quite "out of the running," well knowing that clever acting and bustling
stage management will sometimes make people laugh

at even the most offensive rubbish. But in the case of a serious play the problem is much simpler. If it has no inherent quality to recommend it, the finest acting in the world will not make it a success. Indeed, its fundamental defect is that it makes fine acting impossible.

If Miss Janette Steer, then, had been another Sarah Bernhardt, she could not have infused life into *An American Bride*. I should like to see her in a more possible character before attempting to estimate her qualities. She has presence and earnestness. It is possible that in a part which really touched her emotions she might get rid of some of that harshness of voice and general hardness of contour which detracted from the charm of her Stella. Mr Herbert Waring made all that was possible of the hero, Mr Kerr and Mr Welch were excellent, and Miss Olga Brandon can scarcely be blamed for taking no great interest in the part allotted to her. It is melancholy to see such actors wasting their powers on such work.

"Don't you have a good deal of difficulty with the Licenser of Plays?" said an interviewer to Mr George Edwardes. "No, I don't," was the reply; "and I hope they will never interfere with him at all." No one who saw *A Gaiety Girl* * at the Prince of Wales's

---

* October 14—still running.

on Saturday night will doubt the sincerity of Mr
Edwardes's hope. It is the Censorship that makes
A Gaiety Girl possible, of that there can be no
doubt. It is the Censorship that enables a playwright to represent a well-known Judge as going
about the world gloating over the scabrous details
of the divorce cases which he is called upon to try,
and relating "spicy" anecdotes to parties of young
ladies. It is the Censorship that ordains the alteration of "Sir Francis May" into "Sir Lewis Grey"
(he is still called Sir Francis by most of the performers), and thinks it has thereby safeguarded the
dignity of the Bench.* It is the Censorship that
gives the Royal assent, as it were, to such flowers of
dialogue as this: LADY VIRGINIA, "Marriage is an
ancient institution, divorce is a mere mushroom."
MR JUSTICE GREY (*with a leer*), "And, like a mushroom, it often springs up in a single night." It is the
Censorship that estops, so to speak, the utterance of
our natural sensation of nausea when a clergyman's
daughter, in order to extort her father's consent to
her marriage, induces him, at a carnival ball,
to kiss her, under the impression that she is a
lady professionally prepared for such liberties, and
then threatens him with exposure unless he gives

---

* It would be curious to learn Sir Francis Jeune's opinion of
the Censorship as an institution.

in.*   For all this, and many other mercies (as Mr Edwardes quite justly recognises), we have the Censorship to thank.   Why, O simple-minded interviewer, should Mr Edwardes want the Censor "interfered with," when the Censor never, to any practical purpose, "interferes with" him?   The Censorship is, and must be, the bulwark of frivolity; it is only the serious artist for whom it has any terrors.   Of course I do not profess to have "seen these roads before they were made."   It is possible that the Censor may have purged the play of much "perilous stuff"; but, if so, he simply did the management yeoman's service in averting the intervention of the police.   Be this as it may, the piece, as it now stands, is a lively enough extravaganza of the *In Town* type.   The lyrics are brightly written (by Mr Harry Greenbank), and the music, by Mr Sydney Jones, is distinctly popular, in the sense that the least musical hearer can "catch on" to every air without the slightest difficulty.   Mr Hayden Coffin, who is in excellent voice, sings a slashingly, swaggeringly, patriotic ditty, evidently suggested by Mr Kipling's "Tommy Atkins," and a sentimental ballad which I should think likely to take the drawing-rooms

---

* Early in December, after the play had run more than six weeks, the character was "laicised," in obedience to a protest from some members of the audience, whether addressed to the Censor or direct to the management I do not know.

by storm. Mr Monkhouse is passably funny as the
"criminous clerk"; Miss Decima Moore is exceedingly bright as his daughter; Mr Eric Lewis is capital
as the imbecile judge; and Miss Lottie Venne, though
her part is none of the best, sings her one song with
admirable art.

XXXVIII.

THE PEOPLE'S DRAMA AND THE PEOPLE'S CRITIC: —BY ONE OF THE OTHER PEOPLE.

Pall Mall Gazette, 23rd October.

"WHEN it is proved to me," says Mr Clement Scott,
in his article on "Two Dramatic Revolutions" in
the *North American Review,* "that the public voice
indorses the new drama, then I shall lay down my
arms and quit the field." I am sure the whole play-
going public, majority and minority alike, will with
one voice "indorse" my plea (as Mr Scott puts it),
when I entreat him to reconsider this melancholy
resolution. Its utterance will certainly not arrest the
course of theatrical progress. There will be *a* new
drama (mark, I do not say *the* new drama, for the
world will not stand still at *The Second Mrs Tanqueray* any more than at *Caste* or *Two Roses*);
and *a* public (mark, I do not say *the* public) will
"indorse" it—of that we may rest assured. The
great mundane movement will continue, even though

Mr Scott should solemnly break his pen and throw
its fragments across the track.   But if he should
carry out his threat, and become (as he says Macready did) a " moody recluse," muttering anathemas
from afar, theatrical life would lose half its interest
and charm.   Mr Scott is a character, a personality, a
force.   We know, from recent experience, how dull
things are in his absence, and how promptly, on his
return, the fun recommences.   Therefore this threat
of " quitting the field " fills us with consternation, and
we implore him to retract the vow while he may still
do so with dignity.

In this *North American* article he states his position
with a lucidity not always numbered among the
merits of his style.   " The Stage for the People," he
says, " has ever been my cry."   It was so in 1860.
when the problem was to *make* the stage popular; it
is so in 1893, when the problem is to *keep* it popular.
Nothing could be plainer than this.   Mr Scott represents to a nicety the average middle-class Englishman, or in other words the immense majority of the
playgoing public.   He found the stage, in the 'sixties,
beneath his intellectual level, and sought to raise it.
From 'seventy to 'ninety (roughly speaking) it exactly
came up to his intellectual and artistic requirements,
and he was happy.   In 'ninety it took a fresh start
and left him (and the majority) behind; and he now
shrieks to it to come back and " mark time," for he

cannot follow it into " an atmosphere that is Mephitic."
He is precisely in the position of that hero of Mr
Henry Arthur Jones's who cried (in ballad metre)

> " O God ! roll back Thy universe,
> And give me yesterday ! "

There is only one flaw in this statement of the case
—a flaw which vitiates almost all argument on things
theatrical. I have hinted at it in the first paragraph
of this remonstrance : it is simply the abuse of the
definite article. We talk of *the* Theatre, *the* Drama,
the Public, and forget that these abstractions represent
no real, tangible entity. There is no Theatre, but
many playhouses, no Drama, but many plays, no
Public, but many audiences. Why should we insist
on talking as though there were only one class of
audience demanding one class of play, when we know
quite well that never in the world—not even in the
palmy 'seventies—has such a state of things existed,
and now less than ever ? It is as though we were to
take the average height of an army, make all its
uniforms to that one measure, and declare that the
six-foot men must squeeze into the five-foot-four
tunics and trousers, or else go naked.

" The Stage for the People ! " Yes, by all means.
Mr Scott and the People will always have their stage,
and no one wants to deprive them of it. But why
should not men and women who are not of " the
People " have their stage too, if they are willing to

pay for it? Why should Mr Scott cry, "No, you shall not go to see *The Second Mrs Tanqueray*, and if you do I quit the field"? One would suppose that this terrible Mrs Tanqueray was emptying all the other theatres, so that Mr Scott would presently have never a melodrama or farce in the whole weary world wherewith to solace his soul. Be of good cheer, Mr Scott! *Sursum corda*, as Sir Edwin Arnold phrases it! The universe is not yet given over to Pinero and pessimism. There are still corners where (to use your own metaphor, or metaphors) clean and homely teacups and saucers play on the heartstrings — witness *Liberty Hall* and *Sowing the Wind*. Honest, healthy, breezy, patriotic, idiotic melodrama is not yet dying in its last ditch. Are not *A Woman's Revenge* and *A Life of Pleasure** popular almost beyond precedent? Really, you must not be greedy; you must live and let live. You have between thirty and forty theatres (to say nothing of music-halls) assiduously catering for you; can you not leave us one, two, at the outside three playhouses? —we ask for no more. Why terrorise us by vowing to commit literary suicide, if we, the humble minority, venture to enjoy ourselves in our own quiet way, leaving you and the People quite undisturbed in your

* Drury Lane, September 21. Transferred to the Princess's, December 11, and still running.

more violent delights? The course you threaten
smacks strongly of the Japanese method of con-
troversy known as the *hara kiri* or happy despatch,
which consists (I understand) of seating yourself on
your adversary's door-step and proceeding to rip
yourself open. The method has doubtless its advantages, especially for the adversary ; but I am surprised
that this Japanese institution (and apparently this
alone) should have found favour in your eyes.

No, no! If the sacred British Dinner-Table is
threatened with an invasion of "indecent topics," and
"brutal cynicism," and "pestilent pessimism," that is
surely a very bad reason for its doughtiest defender to
abandon his post and "quit the field." No one else
will take up the battle in his stead ; for no one else,
I am sure, can see why the fitness of a topic for
discussion at a dinner-table should afford the absolute
and final measure of its fitness for treatment on the
stage. Nor is it given to any one else to understand
the fine shades of Mr Scott's code of dinner-table
propriety. He is the foremost champion, for example,
of *A Life of Pleasure*, which deals, as I am credibly
assured, with seduction and prostitution—the theme
of *The Second Mrs Tanqueray* in a rather coarser
form. Is the People's Drama to be deprived of the
fostering care of the People's Critic, merely because
some Other People prefer plays of observation and
thought to plays of convention and sentiment? The

loss to both forms of art would be incalculable.
Melodrama (who knows?) might sicken and pine
away, "caret quia vate sacro," and we Other People
would have to forego the pleasure and instruction of
seeing the drama of to-day criticised from the standpoint of the day before yesterday. Who was it, I
wonder, that "demanded why, when Mr Scott came
home and found *Mrs Tanqueray* a great success, he
could not leave it alone and hold his tongue"? No
one who has the interests of the drama really at
heart would dream of asking such a question. Mr
Scott's "violent opposition," to use his own phrase,
has done *The Second Mrs Tanqueray* a world of
good. The play would not have been the thoughtful
and daring work it is had it failed to find "violent
opponents." Among other things, Mr Scott has
enabled us to realise that we possess in Mr Pinero a
much more original thinker and craftsman than Herr
Paul Lindau, one of the leading dramatists of Germany. And this reminds me that I owe Mr Scott a
personal apology. In common with a great many
other people, I mistook for an accusation of plagiarism
what was, it appears, only a piece of airy badinage,
of raillery, of "banter"! I did not, and, to be quite
frank, I do not to this day, see the joke; but that is
doubtless because I am a Scotchman. I can only
plead that many unimpeachable Englishmen were
equally dense. I even solace my national vanity with

wondering whether it did not take something in the
nature of an operation—legal rather than surgical—
to make Mr Scott himself fully alive to the humour of
the thing.   But this is a bootless speculation.   Finding his humour so little appreciated, Mr Scott will
probably think twice before again having recourse
to such playful medleys of *Dichtung und Wahrheit*
in his defence of the British Dinner-Table.   And
"banter" apart, I am sure we all hope—both the
People and the Other People—that it may be many a
long and lively year before Mr Scott "quits the field,"
and the voice of his enthusiasm and invective is no
longer heard in the land.

XXXIX.

"A QUESTION OF MEMORY"—"LE PATER"—
"THE ORIENT EXPRESS"—"DON JUAN."

1st November.

AT the end of the first act of *A Question of Memory,**
I was inclined to think that in producing this work
of "Michael Field" Mr Grein had made the first
serious mistake of his management, and was playing
into his opponents' hands by converting the Independent Theatre into a *théâtre où l'on s'ennuie.*   As
the play went on, my feeling altered.   It is quite
interesting enough to merit production, for once in

---

* Opera Comique, October 27.

a way. Indeed, one may almost say that the Independent Theatre would have been false to its mission had it refused its hospitality to such a singular piece of work. A dramatic curiosity it certainly is; but a good play it no less certainly is not.

The ladies who choose to be known as "Michael Field" must be numbered among the many victims of the Elizabethan drama. In a note to *Callirhoë*, their earliest production, they thanked their countrymen for greeting them as "a poet," and announced that "it would be the task of their lives to earn the better title of a playwright." Unfortunately, they set about this task in a very mistaken fashion. Beguiled by their passion for the Elizabethans, they conceived that the essence of drama lay, not in the nicely adjusted interplay of action and character, but in the copious effusion of highly figurative rhetoric. That style was the most dramatic which could boast the greatest number of metaphors to the square inch; and the diction and versification of 1590 or thereabouts were reverently accepted as the heaven-ordained stilts on which all lofty drama must move for evermore. Of the appropriateness of speech to character the poets took little thought. All their personages without distinction spoke the same archaic dialect, tense with imagery, and writhed, as it were, in the effort to find the most impossible expression for the most improbable feelings. Imaginative, philosophical, lyrical faculty abounded in their work—everything, in short, except dramatic impulse or inspiration. This worship of a dead convention has produced an infinite mass of still-born literature, and the dramas of "Michael Field" are among its most melancholy results.

In *A Question of Memory* the authors have deserted blank verse, and write a curious short-winded prose, which has somewhat the air of a correct but rather stiff translation from a foreign language. We might conceive this to be a consciously-designed effect if there were the least attempt at verisimilitude in the thoughts expressed by the Hungarian peasants who are the actors in the drama. But they are Hungarian only in name and (more or less) in costume. They are natives of the land of Sentiment, and the dialect they speak is that of Mechanical Introspection. In the first, second, and fourth acts there is scarcely a single natural sequence of thought, feeling, and expression. The dialogue is always flying off at unexpected tangents, and trying to attain sublety by means of incoherence. The authors have observed, quite justly, that feeling *is* incoherent—or, rather, that consciousness is like a swirling stream, in which unexpected and apparently irrelevant objects are always floating to the surface for a moment and then disappearing again, in obedience to laws which we cannot formulate. But they have not observed, or they have studiously ignored, the fact that these freaks and caprices of feeling and thought seldom reproduce themselves in the conversation of sane people, whether cultured or uncultured. Dialogue, therefore, which proceeds hither and thither in a series of grasshopper leaps, and is always alighting on the most unexpected spots, is not the dialogue of life, but of a world evolved from the playwright's inner consciousness. The authors may allege that we cannot get rid of convention, and that this particular style is a convention like another. True ; but I submit that it is an inconvenient and irrational convention. It has certainly this disadvantage, that it obscures the boundary between sanity and madness, the hero's processes of thought being scarcely more fitful when he is out of his senses than when he is in them.

Where, then, lie the merit and interest of the play ? Chiefly in the great situation of the third act. There is no novelty, indeed, in the mere idea of extorting a confession by applying torture, not to the holder of the secret, but to some one whom he loves. Sardou and others have exploited this theme ; but " Michael Field " has imagined an ingenious and really tragic refinement upon it. When Ferencz's mother and sister are led out to execution, the name of the defile where his comrades are hidden is ringing so loudly in his ears that he is in an agony of terror lest he should utter it in spite of himself, or even lest some Austrian thought-reader should hear the unuttered sound that is echoing through his brain. Then, when it comes to his sweetheart's turn to suffer, his resolution breaks down, and, in his frenzy, he is ready to speak the fateful word; but, behold! his tongue cannot shape it, it has vanished from his mind, it has been utterly swept away in the whirl-wind of anguish! Here is a conceivable, a natural, a terribly tragic conjuncture. If only the scene were as well written as it is finely conceived, it would be one of the most moving in English drama. I fancy, too, that there is an idea concealed in the senti-mental casuistry of the last act; but I own it eluded me.

The acting was much stronger on the female than on the male side. Mrs Theodore Wright played the mother with dignity and strength, Miss Hall Caine showed tact and feeling in the difficult part of Thekla, and Miss Mary Keegan made a charming Fina. Mr Acton Bond displayed a good deal of intelligence in the part of Ferencz, but was distinctly overweighted in the third act.

The production in French of François Coppée's *Le Pater* was a daring and not unsuccessful experi-ment. The play is a pretty enough little thing, written in fluent verse, with a good many touches of pathos. Miss Anna Zetterberg, who played the

leading part, showed plenty of force, feeling, and
knowledge of the stage; but her voice was unsympathetic, and there was more than a trace of Teutonic
thickness about several of her consonants.   Mr Ivan
Watson's French seemed to me remarkably good, and
his acting was quiet and effective.

To my great regret, I agree so entirely with all my
colleagues on the subject of *The Orient Express* *
at Daly's Theatre, that there is really nothing left
for me to say about it.   Difference of opinion is
scarcely possible.   An amusing first act, a progres-
sively tedious second and third act, and no part
for Miss Rehan—there is the whole situation in a
nutshell.   Mr James Lewis and Mrs Gilbert are
delightful in their way, Miss Isabel Irving is charming, and Messrs W. G. Elliott and Allan Aynesworth
prove themselves very capable comedians; but what
does it all matter when there is no part for Miss
Rehan?   Mr Burnand, by the way, seems to have
moved with the age in so far that his dialogue is
tolerably free from puns; but he might at the same
time have spared us such prehistoric "wheezes" as
the following :—

"I remember seeing portraits of the brigands just after they
were taken."
"The portraits?"

* October 25—November 11.

" No, the brigands. They were very well executed."

" The brigands ? "

" No, the portraits."

Did any one ever laugh at this trick of speech, I wonder? It has certainly never raised a smile within the memory of man.

It is a mistake to convoke the critics to the first night of a burlesque. As well invite us to admire a rose-bush before it has broken into flower. The pre-arranged words and songs and music and " business " are like the wood and leaf of the shrub, but the aftergrowth of gags and gambols is its true efflorescence. There were some very dull intervals in *Don Juan* * at the Gaiety on Saturday night, all of which will doubtless have disappeared in the course of a week or so; for there are certainly the makings of success in the production. " The new order changeth, yielding place to the old," and *Don Juan* is a " three act burlesque drama " of the good old Gaiety type, not a " musical comedy " after the fashion of *In Town* or *The Gaiety Girl*. There is little in the invention or composition to distinguish it from a score of its predecessors, unless it be the neat turn of some of the verses, by Mr " Adrian Ross"; and altogether it is, perhaps, not quite so pretentiously inept as some former productions of its school. The company is excellent. Mr Arthur

---

* October 28—still running.

Roberts always gives me much more pleasure than did the late Mr Leslie, with all his cleverness. One feels somehow that Mr Roberts is in his natural element, while Mr Leslie was, in some measure, forcing himself to be funny. It certainly cannot be said that Mr Roberts's fun is spontaneous. He works hard enough, in all conscience, for our entertainment; but one feels that it is the work he was born to do. Miss Millie Hylton, who plays Don Juan, seems to me the most graceful and vivacious "principal boy" we have seen for a long time; and Miss Cissy Loftus, as Haidee, possesses the charm of youth and the piquancy of total inexperience. She has a sort of self-possessed helplessness which takes one aback at first, but presently becomes almost fascinating. Miss Sylvia Grey and Miss Katie Seymour dance charmingly, and the male comedians are hard-working and competent. Altogether, I should think *Don Juan* ought to be a joy for ever, or at least for five hundred nights or so, to Mr J. H. McCarthy and other faithful devotees of the Sacred Lamp. If it is not, I cannot but think it is their devotion that is waning, not the lamp that is burning dim.*

---

* The Censor's lot has this season been far from enviable; one woe has trodden on another's heels. His energies were no doubt so absorbed in staving off the threatened "contempt of court" in *A Gaiety Girl* (see Article XXXVII.) that he overlooked a terrible "contempt of Porte" in the third act of *Don Juan*, which led to a vigorous protest from the Turkish Ambassador,

XL.

" DIPLOMACY "—" FROG "—" THE LADY-KILLER "—"TOM, DICK, AND HARRY "—"A SCREW LOOSE."

8th November.

*DIPLOMACY** has never been better acted than on the

and imperilled our ancient amity with the Ottoman Empire. "The Sultan" promptly became "the Pasha" and the storm blew over ; but one cannot help observing that when the Censorship fails to avert such incidents, it thereby nullifies the most plausible argument of its supporters. All the Censorship did in this instance, was to make the Queen and the nation officially responsible, as it were, for an error of taste which, in the absence of any such office, would have lain at the door of the individual management. I am not impugning either the tact or the vigilance of Mr E. F. S. Pigott. He is the best Censor we have ever had, and it is very unlikely that we shall ever find another man of equal diligence, courtesy, and integrity to undertake so laborious and unthankful an office. But Mr Pigott's personal virtues, so far from proving anything in favour of his office, merely show that, even under the best of circumstances, it is futile when it ceases to be noxious. In this very burlesque, Mr Arthur Roberts sang a slangy parody of the story of the Prodigal Son, which could not but offend every one who cares for what is beautiful in literature, to say nothing of those who claim for the parable a still higher sanctity. I have very little doubt that the song would have been soundly hissed had not the Censorship deadened all sense of responsibility on the part of the public. And remember that while, in this case, the very words of Jesus were parodied by a grimacing low comedian, with full official sanction, the same authority had only a few months before absolutely vetoed the production, by the greatest living actress, of Mr Oscar Wilde's beautiful and entirely reverent dramatisation of the legend of John the Baptist !

* November 2—December 16.

night of the Garrick company's return from its provincial tour. To be quite frank, I had gone to the theatre with somewhat meagre anticipations of personal enjoyment; for it is the disadvantage of the well-made play that when once you are familiar with its springs and cog-wheels and escapements, the action of the mannikins whom the clockwork controls is apt to seem as unlifelike as that of the Berne marionettes so vivaciously described by Mrs Bancroft. But, really, this intrigue of Sardou's is such a marvellously delicate piece of mechanism that it is impossible not to admire it, and to watch with interest the subtlety of its arrangements. Here is no figure which, like the Berne "kail-supper," puts the spoon to its left ear instead of its mouth. Every limb, every joint, works with precision; the figures are as large as life and twice as natural. The scene of the three men, admirably acted by Mr Bancroft, Mr Hare, and Mr Forbes Robertson, really moved me, and if the great scene between husband and wife seemed more painful than passionate or pathetic, that was no fault of Mr Forbes Robertson or Miss Kate Rorke. We cannot sympathise very acutely with passion which is obviously conditioned by the playwright's frugal determination to leave himself matter enough for an effective fourth act. The only new member of the cast was Miss Elizabeth Robins, who played the Countess Zicka. It is not a part which

brings out the best side of Miss Robins's talent, but
her performance was nevertheless very interesting.

A much better play than that which Dr Edward
Aveling presented at the Royalty last week would
have been ruined, to my thinking, or rather feeling,
by the title—*Frog*.* Every time it occurred in the
dialogue it gave me a little shiver. The very sound
of the word is ugly and clammy, and the idea, the
invention, is frigid. And my uneasiness increased
with each repetition of the word. It was like an
error of tact or breach of manners, pardonable for
once in a way, but intolerable when repeated and
rubbed-in. For the rest, the play contained some
really bright dialogue, but was ruined by seemingly
wilful conventionality, both in the theme and in the
execution. The conjugal difficulties of the husband
who "knows nothing about poetry and painting and
sculpture," and the wife who is supposed, on very insufficient evidence, to be an adept in these graceful
pursuits, must be treated now-a-days with a very light
and skilful hand if they are to begin to interest us.
Dr Aveling has, unfortunately, served up the theme
with the mustiest of dressings. Christmas sentimentality, carols *à la cantonnade*, an old gentleman whose
conversation is mainly composed of quotations from
Shakespeare, a romantic French lover, an intervention

---

* October 30—November 4.

of Providence by which the wife is made to "sin only in intent"—all this is positively archaic.   It really seems as though Dr Aveling must have exhumed this *Frog* from the legendary rock, and from a pretty deep-down bed.   Miss Annie Rose played the comic heroine (not the lady of the sinful intent) with a good deal of archness and grace.   Mrs Theodore Wright was very amiable as the hero's widowed mother, and Mr Edmund Gurney showed real feeling in the part of the unhappily-named hero.

Of the three three-act farces (nine acts of farce !) enumerated in the heading of this article, the first, *The Lady Killer*,* at the Strand, is a commonplace but amusing adaptation from the French, while the other two are flagrantly Anglo-Saxon.   Bisson's *115 Rue Pigalle*, the original of the Strand farce, is evidently a wild piece of buffoonery, which becomes all the more inconceivable when the scene is transferred to England ; but there is a certain amount of constructive skill in the articulation of the play, and Messrs Harry Paulton and Willie Edouin have characters, of a sort, to impersonate—conventional grotesques if you will, but not entirely denuded of traits of observation.   The English (or Anglo-American) farces, on the other hand, leave observation and constructive thought a thousand miles behind.   The

---

* October 17—November 17.

drama seems to have abjured its function of representing, or even misrepresenting, life, and to be fantasticating in a region where two and two make anything but four, and the Court of Common Sense has no jurisdiction. There is some indefinable quality in them which rescues them from sheer idiocy. They amuse their public royally, and for my part I laughed several times at both of them. But it would be impossible to imagine a form of art more innocent of reason or coherence.

I would even invite the attention of students to *Tom, Dick, and Harry*,* by Mrs R. Pacheco, as a consummate and memorable example of the pitch to which sheer unreason can be carried on the stage, without exciting any sort of protest on the part of presumably sane audiences. It is a Comedy of Errors raised to the third power. Dick and Harry are indistinguishable twins, and Tom, who, to gain his private ends, disguises himself in a false wig and beard, chooses, for no particular reason, to make-up after a photograph of one of the twins, thus rendering himself indistinguishable from Dick and Harry. All three turn up, by pure chance, at the same hotel on the same day, all three, by pure chance, dressed precisely alike, so that, of course, every one mistakes Tom for Dick, Dick for Harry,

---

* November 2—still running.

and so forth, in an endless series of permutations. Now all this is preposterous enough ; indeed it would be hard to invent a more incredible intrigue. Even to show us four, five, or six indistinguishable characters would not heighten the absurdity, for we can as easily believe in six as in three, in sixty as in six. But now comes the curious part of it. Not only is the public willing to accept these monstrous postulates—it is even willing to let its imagination nullify the evidence of its senses, and to pretend that the three men are alike, when as a matter of fact no one with eyes in his head could possibly mistake one for the other. All the art of the perruquier cannot make Messrs Hawtrey, Percy, and Playfair even plausibly like one another; yet the audience consents to make-believe to the bitter end, and is not in the least put about when Tom's sweetheart or Dick's wife mistakes Harry for Tom, or Tom for Dick, though every one, from the front of the stalls to the back of the gallery, can tell at a glance which is which. It is simply a case of *populus vult decipi ;* we are so avid of easy laughter that we will " play at " anything in order to enjoy it, and submit to any insult to our intelligence for the sake of a momentary tickling of the diaphragm. Monsieur Sarcey ought to pay a special visit to England, in order to study *Tom, Dick, and Harry*. He would find in it the crowning proof of his pet theory, that there is nothing the public will

not swallow, if only you have the knack of enlisting
its will on your side. Mr Hawtrey and his coad-
jutors certainly enlisted the will of the Trafalgar
Square audience on the night when I was present.
Their enjoyment seemed to be quite genuine and
spontaneous.

Mr Mark Melford's farce, *A Screw Loose*,* belongs
essentially to the same order of art, though it perhaps does not put quite so gigantic a strain on our
powers of make-believe. The problem Mr Melford
has set himself is briefly this:—Given one lunatic and
a number of sane persons, to make all the sane
persons be mistaken for madmen, while the lunatic is
accepted as sane. The solution is very simple. You
have only to let the sane people behave more idioti-
cally than the lunatic, and the trick is done. This
is precisely how Mr Melford does the trick, to the
unbounded delight of the Vaudeville audience. Mr
Frank Wyatt, who plays the lunatic, must be congratulated on minimising the inherent painfulness of
his part by his airy whimsicality. He is very ably
seconded by Mr Arthur Elwood, Mr Abingdon, Mr
Fred Thorne, and Miss Gertrude Kingston.

---

* November 4—December 2.

XLI.

" MEASURE FOR MEASURE "—" GUDGEONS "— " MRS OTHELLO."

15th November.

IT is to be hoped that some means may be found of preserving for future use the excellently painted scene, representing the interior of an Elizabethan theatre, in which the Shakespeare Reading Society gave their performances of *Measure for Measure** at the Royalty last week. According to Mr Arthur Dillon's handbook, it was the Fortune Theatre that the designer, Mr Minton Taylor, had in his eye; but he had evidently borrowed the general outline of the structure from the pen-and-ink drawing of the Swan Theatre (also a " public," or unroofed house) recently unearthed in the MS. note-book of a Dutch traveller, Johannes de Witt. I am inclined to doubt whether this was really a typical structure. In De Witt's drawing, for example, there is no upper stage, no provision for Juliet's balcony, or the walls of Angiers in *King John ;* unless we are to suppose that one or two boxes of the tier at the back could on occasion be utilised for such purposes. This conjecture is supported by a stage-direction in one of Marston's tragedies, *Antonio and Mellida :* " Andrugio's Ghost

---

* November 9, 10, and 11, and matinée.

is placed betwixt the music-houses"—the "music-houses" or "rooms" being undoubtedly boxes at the back of the stage. There is no question, however, that a projecting platform, with a space underneath it, was one of the common appurtenances of the Elizabethan stage, and Mr Taylor, has done rightly in introducing it ; but in so doing he masks the doors shown in De Witt's drawings. Now these doors of entrance and exit were certainly among the most characteristic features of the Elizabethan stage, and we cannot suppose that the word "door" was applied to a mere curtained opening. Indeed, in pictures of Restoration theatres (connecting-links in the process of evolution between the Elizabethan and the modern playhouse) we see the doors quite distinctly in the deep proscenium. In this very play, *Measure for Measure*, we have the direction, "Enter Duke, Varrius, Lords ; Angelo, Escalus, &c., *at several doors*," meaning, of course, that the two parties entered from opposite sides. Again, I cannot believe that in a theatre which had "rooms" or boxes at the back of the stage, any "traverse" (curtain) was drawn so far forward as that between the pillars supporting the pent-house roof at the Royalty, seeing that it entirely shut out every front scene from the view of the masked ladies in the "rooms." A whole essay, nay, a whole book, might be written in criticism of details of the Royalty scene. I may even confess that I have made some collections towards such a book, and am therefore in a position to say, with a certain confidence, that Mr Minton Taylor has shown both learning and ingenuity in his reconstructive effort. On the whole, and taking into account the somewhat restricted space at his command, I doubt if he could have done better. The gallants, smoking their Elizabethan clay pipes on their sixpenny stools on the stage, certainly contributed to the illusion ; but I fear it was very seldom that the ruffling blades of the Court and the Inns of Court conducted themselves with such propriety. To make the realism perfect they should have called for and consumed burnt sack in the midst of the performance, exchanged banter with the citizens in the "yard," and between-whiles quarrelled among themselves. It would not have been amiss if one of them had casually run another through the body.

So much for the scene. As for the play, *Measure for Measure* was certainly not the best that could have been selected to illustrate the artistic advantages and drawbacks of the early theatre. In the first place, the Elizabethan costumes worn by the actors were not essentially different from those in which a manager of to-day would dress the play. It would have been much better (if possible) to have selected, say, a Roman play, and let us see how Brutus and Antony looked in slashed doublets and trunk-hose.

(But soft! Did they already use "shapes" in classical pieces on the Elizabethan stage? I really forget, and my authorities are not at hand.) In the second place, there is no other play of Shakespeare's in which so much of the dialogue is absolutely unspeakable before a modern audience. Therefore large cuts were inevitable ; and having begun to cut, the actors went on with a sweeping hand, and made huge excisions for the mere sake of brevity. Now the chief interest of such an experiment would have been to speak as nearly as possible the whole text of the play, and see how close the performance could be brought to the traditional "two hours' traffic" of the Shakespearian stage. It was noteworthy that, despite the enormous excisions, and despite the fact that "business" was (quite properly) reduced to a minimum, and that some of the actors (quite improperly) recited their verses so fast as to be totally unintelligible, the two hours' limit was on Thursday night exceeded by five or ten minutes. In the third place, *Measure for Measure* happens to be one of the plays in which there is no necessity for using the upper stage. There is not a single stage-direction : "Enter So-and-so, above," nor is there any passage in which it seems in the least degree probable that a stage-manager of the period would have brought the upper stage into requisition. On Thursday night, then, it was used in a quite arbitrary fashion, and once or twice in contradiction to the text. This was, of course, a pity. It would have been much more interesting to have seen the upper stage employed in one of the numerous scenes to which it belongs of necessity.

As the performers withhold their names on the playbill, it is to be presumed that they deprecate criticism of their individual efforts. I shall only remark, then, that a Shakespeare Reading Society ought surely to set an example to the professional stage in meticulous respect for the poet's text; whereas several of the performers simply improvised at will when their memory failed them, and not one paid any great attention to the metre. For the rest, the Duke and Lucio both looked and spoke well, the Isabella showed intelligence and sincerity, and the Claudio was strikingly handsome, both in features and figure. His admirable stage-face reminded me strongly of the portraits of Charles Kemble.

Mr Louis N. Parker has at last achieved the success which he has done so much—yet hitherto not quite enough—to deserve. *Gudgeons*,* produced with much applause at Terry's Theatre last Friday evening (let the superstitious take note!) is a very clever and entertaining play, showing in every scene the touch of the true dramatist. Do not let us exaggerate

---

* November 10—still running.

its merits ; to do so would be to render an ill service
to Mr Parker and his collaborator, Mr " Thornton
Clark." It does not stand on the highest plane even
of English dramatic work ; but it takes a distinguished place on the second level. Its balance-sheet
may be drawn up somewhat as follows :—

Debit.	Credit.
Plot—what there is of it—improbable towards close.	Plot subordinated to character-study.
Chief character belongs to familiar, and even conventional, type.	Chief character nicely differentiated from others of same type.
Psychology rather summary and superficial. The two principal characters' moral self-consciousness (or self-estimation) left undefined.	Adventurer's wife novel and even pathetic conception.
High lights in dialogue a good deal too high. Adventurer's duplicity emphasised, at times, in defiance of plausibility or possibility.	Dialogue brilliant and *dramatically* brilliant—that is, not dependent on irrelevant verbal wit.

That the balance, when struck, is largely in favour
of the play, was proved by the reception accorded to
it ; but that is no reason why we should not urge Mr
Parker, in his future work, to minimise the number
and importance of the items on the debit side. He
has not yet forsworn that license of unreality which
has been so noxious a tradition in English dramaturgy.
He makes far too many sacrifices to that obsolete idol,
the Optic of the Theatre. He is too often content to

ask himself, "Would this thought occur to this personage?" without putting the further and no less
essential query, "Would this personage utter this
thought?" The result is a great number of speeches
"brought in without discretion," as Milton phrases
it, "corruptly to gratify the people." In other words,
the play is a character-comedy shot with farce.

There were moments when I felt that Mr Herbert
Waring was not enough of a *comedian*, in the specific
sense of the word, for the character of James Ffolliott-
Treherne ; but these were the authors' worser moments.
Where the authors are at their best, Mr Waring was
beyond praise. His performance, indeed, was something of a revelation, precisely because of the admirable sobriety with which he treated a character in
which the conventional comedian would have looked
for, and found, opportunities for facile caricature.
Even in his make-up—in the livid hollows beneath
his eyes—Mr Waring was perfect. He raised the
character almost to a tragic level, and presented a
memorable embodiment of remorseless and ravenous
egoism. Miss Janette Steer showed intelligence and
originality in the very fact that, being the manageress,
she accepted so subdued a part as Mrs Treherne ; and
her execution of it was no less to her credit. The
character, with its dog-like devotion, is curiously
effective, but I confess I do not quite grasp the
authors' idea in it. What sort of woman is this,

anyway? She is obviously of gentle birth and breeding, and her nature does not seem to be, like her husband's, radically false; yet she has apparently no shred of moral feeling, and regards Treherne's feats of rascality with childish admiration, or rather adoration. It almost seems as though he had hypnotised her, so that she was no longer responsible for her thoughts and actions. Her state of mind may not be inexplicable, but the authors certainly leave it unexplained. Mr Murray Carson is excellent as the Universal Agent, who reminds one of Mr Stevenson's Pinkerton, and still more of the original from whom Pinkerton is said to have been drawn. Mr Carson's American, especially in the first act, is the best I ever heard an Englishman speak. Mr W. T. Lovell and Miss Sybil Carlisle play the lovers very prettily, and Messrs Charles Fulton and James Welch complete a most satisfactory cast.

There is really nothing to be said of *Mrs Othello*,* at Toole's, except that it is a rattling adaptation (by the late Mr Fred Leslie and Mr Arthur Shirley) of a third-rate French farce, and that it charmed the first-night audience. The enormous buffoonery of the third act is, indeed, quite irresistible. It sent us all into shrieks of laughter. The farce is played with

---

* November 11. Transferred to Vaudeville, December 26— still running.

unlimited "go" by Miss Fanny Brough, Miss Cicely Richards, Mr Charles Glenney, Mr George Raiemond, Mr W. H. Day, Mr Julian Cross, and Mr Cecil Crofton. No entertainment could well be more unpretending. One cannot precisely say that is "funny without being vulgar;" but, at least, it is not vulgar without being funny.

XLII.

"THE SCHOOL FOR SCANDAL."

22nd November.

WE are all languishing to applaud without reservation a production at Daly's Theatre; but Mr Daly obstinately denies us the opportunity. His managerial instinct seems, for the time, to have deserted him. As he sat in front of the house at the dress-rehearsal of *The School for Scandal,** and looked at it with the dispassionate eye of a playgoer and student of the theatre, did he really find in it such merits as could possibly be expected to render it attractive to the English public? Miss Rehan's Lady Teazle, we may assume, represents more or less exactly his own views of the character; but can he be under any illusion as to Mr George Clarke's Joseph Surface? The part, no doubt, is a difficult one to cast; but I venture to suggest that if he could not lay his hand on a better

---

* November 13—December 30.

Joseph, Mr Daly would have done much more wisely
to have withdrawn the play before production, even at
the last moment. Mr Clarke is a capable and experi-
enced actor, excellent as an American stockbroker,
and passable (to British eyes at any rate) even as an
American Secretary of State; but his Richard Cœur
de Lion was not more pathetically impossible than his
Joseph Surface. With his ill-fitting wig, and his face
made-up to a uniform salmon-colour, he looked and
acted like the conventional Joseph of a second-rate
provincial company of five-and-twenty years ago. Mr
William Farren's Sir Peter, again, is a sterling bit of
acting, with which, especially in its present surroundings, it would be ungracious to quarrel; but as Mr
Farren has been practically our only Sir Peter since
the death of Phelps and dear old Chippendale, his
performance—I am trying to look at the thing from
the managerial point of view—obviously lacks the
attraction of novelty. Mr Arthur Bourchier makes an
exceedingly creditable, but not precisely a fascinating,
Charles; and Careless, Backbite, Crabtree, and the
rest can at most be ranked as "fair to middling."
Then we have Mr James Lewis in the small part of
Moses, neither more nor less amusing than any other
competent comedian who knows the traditions; and
Mrs Gilbert, presenting the possibilities of the best Mrs
Candour of our day, but reduced to the merest shadow
by the bowdlerisation of the dialogue. I am the last

to complain of the suppression of questionable " gags,"
but I see no reason for cutting out lines which
Sheridan wrote, and which belong to the manners
of the time.   Thus we have one important character very inadequately filled, and others without any
pretension to such remarkable excellence as could
reasonably be expected to lend a novel attractiveness
to the delightful but fatally familiar comedy.   Remains,
then, Miss Rehan's Lady Teazle—can Mr Daly have
fancied it so dazzling a creation as to blind us to all
flaws and failings in the rest of the performance?
Brilliantly coloured it certainly is, but the colours are
laid on, for the most part, without taste or discrimination.   This Lady Teazle is neither a fine lady to the
manner born, nor a country girl aping the fine lady.
She is simply a nervous, restless, self-conscious woman,
always striving after effect, never still for a moment,
and never natural.   She skips, trips, and frolics through
the part ; she does nothing, in Lewis Carroll's phrase,
but " gyre and gimble."   By dint of pauses, suspen-
sions, nods, becks, and elaborate eye-play and by-play,
she tries to throw each line into special relief, as
though Sheridan's wit would otherwise be apt to escape
notice.   Did you ever try to read a book through
a small and powerful magnifying glass, enabling the
eye to take in only two or three words at a time?
Miss Rehan's treatment of her dialogue reminded me
strongly of this slow and jerky process.   Slowness,

indeed, was the general defect of the revival. Every bit of business, every laugh, every chuckle, was indefinitely protracted, so that, despite the free curtailment of certain scenes, the fourth act was not over on the first night until eleven o'clock. With all sympathy for Mr Daly and all admiration for Miss Rehan, it is impossible to regard this revival as well advised or well executed. Nothing pleased me so much, I grieve to confess, as the elaborate and beautiful dance in the first act. It is only right to add, however, that the first-night audience were of a different opinion, and applauded the whole performance without reserve.

XLIII.

"Good-Bye"—"A Venetian Singer"— "Under the Clock."

Under the Clock, by Messrs Brookfield and Seymour Hicks, is like *l'acte des théâtres* in a French *revue* rather than one of the ordinary English travesties to which we are accustomed. The innovation is a pleasant one, and may, perhaps, set a fashion. In a long-drawn parody of a single play the fun almost always flags before the end ; but when half-a-dozen plays are passed in rapid review, even if one scene misses fire, we need not despair of the next. Not one of the scenes in *Under the Clock* can be said to miss fire ; but I own that a good many of the authors' minor allusions were lost upon me. I wonder how many of the audience understood the apparition of the "Third Mrs Tanqueray," with the remark "Gone wrong at the eleventh hour"? It baffled me at the moment; but in the silent watches of the night I wrestled with it and overcame. Like the legendary Scotchman, I feel inclined to dig Mr Brookfield in the ribs and say, "I hae ye noo!" but it is my painful conviction that the majority of the audience will go to their graves without having seen the joke.* There are a few episodes, then, that should either be clarified or cut; but, on the whole, the extravaganza goes very merrily, and is well worth seeing. Mimicry is not precisely the strong point of Mr Brookfield, Mr Seymour Hicks, or even of Miss Lottie Venne; but in these thumb-nail caricatures, so to speak, it is sufficient if the likeness be recognisable, even if it be less than exact. Mr Brookfield was at his best, to my thinking, in his imitation of Mr Penley, while Miss Lottie Venne was happiest as Miss Julia Neilson; but both artists kept the fun going throughout with inexhaustible spirit. Neither of the other items in the "triple bill"†—*Good-bye*, by Mr Seymour

---

* It appears to have been an allusion to Mrs Kendal's performance of the erring Mrs Tanqueray.

† Court Theatre, November 25. *Faithful James*, by Mr B. C. Stephenson, was soon afterwards substituted for *A Venetian Singer*. It appears that *Good-bye*, by Mr Seymour Hicks, which I here pass over somewhat cavalierly, was in reality a work of distinguished merit, and even greater promise. I am sorry not to

Hicks, and *A Venetian Singer*, by Messrs Stephenson and Jakobowski—calls for special notice. They are inoffensive trifles, no more.

---

have been the first to hail the rising sun, but hasten to make what atonement lies in my power by quoting a part of the article in which Mr Clement Scott performs that pleasing duty. Mr Seymour Hicks, according to Mr Scott, is coming to the front very rapidly:—" His animal spirits carry him away, and he is apt to kick over the traces. But that is a fault easily to be forgiven in this bored and *blasé* and jaundiced age, when, for the most part, our young authors write like miserable, little, wizened old men and pose as Tottenham Court Road Voltaires! These sickly, and I regret to say to me personally sickening, little old young gentlemen will probably fall foul of manly, boyish, natural young Seymour Hicks because he has written a pretty little play called *Good-bye*, which does not disdain sentiment. . . . They will squirt at poor young Seymour Hicks their acrid and acid and venomous juices, they will babble to him about 'sentiment' and 'convention' and the 'drama of the day before yesterday,' and they will beg him to poison his heroine and asphyxiate his lover, and urge him to put a pistol in the hands of his husband-hero and bespatter the drawing-room carpet with his brains; but, good, honest, boyish Mr Seymour Hicks, do not listen to the voice of these charmers, charm they never so wisely. You are on the right tack, Mr Seymour Hicks—believe me, you are on the right tack. The women are with you, and the women are the real influence of the playhouse. The people are with you, and the people will never desert you if you delight them. Go on, young author, buoyed up by youth and the best of youth's assistants—faith. Write your honest, touching little plays. Believe in soldiers, believe in loyalty to women. Take up your Browning and read—

> ' God be thanked, the meanest of His creatures
> Boasts two soul-sides—one to face the world with,
> One to show a woman when he loves her ! '

XLIV.

"CAPTAIN SWIFT."

6th December.

IF Mr Haddon Chambers has not as yet enriched
English literature with an immortal play, he has at
least added a classic phrase to the language, and
it is not every one who has done that. "The long
arm of coincidence" will hand his name down to
generations yet unborn. And yet the image is not
a very consistent one. "The many arms of coincidence" would be more accurate. *Captain Swift* *
presupposes a four-armed Briareus to bring together
(1) the Bushranger, (2) his Erring Mother, (3) his
Vindictive Foster - Brother, (4) the Magnanimous
Squatter who feels that he owes his life to the Bush-
ranger, who might have shot him, but didn't. And
then, even with this fourfold coincidence to aid him,
eked out by starts, gasps, slips of the tongue, and
strawberry-marks on the left arm, Mr Chambers
has still to call in the help of the common or Adelphi

"Enjoy life, clever young author, while it lasts for you.
Dance your breakdowns, imitate your companions, frolic and be
funny. You will write a far better play than *Good-bye* by and
by. But don't be disheartened by these dreadful little old mannikins who would poison your enthusiasm and reverence. You
are doing well, and you will do better. Meanwhile, in the
words of the old, dreadfully *conventional* theatrical cry, ' Brayvo,
Hicks ! '"—*Illustrated London News*, December 2.

* Haymarket, December 2—still running.

detective in order to work out his tragedy! The play belongs to the infancy of art, but there is a certain amiability about its youthfulness, and it is much less tedious than many a more rational piece of work. Mr Tree is still the ideal drawing-room bush-ranger. He "fills the bill," if ever man did. But I am still harassed by a problem which used to puzzle me five years ago : why, at the end of the first act, does Swift say to Gardiner, with the most significant emphasis, "No, we have never met—*before*"? Does he mean that they have met afterwards, in the sweet by-and-by? Reason recoils from such an interpretation, but I can conceive no other. Miss Carlotta Addison succeeded, with admirable art, in awakening our sympathies for the erring mother; Miss Fanny Coleman was good as her cynical sister ; Mrs Tree made a pleasant Stella ; Mr Holman Clark was clever as the foster-brother; and altogether the cast was quite up to the former level.

XLV.

" THE BLACK CAT."

13th December.

" E PUR si muove ! " Not only does the solar system move, but, incredible as it may seem, Mr Clement Scott actually moves with it—unconsciously and in-voluntarily, of course, but quite unmistakably. Even while he is striking the attitude of Joshua at Ajalon, and bidding the sun stand still, the force he seeks to control has laid its grip on him and swept him along, until he sees things at a totally new angle and in totally new relations. Three years ago—nay, less, much less than three—*The Black Cat** would have outraged every holiest feeling in his manly bosom. He would have arisen in his wrath, and rent it limb from limb. I can see in my mind's eye the opening sentences of his denunciation. They would have run as follows :—" It was indeed a gruesome spectacle to which we were convoked by the faddists and fanatics of the Independent Theatre on Friday last. Under the ægis of the disinterested Dutchman who has made it his self-imposed mission to personally conduct the British drama into the paths of pestilent pessimism, Dr John Todhunter converted the Opera Comique stage into a dissecting-room and treated the weird but scanty audience of long-haired atheists, sexless Socialists, agnostics, Ibsenites, Anarchists, and egoists to a demonstration in morbid anatomy so appalling and sickening as to delight their carrion-loving souls. There they all lay on their zinc slabs, the three 'subjects' of this ghastly post-mortem, while the doughty doctor tucked up his sleeves, brandished his scalpel, and set about his terrible task with grim and

---

* Opera Comique, December 8.

ghoulish gusto. It is hard to say which of the corpses presented the most loathsome spectacle—the moping, maundering, misanthropic wife, teazing her husband, torturing her child, and at last driven to the sin of suicide in order to escape from her own ill-temper; the nerveless, niminy-piminy, nincompoop husband, without an atom of true British manhood in him, feebly squirting his envenomed epigrams at all that is sweet and sacred in life; or the Duessa of the Divorce Court, darting her basilisk glances at every man she meets, and unblushingly preaching the brazen gospel of egoism, socialism, individualism, agnosticism, and free-love. Hitherto our purveyors of putrescence have had to go abroad for their clinical lectures, their dead-house demonstrations. Now, at last, the contagion has reached our own shores, and it behoves every one of us, who has any remnant of faith left in the manliness of man and the womanliness of woman, to take up arms against it. We must put our foot down on the miasma. We must boycott the bacillus. We must nip the cancer in the bud. Let us boldly assure our Dr Todhunters, Dr Ibsens, Dr Dulcamaras, *et hoc genus omne*, that we will not tolerate upon the English stage the jargon of morbid pathology. It has ever been the glory of the British drama to shrink from the discussion of all topics save such as can be brought on the *tapis* of the domestic dinner-table after the children have come down to dessert. And shall we renounce this golden rule at the *ipse dixit* of a clique of long-haired Socialists, effete egoists, and pessimistic prigs? Are we to suffer our Imogens and our Rosalinds, our Polly Eccleses and Mary Melroses, to be driven from the stage by a Blanche Tremaine and a Constance Denham—one the avatar of free-love, the other the evangel of self-slaughter? No! There are still some of us who prefer to believe, with Browning, that— [The reader can supply for himself the indispensable quotation from Browning. Any scrap of metrical Mark - Tapleyism will do.] The faddists and the pessimists have not yet carried the day. The Women are against them; the great heart of the Great Public still beats in the right place. Dr Ibsen we have long ago sent about his business, like the egoist and bungler he is. Let Dr Todhunter follow his fellow-quack to the suburban solitudes of scabrous Scandinavia. There, perhaps, his clinical demonstrations may find their admirers. Here we have no use for them."

Who can doubt that this, or something like it, would have been Mr Scott's deliverance upon *The Black Cat* a few years, or even a few months, ago? For, whatever its merits, Dr Todhunter's play is certainly not a pleasant one. It does not vindicate the inviolable British hearth or the immaculate British dinner-table. The sympathetic personage is conspicuous by his absence. There is no virtue to be rewarded, and vice meets with no very exemplary punishment. Yet, so far from denouncing it, Mr Scott assures us that "it is within an ace of being not only a very admirable but most practicable drama. It interested and pleased the few ; with a little care it might have delighted the many." "Interesting," "fresh," "alluring," "appetising," are among the epithets he bestows upon it. The only thing he does not approve is the final suicide, and even that he declares inartistic and inexpedient rather than immoral and irreligious. All this indicates a serious displacement of Mr Scott's ethical and æsthetic point of view. He no longer stands where he did, in the forefront of the compact majority. His palate is evidently being depraved, so that he can swallow without so much as a wry face decoctions which, only a little while ago, would have made him choke and sputter with loathing. And he is not alone in his change of front. Other critics, who would at one time have had nothing but contumely for *The Black Cat*, now treat it with courtesy, and almost with enthusiasm. In this fact lies the chief interest and significance of the production. It shows how the cat is jumping.

Dr Todhunter's play is unquestionably very able and even brilliant, simple in motive, strong in handling, full of suggestive intelligence, and yet free from deliberate theorising. It is a tragedy of character, in

which the action, such as it is, can be very easily foreseen, and the interest is sustained by pure analysis
of motive and conflict of passion. Note how, in the
first and second acts, the dramatist deliberately brings
down his curtain upon the same incident, and that an
incident of no importance. We are miles away from
the old tableau-hunting technique — yet Mr Scott
appears to have noticed nothing amiss. One or two
scenes became a little tedious, because the conversation seemed to rotate on its own axis instead of carrying forward the process of thought and emotion ; but
on the whole the first two acts were entirely successful. In the third act, we became conscious of a
weakness which had hitherto escaped us. As soon
as the tragic solution of the problem began to loom
ahead, we realised—at least that is how I account for
what seems to have been a very general feeling—we
realised that we did not know or care enough about
these people to want to have our sensibilities harrowed
on their account. It was not that Constance Denham's suicide seemed improbable or out of keeping
—only somehow we were not in the mood for it.
Speaking for myself, I must own that it did not move
or impress me in the least. On the contrary, I was
chiefly occupied in wishing that Constance would
poison Blanche Tremaine as well, and wondering
whether she took cream and sugar with her prussic
acid. The moral is, I fancy, that the author who,

through two acts, has appealed solely to the intellect
of his audience, must not without warning, as it were,
make a large draft on their emotions. No doubt the
character of Constance was intended to arouse our
pity throughout, and in a sense it did ; but the
struggle in her sickly soul was not vividly enough
depicted to awaken more than an intellectual interest.
Blanche, too, is imperfectly realised. She is all right
so far as she goes, but she goes only to the brain, not
to the heart. In a word, we do not care at all what
happens to this trio of bungled lives. Nothing that
could possibly befall would give us keen satisfaction
or deeply afflict us ; therefore the violent and tragic
ending is like an appeal to which we cannot respond.
Dr Todhunter has conceived his characters well, but
has not projected them quite vigorously enough.
Nevertheless, *The Black Cat* secures him a prominent
place in the little group of dramatists to whom we
may look for good work in the future. One technical
hint, by the way, for his next essay—let him, so far
as possible, eschew the soliloquy.

The performance was entirely creditable to the
Independent Theatre. Miss Hall Caine showed tact
and skill in the very difficult part of Constance, and
Miss Mary Keegan lent just the right sort of charm
to Blanche Tremaine—an easier, yet by no means
easy, part. Mr Bucklaw was perhaps a trifle
commonplace as Denham, but played with intelli-

gence and sincerity; Mr Orlando Barnett and Mr Neville Doone were both excellent; and Miss Dora Barton was one of the prettiest and most natural children I ever saw on the stage.

A few evenings ago I paid a second visit to *Gudgeons* at Terry's Theatre, and thought even more highly of the play and the performance than I did on the first night. Messrs Parker and Carson have certainly produced the most entertaining comedy of the season. The second and third acts, despite some breaches of verisimilitude, are altogether delightful, and even the first act is far from dull. Mr Waring's performance of James Ffolliott-Treherne is a really memorable character-creation, Mr Carson's Hooper is a clever sketch, and Miss Janette Steer's Mrs Treherne shows a very high order of dramatic intelligence. *Gudgeons* is unquestionably a play not to be missed.

XLVI.

"The Headless Man"—"Six Persons"— "Beauty's Toils"—"Don Quixote"— "The Second Mrs Tanqueray."

27th December.

In *The Headless Man*,* Mr Burnand has worked out in three acts that happy thought: "Fancy having to

---

* Criterion, December 21—still running.

consult an idiot solicitor!" which occurs, if I mistake not, somewhere in *Happy Thoughts*. The working-out is a trifle too complex for my poor understanding. The business of the photographs and the portmanteaus bewilders me like thimble-rigging or the three‑card trick. But it is not in the least essential that any one should fully unravel these complications. The whole point of the piece lies in the delightful inconsequences of Sam Hedley, and these Mr Wyndham delivers with a light-hearted conviction which renders them quite irresistible. It is no derogation to Mr Wyndham's more serious powers to say that he remains easily first among the light comedians of this generation. He is ably seconded by Mr Blakeley and Mr J. G. Taylor, Miss Ellis Jeffreys and Miss F. Frances, so that it seems likely we may have some time to wait for the promised comedy by Lady Violet Greville.

Mr Zangwill's bright little duologue at the Haymarket is overweighted by its too pretentious title— *Six Persons,**—and the quotation from *The Autocrat of the Breakfast-Table*, which accounts for it. We are led to expect some subtle discrimination between the three personalities implicit in each of the interlocutors; whereas the three Charleses and three Eugenias are no more clearly developed than in any dialogue

---

* December 22—still running.

which turns on a mutual misunderstanding. Until the very last moment, indeed, we have no hint of what I suppose Mr Zangwill intends for the real Charles and Eugenia. The concluding incident suggests, no doubt, that they have in reality been in love with each other all the time; but they have concealed the fact from the audience quite as successfully as from themselves. Thus we have seen only two Eugenias and Charleses during the whole course of the play; and he would be a dull dog indeed who could not, by the aid of copious soliloquies and frequent asides, distinguish Eugenia's Eugenia from Charles's Eugenia, Charles's Charles from Eugenia's Charles. That is the very child's-play of analysis. Mr Zangwill, as we all know, is anything but a dull dog, and his little play is a sparkling and spirited piece of writing of the old Theyre-Smith school. It is capitally acted by Miss Irene Vanbrugh and Mr Frederick Kerr.

There is an excellent comic idea in *Beauty's Toils*,* by Mr Charles S. Fawcett, founded on a story named *Her Fatal Beauty*, by Mr W. B. Maxwell, and produced last week at the Strand Theatre. Plenty of fun, it is clear, might have been got out of the fascinating and accomplished housemaid, and the havoc wrought by "her fatal beauty" in the palaces of dukes and the premises of dentists. A good deal of the fun Mr

---

* December 21—still running.

Fawcett has actually managed to extract, but it was sadly obscured on the night when I saw the piece (the second night) by an intolerably slow and slovenly performance. By this time it probably plays more closely, and ought to be just the thing for the Strand public. Mr Edouin was himself the chief culprit in the matter of slowness. Mr Giddens was excellent, and Mr Gerald Moore's imperturbable drawl became funny by dint of sheer persistence. As the goddess in cap and apron, Miss Miriam Clements had little to do but to look handsome, and that she did to perfection.

Don Quixote * at the Alhambra is a scintillant and kaleidoscopic ballet, quite up to the highest standard of this popular establishment. Those who have any affection for the Knight of the Rueful Visage had better divert their attention from the so-called dramatic element in the production, and concentrate their mind on the mere divertisement. It is not altogether agreeable to see the excellent hidalgo, in the person of Mr Fred Storey, comporting himself like the late Mr F. Vokes in the wildest of his antics ; but then it is so easy to disconnect the Don from the dancer, who, simply as a dancer, is undoubtedly clever. Signora Salmoiraghi, the principal *danseuse*, is a performer of skill and method rather than

---

* December 11—still running.

inspiration ; but she knows her business thoroughly, and appears to have won the heart of the Alhambra audience.   The great charm of the production, however, lies in the Vintage Festival of the second scene, and the final diversions at the court of the Duchess, which are really brilliant spectacles.

In recording my first-night impressions of *The Second Mrs Tanqueray*, I said that it was not a play I hankered after seeing again.   Well, I saw it the other night for the fourth time, with renewed interest and admiration, but still with the feeling that it cannot be called a *pleasant* play, an exhilarating or diverting entertainment.   It is precisely this fact which renders its popularity so remarkable and so encouraging.   It has been the great, almost the only, success (burlesques apart) of a not over-prosperous season ; and no happier augury for the future of the stage could well be conceived.   One could almost parody the remark of the Edinburgh gallery-boy, and ask, "Whaur's your 'British Public' noo ?"—that British Public which would accept nothing at the theatre but a mild narcotic after its day's work, which brought its young ladies of fifteen to the dress-circle, and resented the slightest shock to their innocent ignorance, or ignorant innocence, which regarded the drama as a mere *chasse* to its after-dinner coffee,* and demanded, not to

* My friend Mr A. B. Walkley, in the *Speaker* for December

think about life, but to have its mind distracted from all serious thought whatsoever? Where, I say, is this British Public? It seems to have "softly and suddenly vanished away." Now that the Ardlamont sensation has run out, the evening papers might find

MYSTERIOUS DISAPPEARANCE OF THE

BRITISH PUBLIC

a taking line for their bills. I have my own theory to account for it. I think the ideal British public, if it ever existed at all, has emigrated to America, and devoted itself to dramatic criticism. The American critics prefer *The Silver Shell* to *The Second Mrs Tanqueray,* and cannot forgive Mrs Kendal for having polluted their chaste stage with so improper a character. The American public, meanwhile, fills the theatre eight times a week; so it seems that the ideal

---

30, no doubt with this passage in his mind, talks of "the playgoer who (to Mr William Archer's annoyance, apparently) likes to take a play as he takes a *chasse* to his coffee." Not at all, my dear A. B. W.; this attitude of mind does not "annoy" me in the least; only I think it irrational and uncritical to make your *chasse* the sole measure of ALL drama, and condemn a play merely because it won't go into your liqueur-glass. Let me add that Mr Walkley's able championship of *The Second Mrs Tanqueray* proves that his devotion to the *chasse* ideal is not so bigoted as he would have us think.

Public has "no show" on either side of the Atlantic. The whole truth, of course, is that there no one Public, but that in every great city there are many strata, so to speak, of theatre-goers. What *The Second Mrs Tanqueray* has done is to prove that among them there is one stratum, and not a small one, which takes its intelligence with it to the play. That clearly ascertained, there is no longer any reason why our dramatists should leave *their* intelligence at the stage-door.

At this season of solemn meditation, one passes in review, among other things, the enthusiasms and illusions of the bygone year. Very often the two are synonymous; but in the case of *The Second Mrs Tanqueray*, after seven months' reflection and discussion, I have not the slightest disposition to repent my enthusiasm. On the contrary, all the criticisms I have heard of it have merely confirmed my admiration for Mr Pinero's work. Not that they have all been unjust or irrelevant; some, indeed, have been remarkably acute; but the very fact that it is a play on which none but really acute criticisms even begin to "bite" proves its immense superiority to anything (except perhaps *Beau Austin*) we have hitherto had to deal with. For instance, I have heard ladies object to the character of Aubrey Tanqueray, not merely because (as we all acknowledged from the first) he is

a trifle vague and colourless, but because of the
alleged stupidity of his attitude, and clumsiness of his
conduct, towards Paula. Well, there may be a good
deal in this. I should like very much (and so, I am
sure, would Mr Pinero) to see a full analysis of the
character of Aubrey from a woman's point of view.
But how many English plays have been produced
within the memory of man that raised any such
delicate question of character and conduct as to require what we may call specialist criticism, or to arouse
the party-spirit of sex? A novel occasionally does
so,—witness *Tess of the D'Urbervilles*,—but the rudimentary psychology of the average drama is a thing
no clever woman would dream of troubling her head
about. *The Second Mrs Tanqueray*, in a word, is the
only modern play which stands on the same artistic
level with such a work as *Tess of the D'Urbervilles*.
Many people dislike the play—many people dislike
the novel—but no one whose judgment is worth a
moment's attention would treat either one or other
with mere contempt. There is even a curious analogy
between the two works, in so far that in each case a
masculine writer has succeeded brilliantly with his
woman and made a comparative failure of his man.
Of course there is "more in" Angel Clare than in
Aubrey Tanqueray; but then Mr Hardy had at his
command just about ten times as much space as Mr

Pinero. I am not arguing, however, that the play is as fine an achievement as the novel—it may or may not be. All I insist is that even those who dislike it instinctively apply to Paula and Tanqueray the same standards which they would apply to Tess and her husband, and that no other modern English play (again with the exception of *Beau Austin*, which remains, unhappily, "sans lendemain"), could be brought into any sort of relation with such standards. It is noteworthy that among the very severest critics of *The Second Mrs Tanqueray* we should find the authors of *The Strike at Arlingford* and *Widowers' Houses;* but I would not have Mr Pinero unduly abashed by their disesteem. There is a species of technical criticism which is in its essence unjust. The craftsman, especially if he is new to his craft, and, having more or less overcome some of its initial difficulties, is revelling in the "anch' io sono pittore" stage of self-complacency, has an inclination to look at the work of other craftsmen and think, "Now I would have done that differently—therefore it is bad." (Observe that the major premise of the syllogism is modestly suppressed.) Their disapproval of the mere brush-work of the picture blinds them to its more essential qualities. Thus, at any rate, I am fain to account for the absence from their judgments of all reasonable sense of proportion. Mrs Patrick

Campbell, by the by, has distinctly improved since the earlier performances of the play. I am cannily inclined to await her appearance in some other character before committing myself to the word "genius," which has been freely flourished in this connection; but there is not the least doubt that her Paula is a very remarkable creation or incarnation.

INDEX.

—•—

THEATRES.

PLAYS.

300   INDEX.

AUTHORS.

ACTORS.